ARISA

3

Natsumi Ando

Translated and adapted by
Andria Cheng

Lettered by
North Market Street Graphics

KC
KODANSHA
COMICS

A Kodansha Comics Trade Paperback Original.

Arisa volume 3 copyright © 2009 by Natsumi Ando
English translation copyright © 2011 by Natsumi Ando

Published in the United States by Kodansha Comics, an imprint of Kodansha USA Publishing, LLC., New York.

Publication rights for this English edition arranged through Kodansha Ltd., Tokyo.

First published in Japan in 2009 by Kodansha Ltd., Tokyo.

ISBN 978-1-935-42917-3

Printed in the United States of America.

www.kodanshacomics.com

2 4 6 8 9 7 5 3

Translator/Adapter: Andria Cheng
Lettering: North Market Street Graphics

CONTENTS

Honorifics Explained..... v

Arisa Volume 3 1

Bonus Content 165

Translation Notes 167

HONORIFICS EXPLAINED

Throughout the Kodansha Comics books, you will find Japanese honorifics left intact in the translations. For those not familiar with how the Japanese use honorifics and, more important, how they differ from American honorifics, we present this brief overview.

Politeness has always been a critical facet of Japanese culture. Ever since the feudal era, when Japan was a highly stratified society, use of honorifics—which can be defined as polite speech that indicates relationship or status—has played an essential role in the Japanese language. When addressing someone in Japanese, an honorific usually takes the form of a suffix attached to one's name (example: "Asuna-san"), is used as a title at the end of one's name, or appears in place of the name itself (example: "Negi-sensei," or simply "Sensei!").

Honorifics can be expressions of respect or endearment. In the context of manga and anime, honorifics give insight into the nature of the relationship between characters. Many English translations leave out these important honorifics and therefore distort the feel of the original Japanese. Because Japanese honorifics contain nuances that English honorifics lack, it is our policy at Kodansha Comics not to translate them. Here, instead, is a guide to some of the honorifics you may encounter in Kodansha Comics books.

-san: This is the most common honorific and is equivalent to Mr., Miss, Ms., or Mrs. It is the all-purpose honorific and can be used in any situation where politeness is required.

-sama: This is one level higher than "-san" and is used to confer great respect.

-dono: This comes from the word "tono," which means "lord." It is an even higher level than "-sama" and confers utmost respect.

-kun: This suffix is used at the end of boys' names to express familiarity or endearment. It is also sometimes used by men among friends, or when addressing someone younger or of a lower station.

-*chan:*   This is used to express endearment, mostly toward girls. It is also used for little boys, pets, and even among lovers. It gives a sense of childish cuteness.

Bozu: This is an informal way to refer to a boy, similar to the English terms "kid" and "squirt."

Sempai/
Senpai: This title suggests that the addressee is one's senior in a group or organization. It is most often used in a school setting, where underclassmen refer to their upperclassmen as "sempai." It can also be used in the workplace, such as when a newer employee addresses an employee who has seniority in the company.

Kohai: This is the opposite of "sempai" and is used toward underclassmen in school or newcomers in the workplace. It connotes that the addressee is of a lower station.

Sensei: Literally meaning "one who has come before," this title is used for teachers, doctors, or masters of any profession or art.

-*[blank]:*   This is usually forgotten in these lists, but it is perhaps the most significant difference between Japanese and English. The lack of honorific means that the speaker has permission to address the person in a very intimate way. Usually, only family, spouses, or very close friends have this kind of permission. Known as *yobisute*, it can be gratifying when someone who has earned the intimacy starts to call one by one's name without an honorific. But when that intimacy hasn't been earned, it can be very insulting.

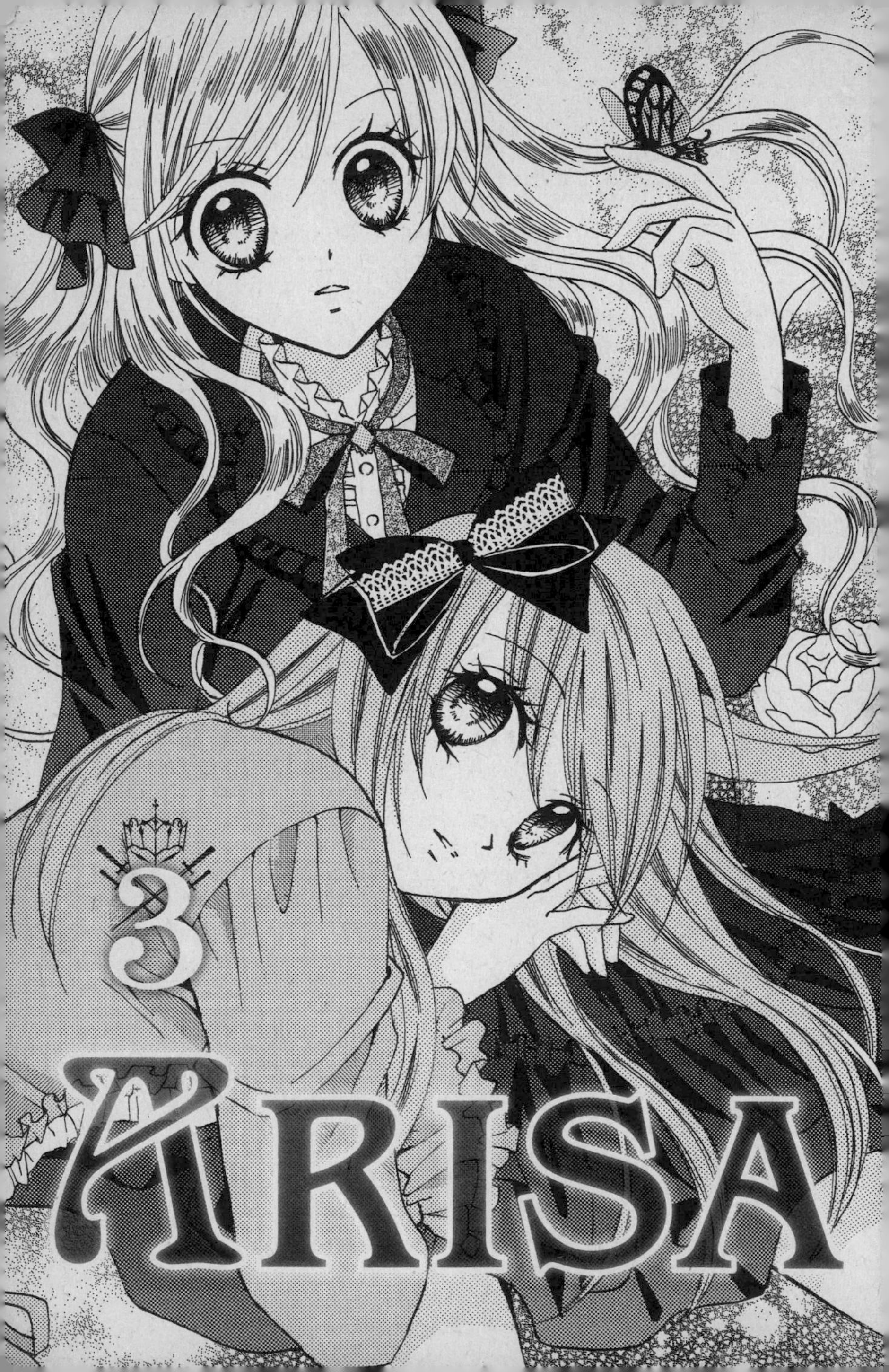
3
ARISA

Contents

ARISA

Chapter 9
Planetarium..............................4

Chapter 10
Mariko Takagi..........................45

Chapter 11
The Owner of the Number...85

Chapter 12
Transfer Student...................124

The story so far

Tsubasa and Arisa are twin sisters separated by their parents' divorce. They finally reunited after three years of being apart, but their happy time together came to a sudden end when Arisa jumped out her bedroom window right in front of Tsubasa, leaving behind a mysterious card...

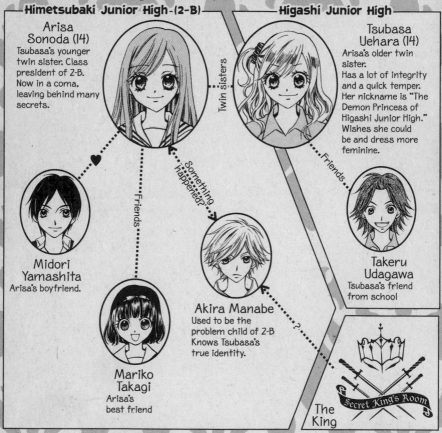

Himetsubaki Junior High-(2-B)
Higashi Junior High
Tsubasa Uehara (14)
Arisa's older twin sister.
Has a lot of integrity and a quick temper.
Her nickname is "The Demon Princess of Higashi Junior High."
Wishes she could be and dress more feminine.
Twin sisters
Arisa Sonoda (14)
Tsubasa's younger twin sister. Class president of 2-B.
Now in a coma, leaving behind many secrets.
Friends
Takeru Udagawa
Tsubasa's friend from school
Something happened?
Friends
Midori Yamashita
Arisa's boyfriend.
Akira Manabe
Used to be the problem child of 2-B
Knows Tsubasa's true identity.
?
Mariko Takagi
Arisa's best friend
Secret King's Room
The King

In order to discover the secrets Arisa was hiding, Tsubasa pretended to be her and attended Himetsubaki Junior High. In Class 2-B, a mysterious internet presence called "The King" led strange incidents and bullying. It turns out that Arisa was the original "King," but someone else took over in order to control her classmates. Tsubasa decided to team up with Manabe to find the true identity of the "King," but now there is a new "King Time" in the planetarium, bringing along with it new troubles for Class 2-B...

Today...
...is Friday.

Let's catch this new "King."
During the next "King Time."

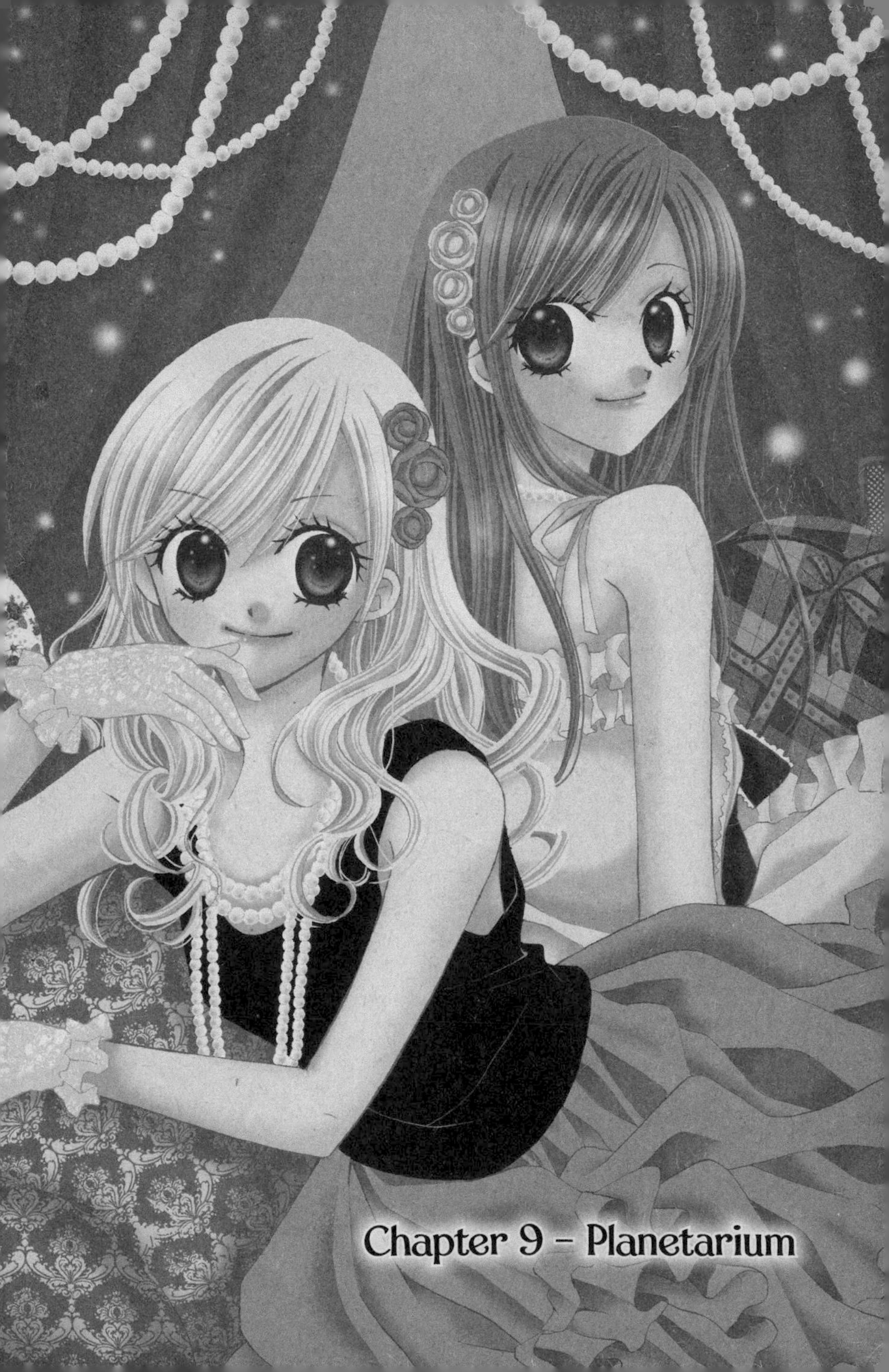
Chapter 9 - Planetarium

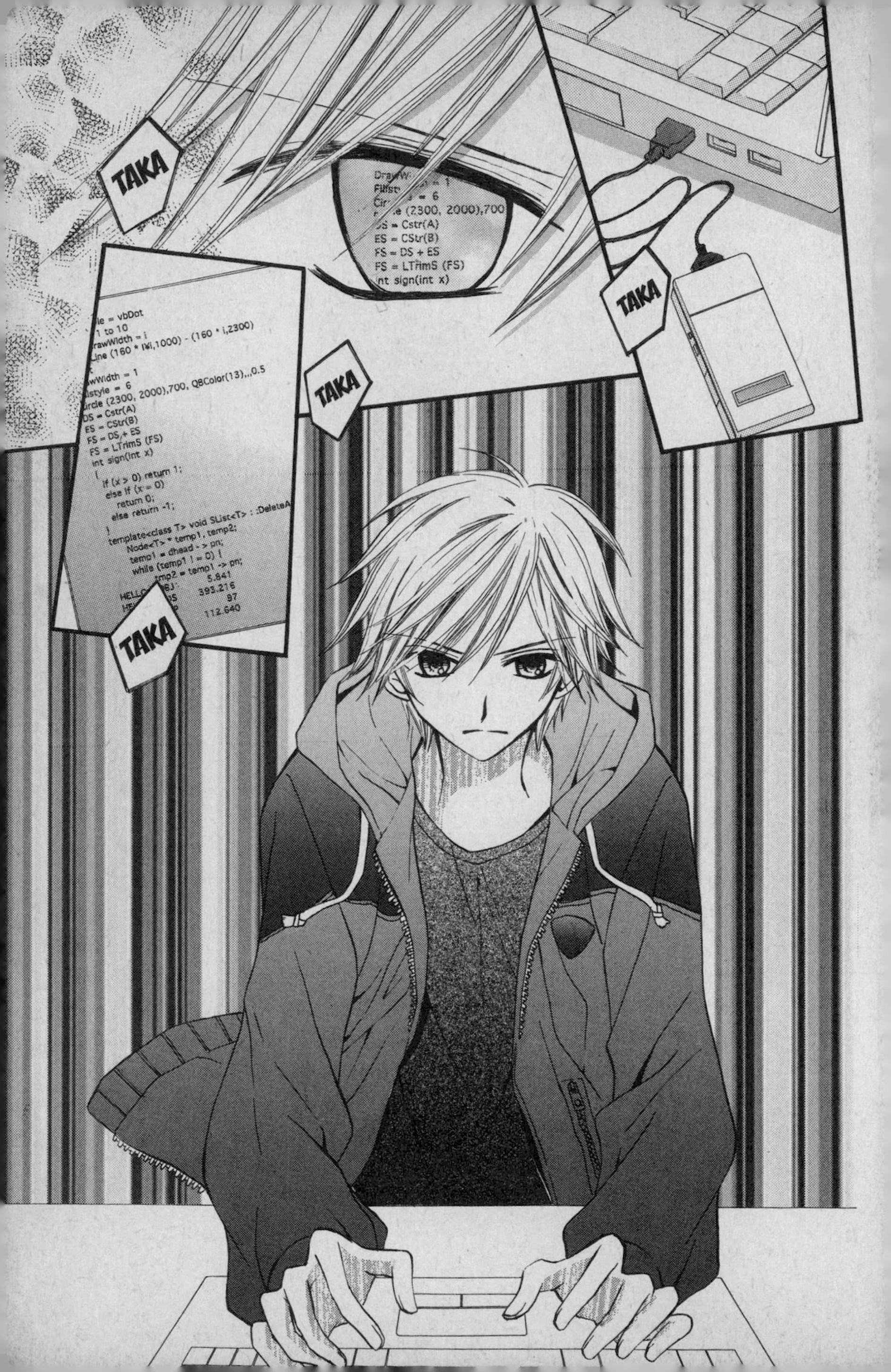

TAKA
ES = CStr(B)
FS = DS + ES
FS = LTrimS (FS)
int sign(int x)
TAKA
TAKA
if (x > 0) return 1;
else if (x = 0)
return 0;
else return -1;
Node<T> * temp1, temp2;
temp1 = dhead - > pn;
while (temp1 ! = 0) {
tmp2 = temp1 -> pn;
5.841
393.216
97
112.640
TAKA

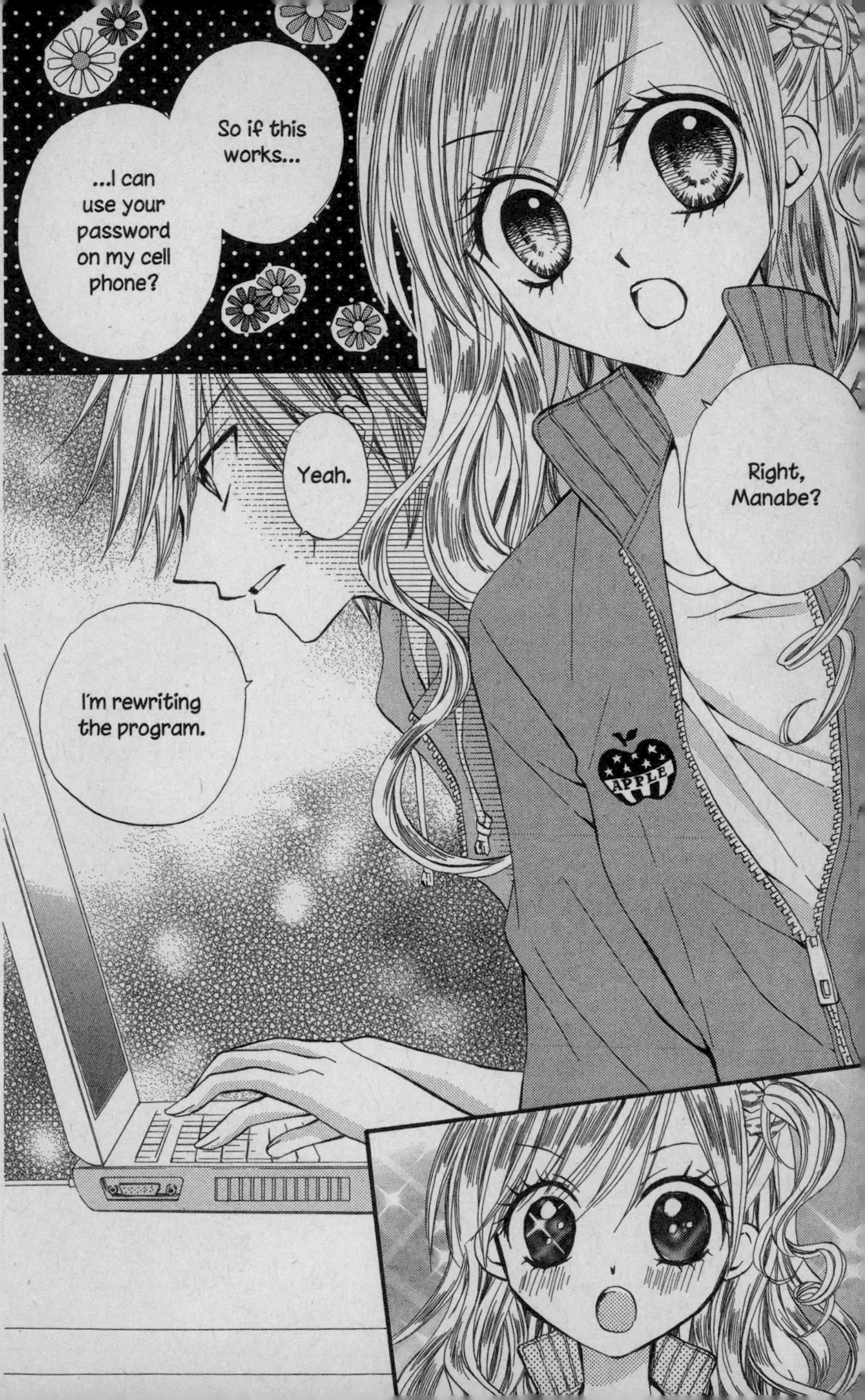
So if this works...
...I can use your password on my cell phone?
Right, Manabe?
APPLE
Yeah.
I'm rewriting the program.

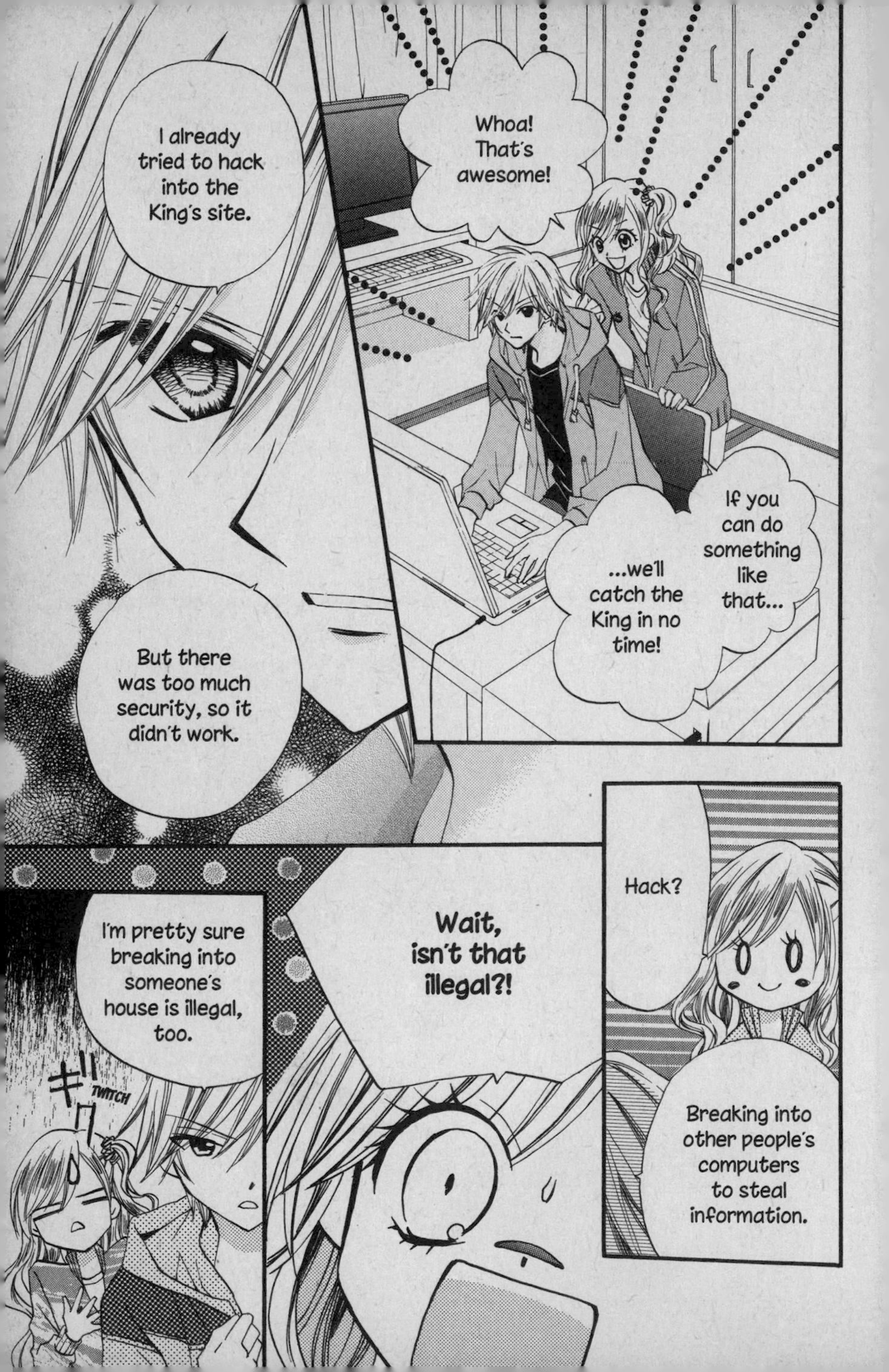

Whoa! That's awesome!
If you can do something like that...
...we'll catch the King in no time!
I already tried to hack into the King's site.
But there was too much security, so it didn't work.
Hack?
Breaking into other people's computers to steal information.
Wait, isn't that illegal?!
I'm pretty sure breaking into someone's house is illegal, too.
TWITCH

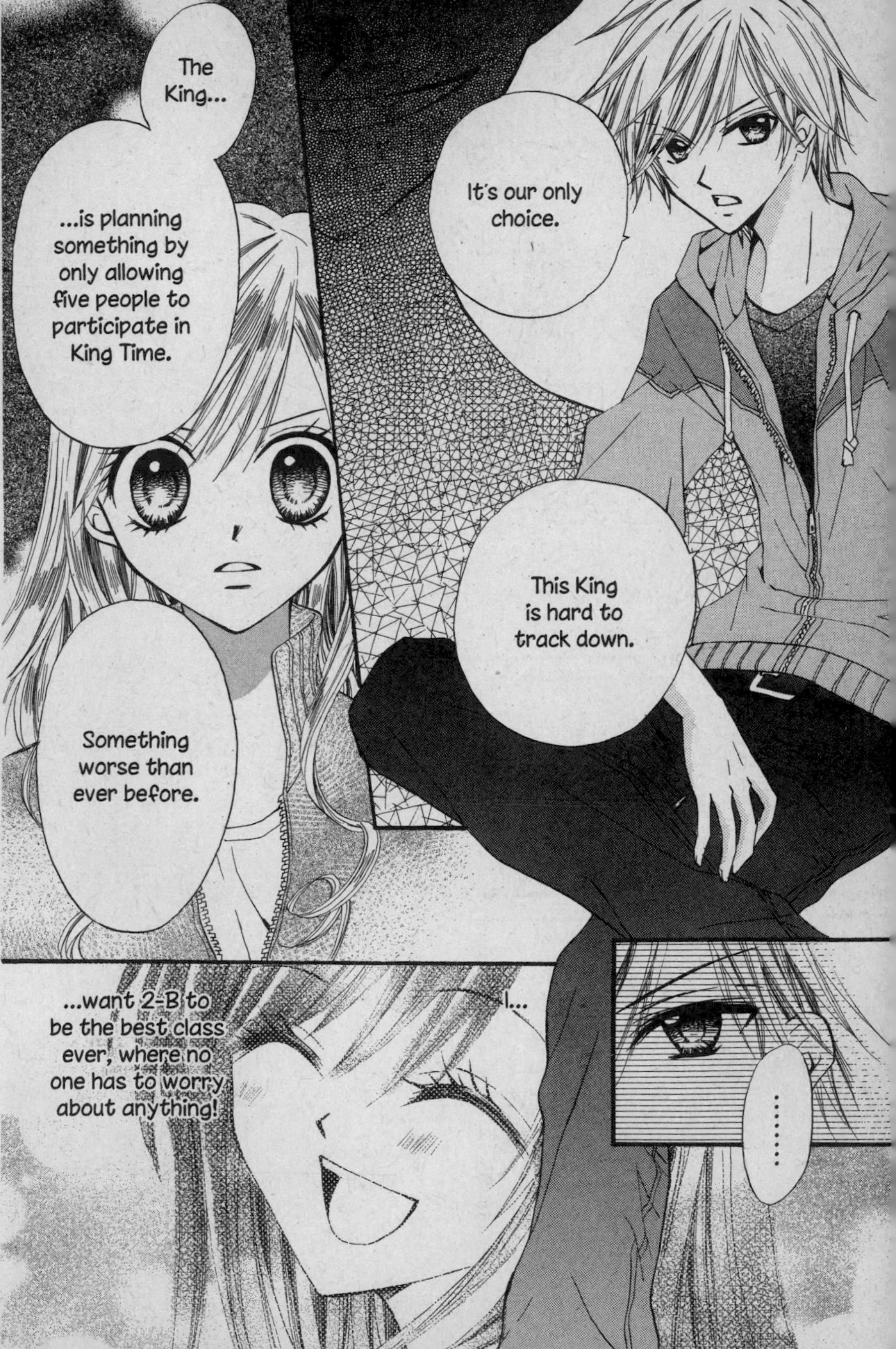
It's our only choice.
This King is hard to track down.
The King...
...is planning something by only allowing five people to participate in King Time.
Something worse than ever before.
......
I...
...want 2-B to be the best class ever, where no one has to worry about anything!

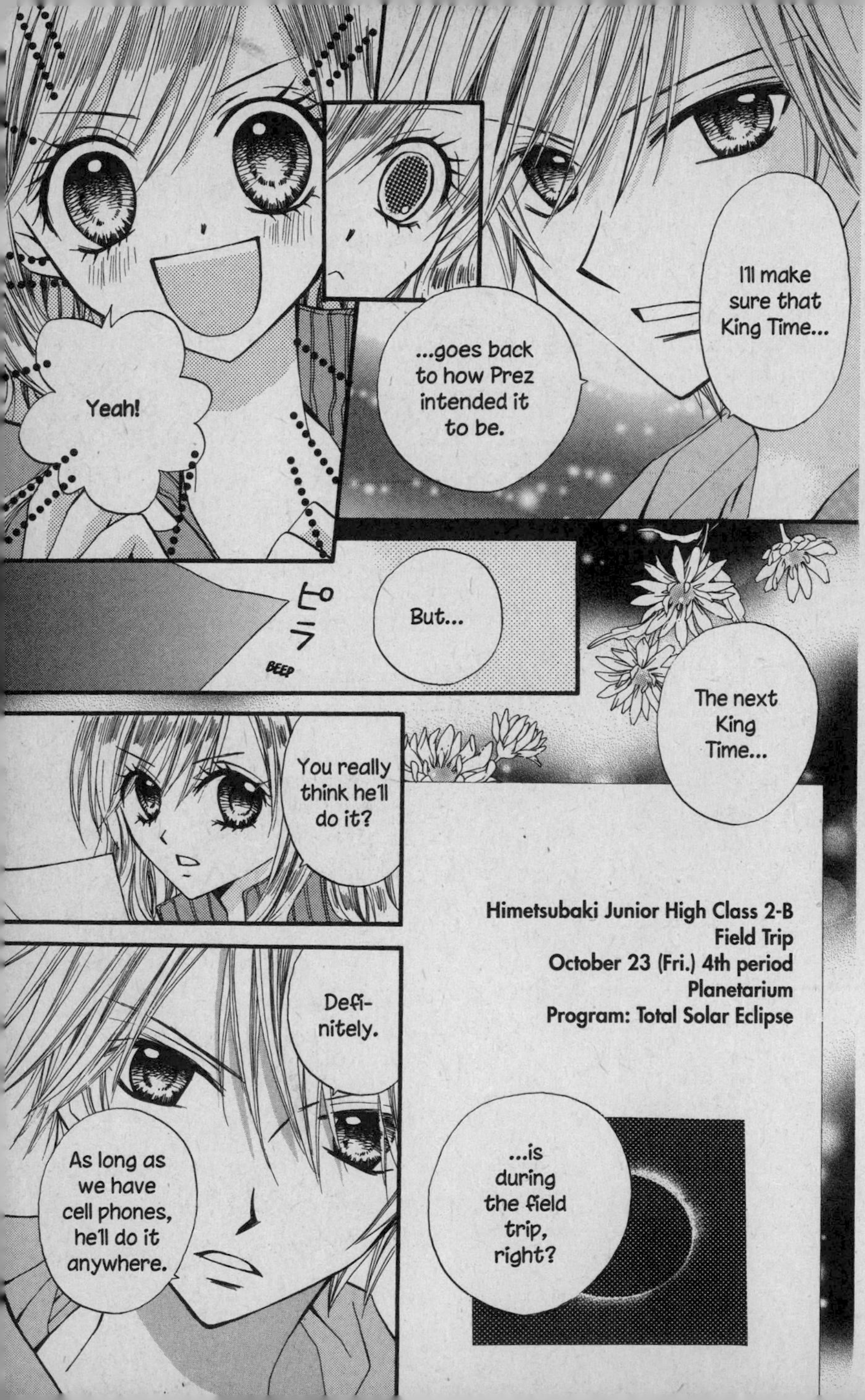
I'll make sure that King Time...
...goes back to how Prez intended it to be.
Yeah!
The next King Time...
Himetsubaki Junior High Class 2-B
Field Trip
October 23 (Fri.) 4th period
Planetarium
Program: Total Solar Eclipse
...is during the field trip, right?
ピラ
BEEP
But...
You really think he'll do it?
Defi-nitely.
As long as we have cell phones, he'll do it anywhere.

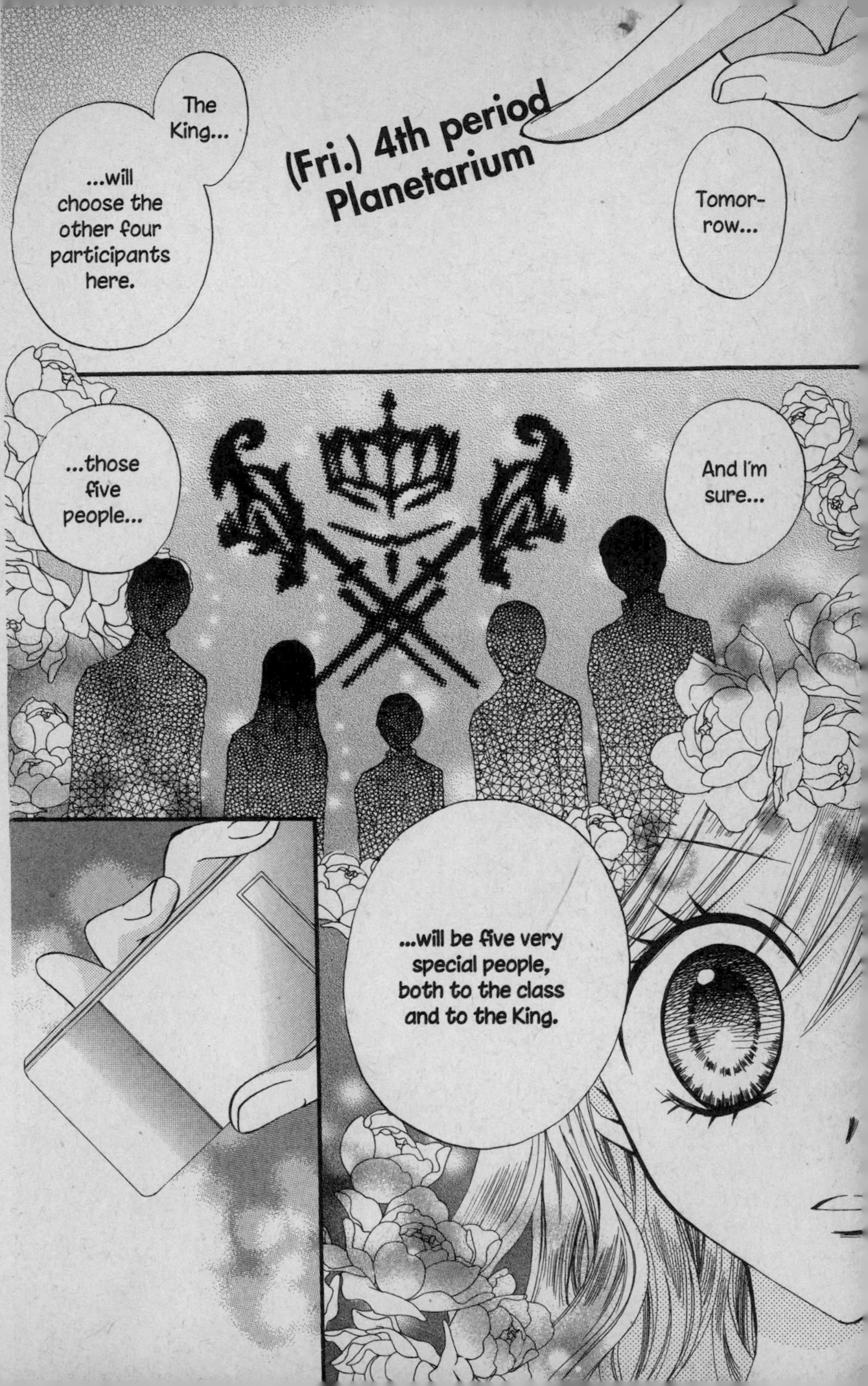
Tomorrow...
(Fri.) 4th period Planetarium
The King...
...will choose the other four participants here.
And I'm sure...
...those five people...
...will be five very special people, both to the class and to the King.

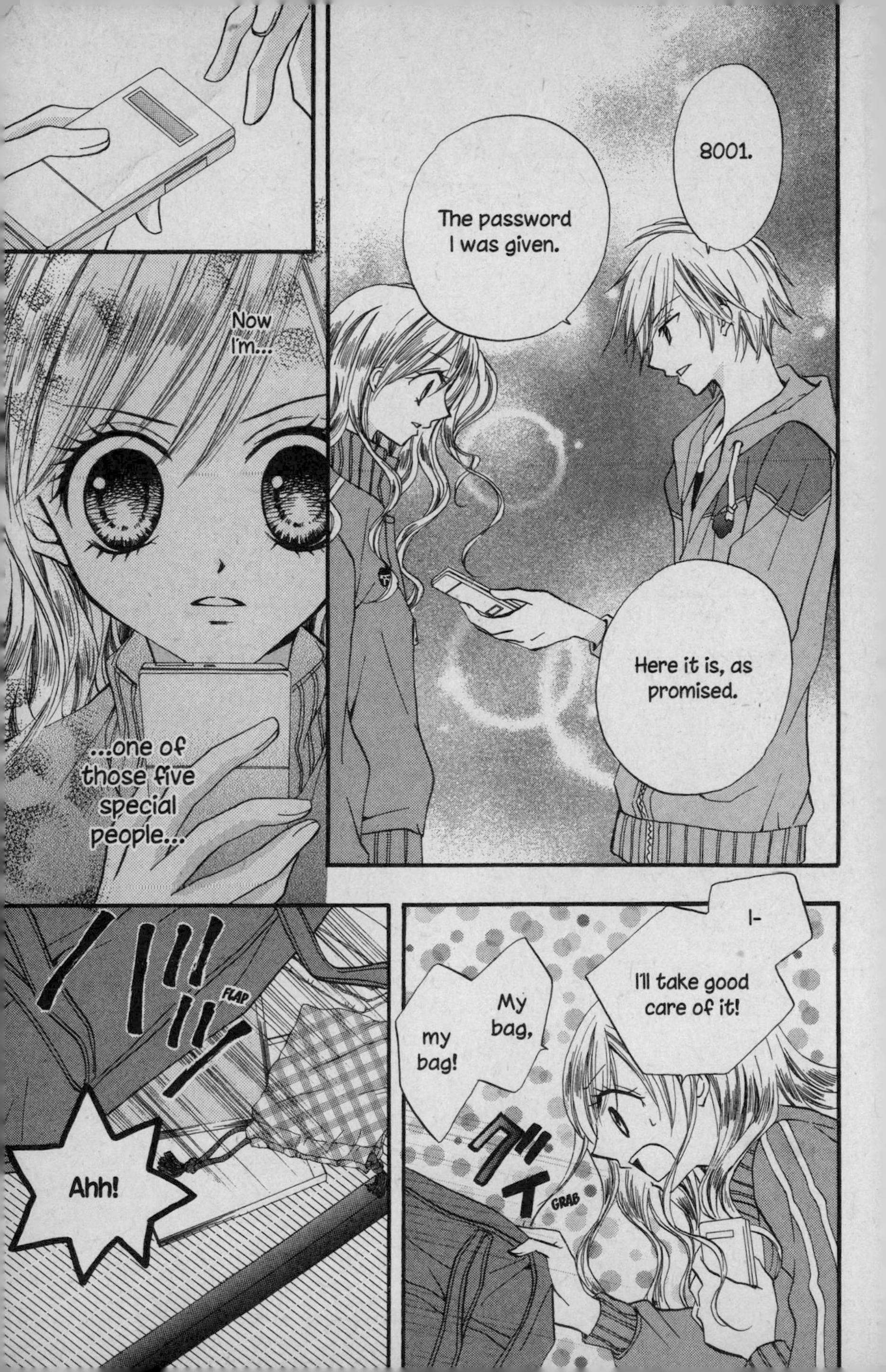
8001.
The password I was given.
Here it is, as promised.
Now I'm...
...one of those five special people...
I-
I'll take good care of it!
My bag,
my bag!
GRAB
FLAP
Ahh!

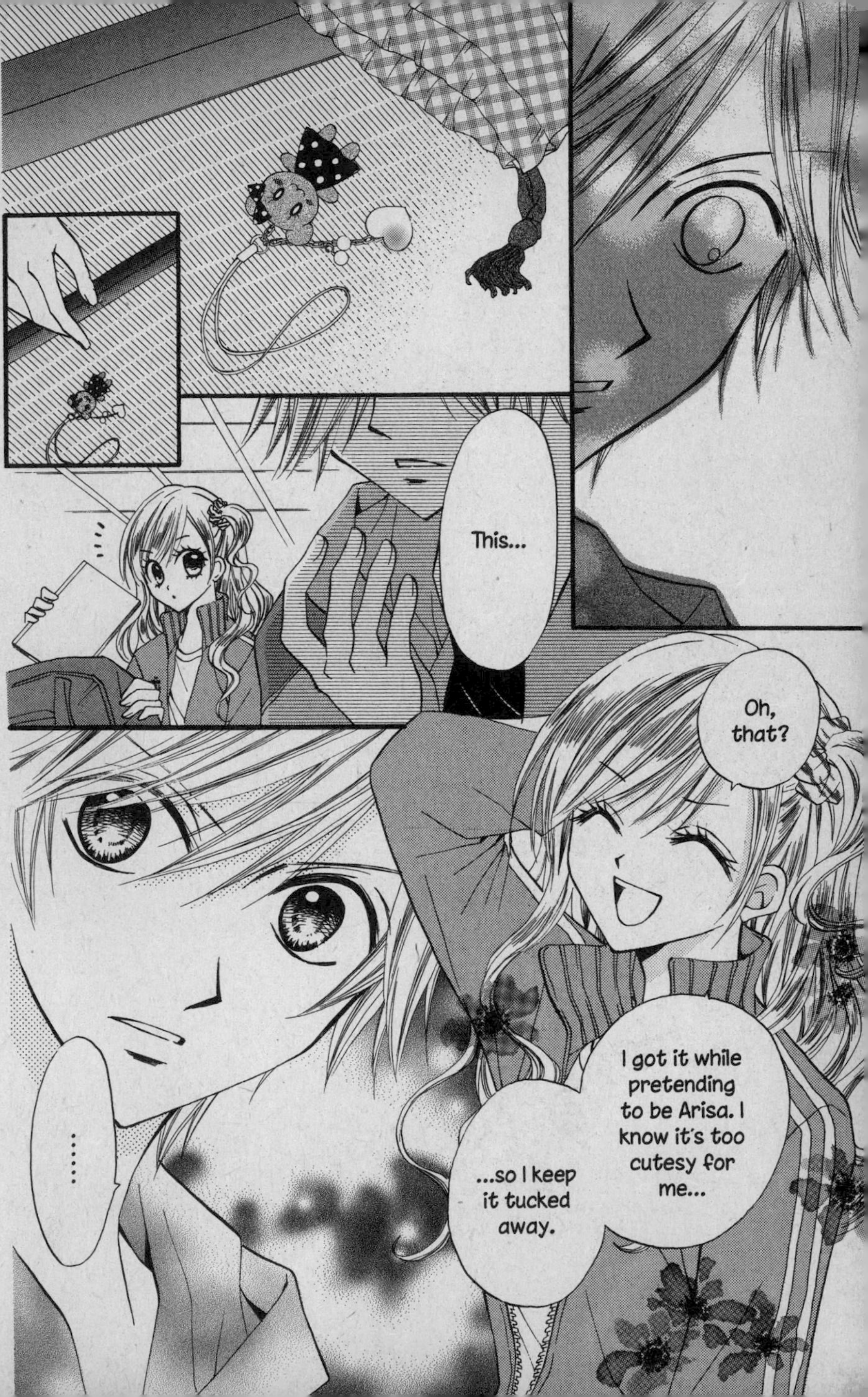
This...
Oh, that?
I got it while pretending to be Arisa. I know it's too cutesy for me...
...so I keep it tucked away.
......

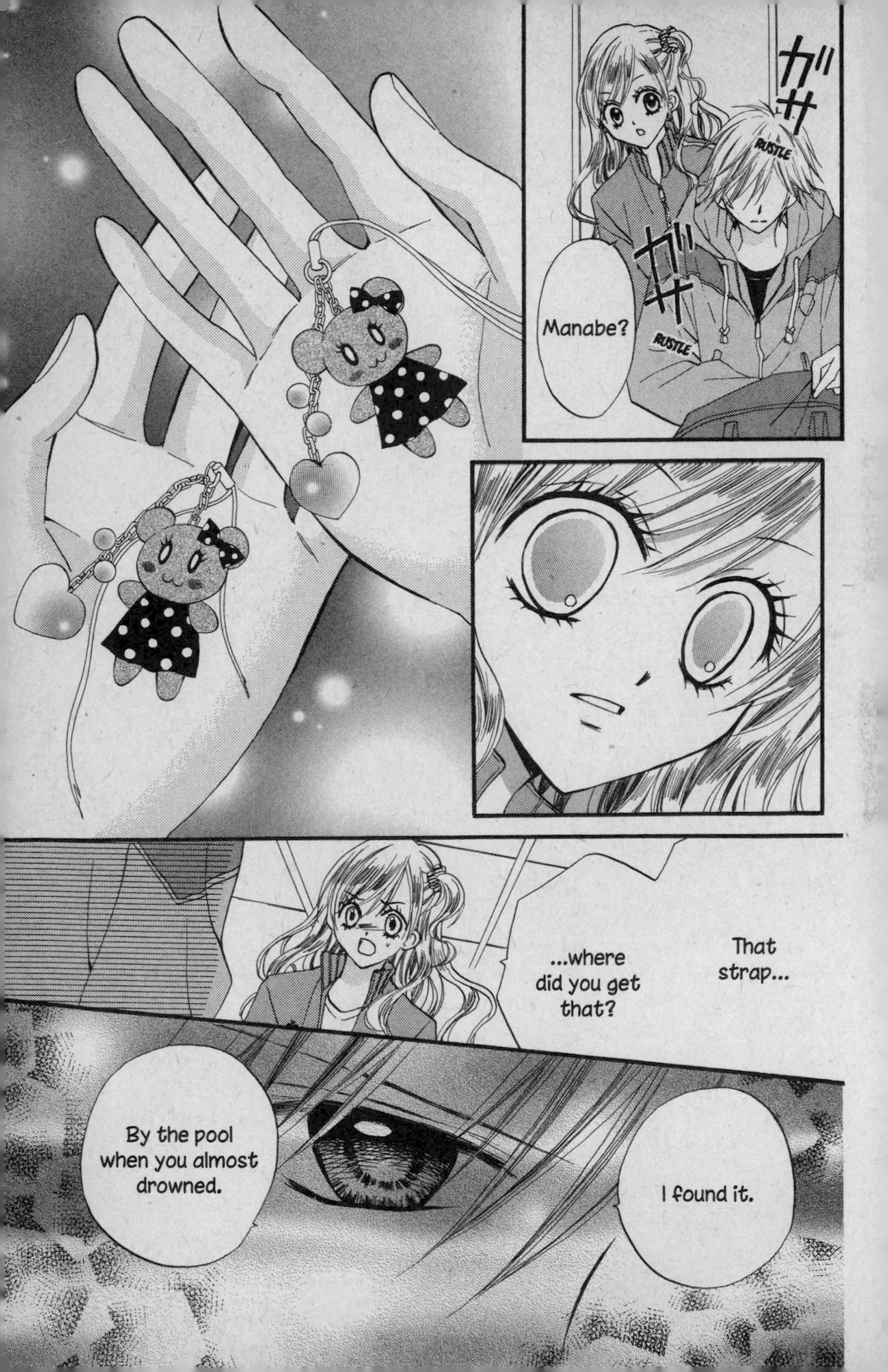
ガサ
RUSTLE
ガサ
Manabe?
RUSTLE
That strap...
...where did you get that?
I found it.
By the pool when you almost drowned.

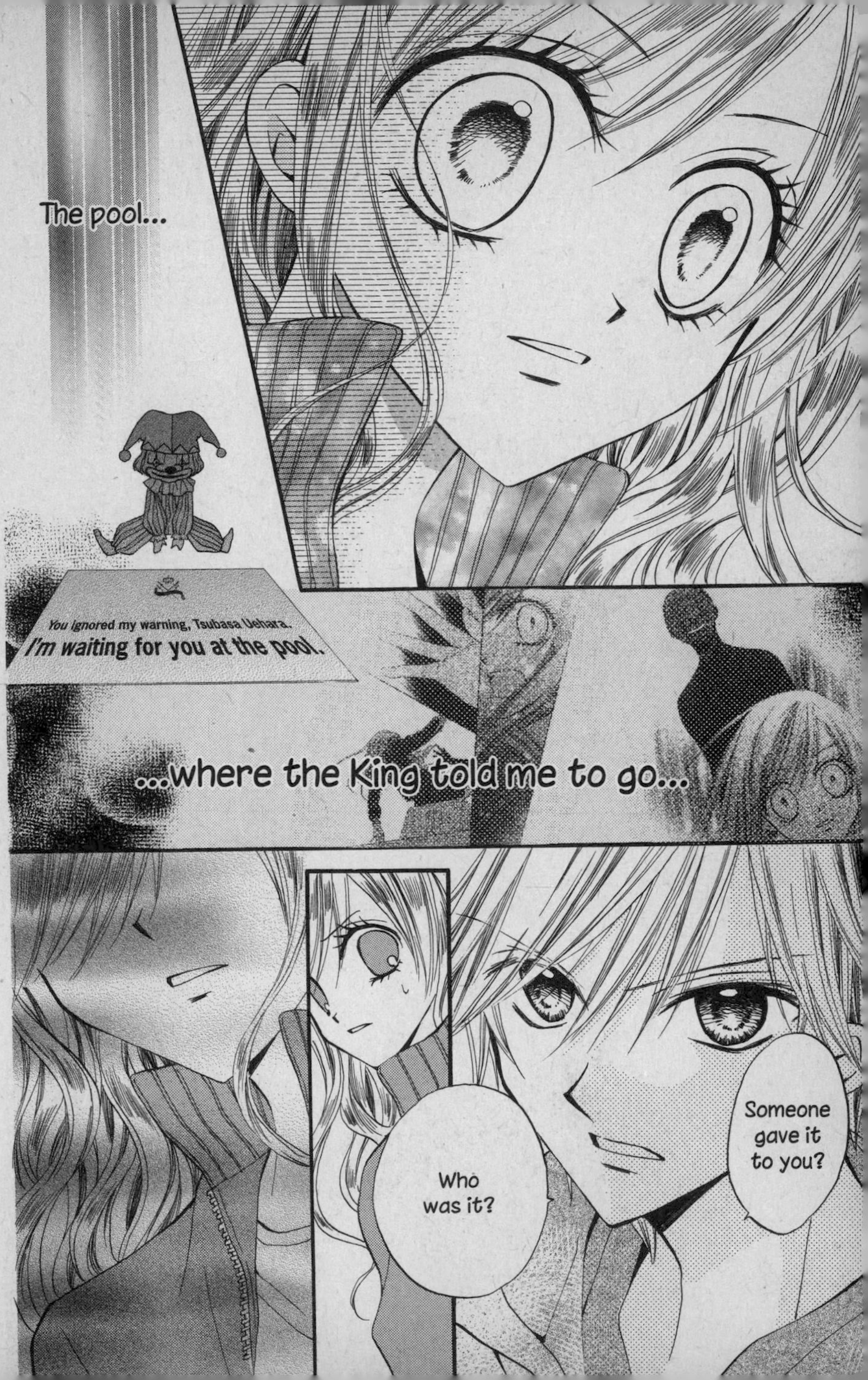
The pool...
You ignored my warning, Tsubasa Uehara.
I'm waiting for you at the pool.
...where the King told me to go...
Someone gave it to you?
Who was it?

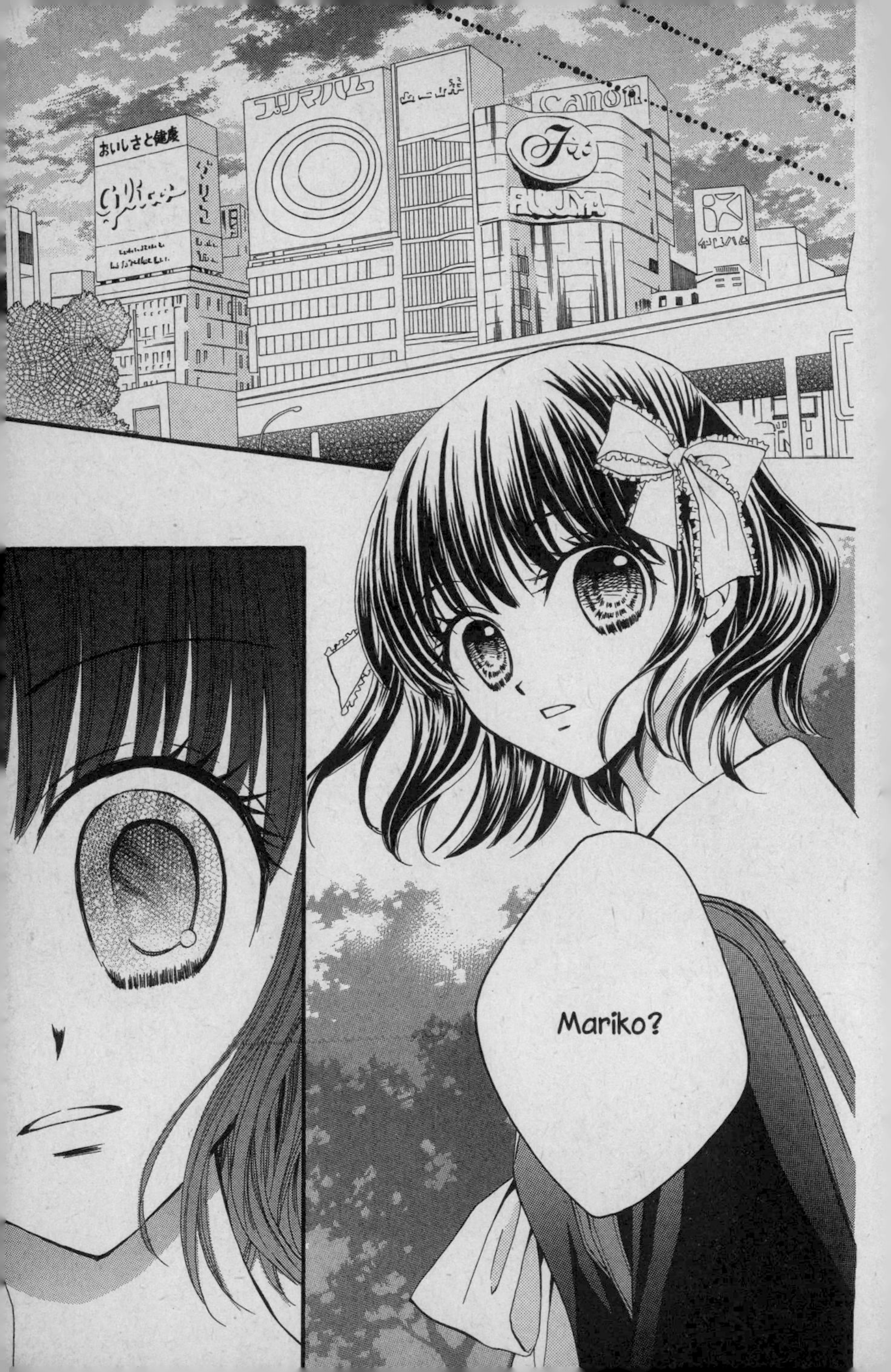
Canon
プリマハム
おいしさと健康
Mariko?

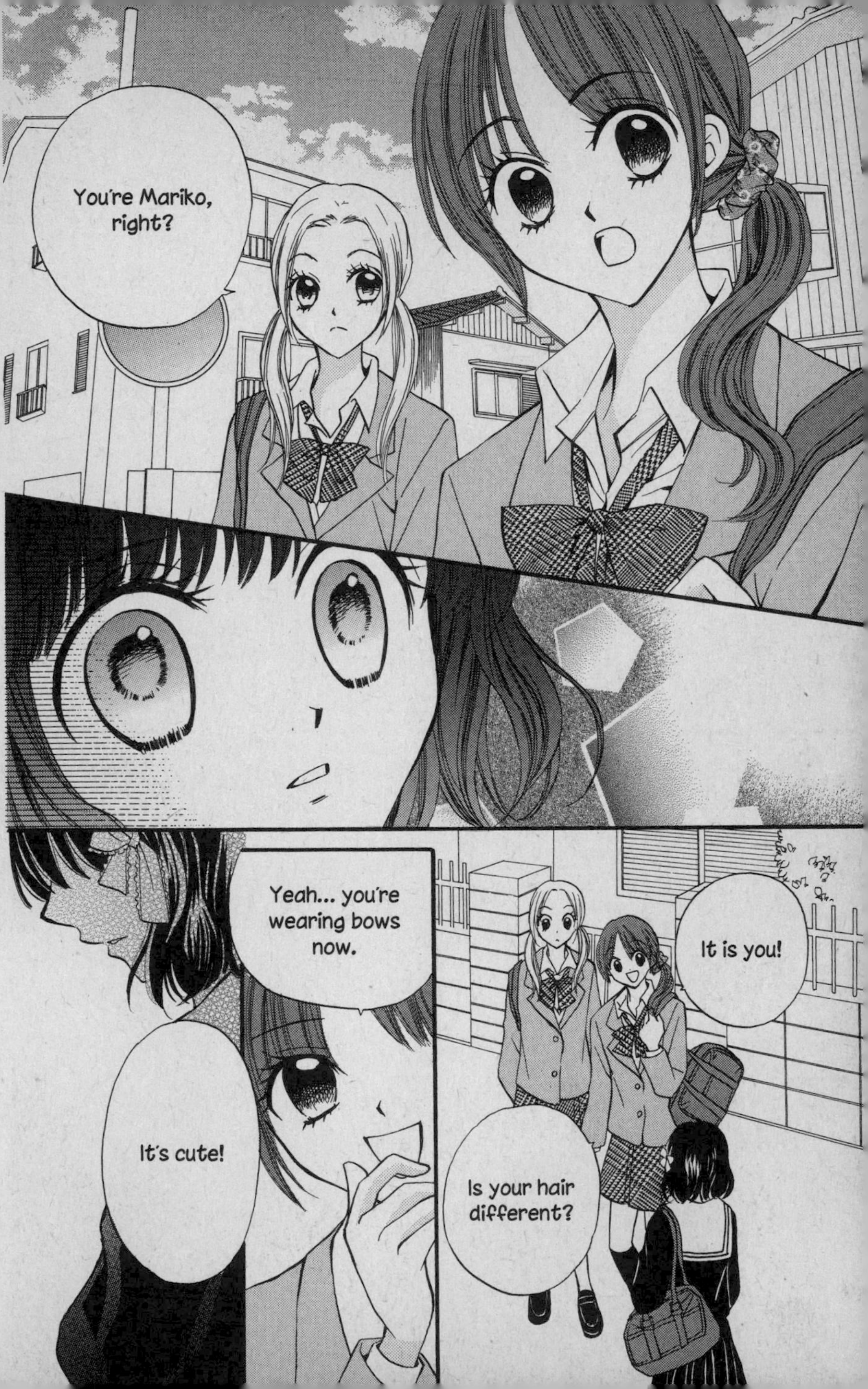
You're Mariko, right?
It is you!
Is your hair different?
Yeah... you're wearing bows now.
It's cute!

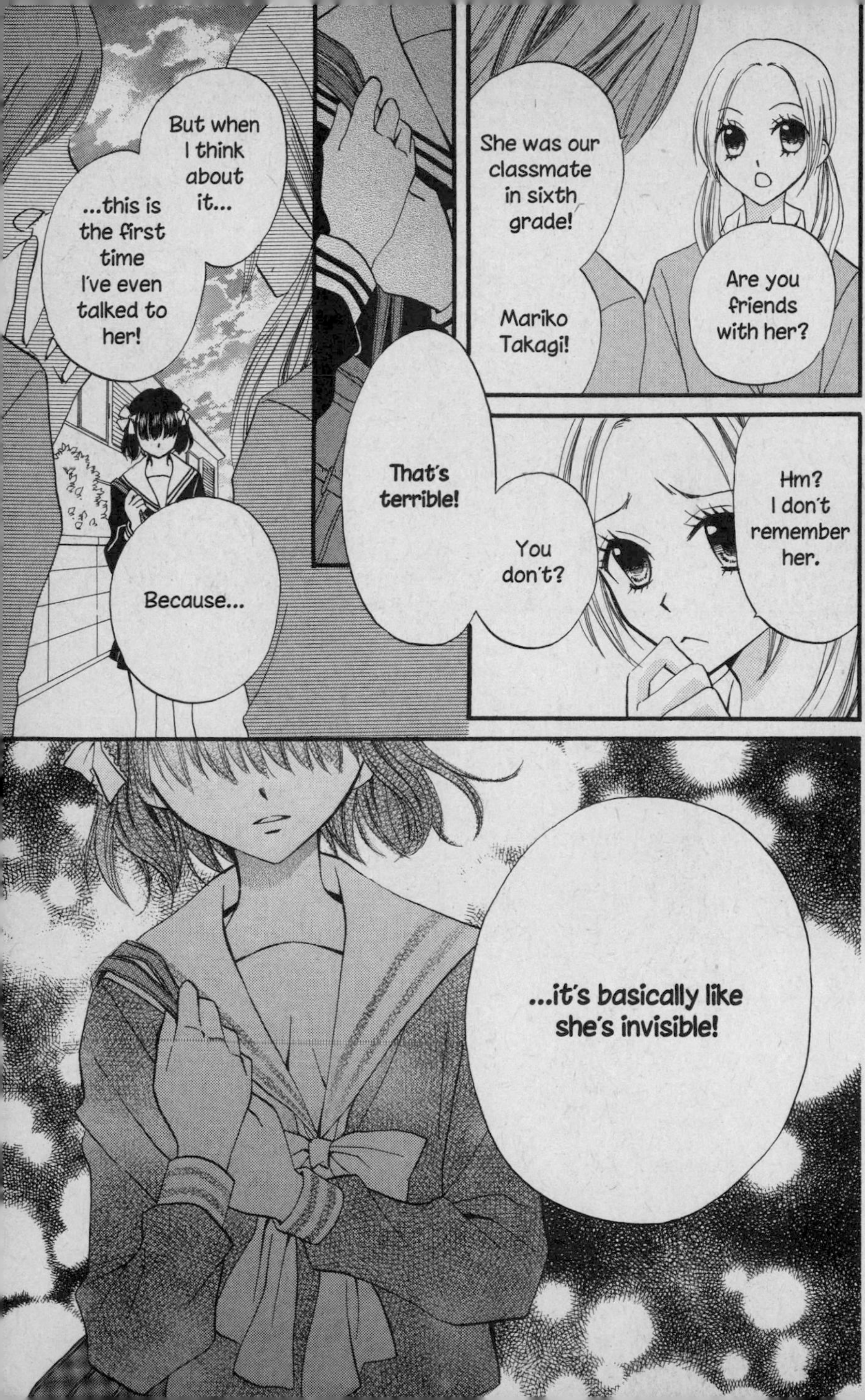
She was our classmate in sixth grade!
Mariko Takagi!
Are you friends with her?
Hm? I don't remember her.
You don't?
That's terrible!
But when I think about it...
...this is the first time I've even talked to her!
Because...
...it's basically like she's invisible!

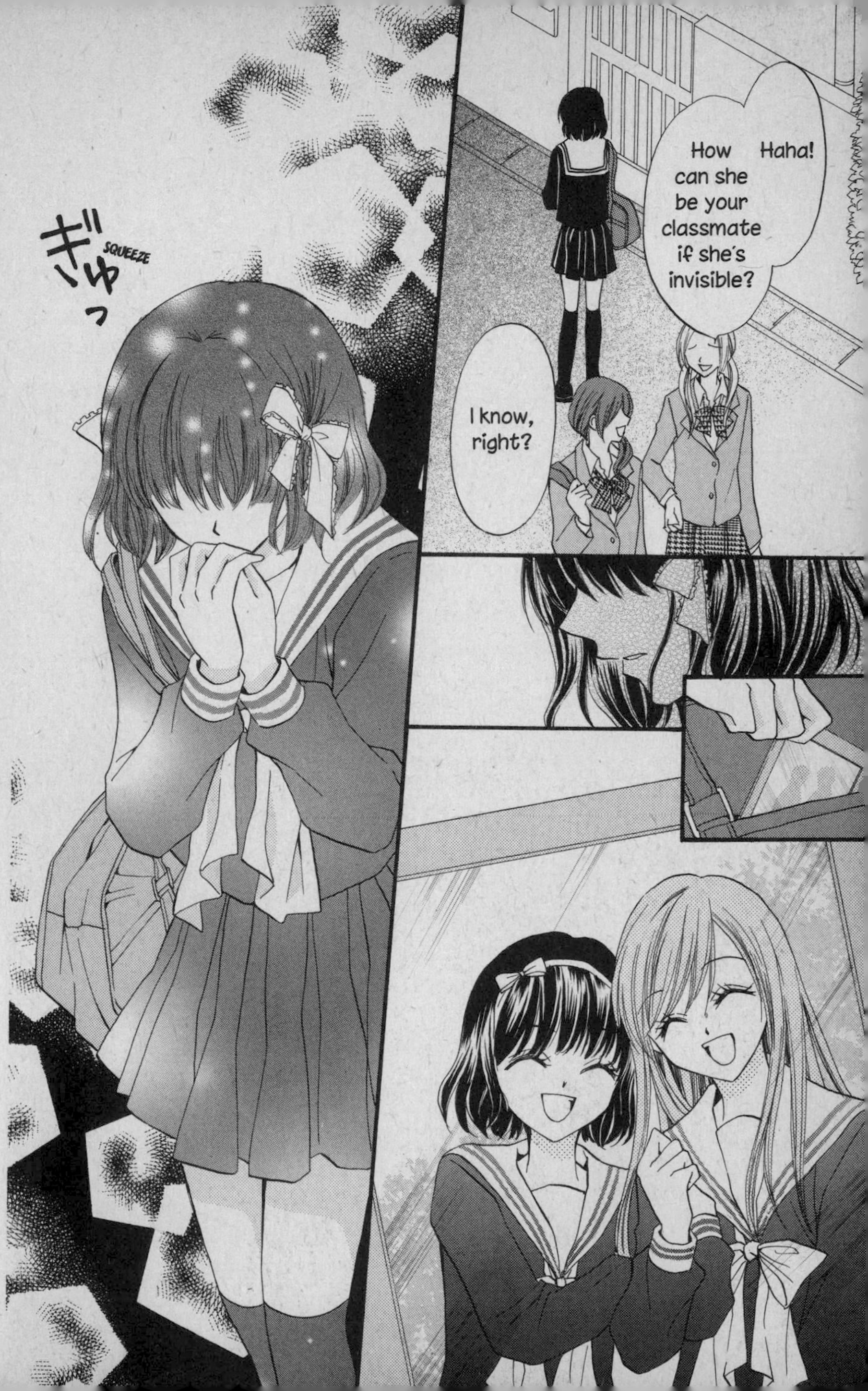
Haha!
How can she be your classmate if she's invisible?
I know, right?
ぎゅっ
SQUEEZE

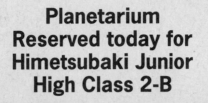

**Planetarium
Reserved today for
Himetsubaki Junior
High Class 2-B**

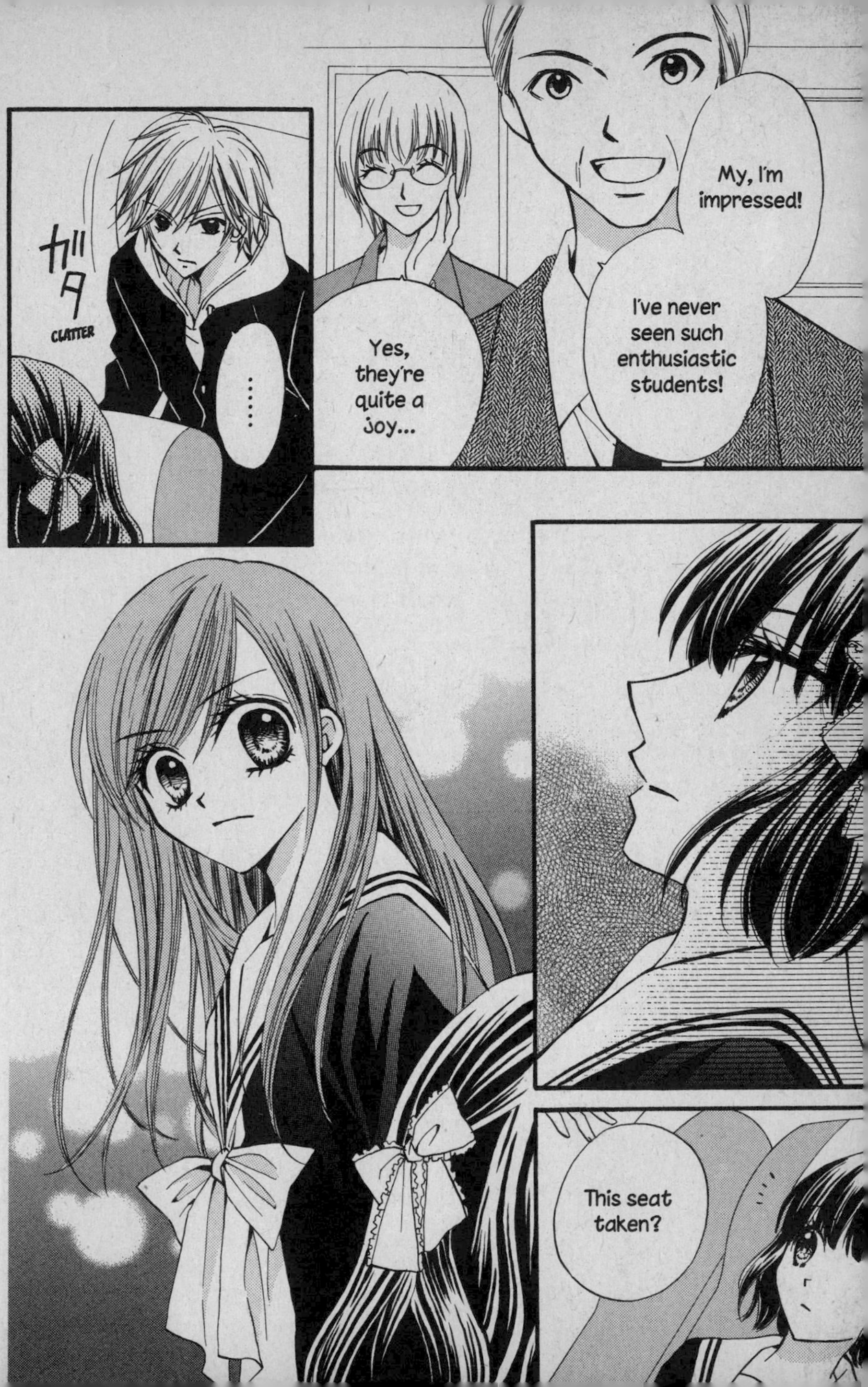
My, I'm impressed!
I've never seen such enthusiastic students!
Yes, they're quite a joy...
ガタ
CLATTER
......
This seat taken?
...

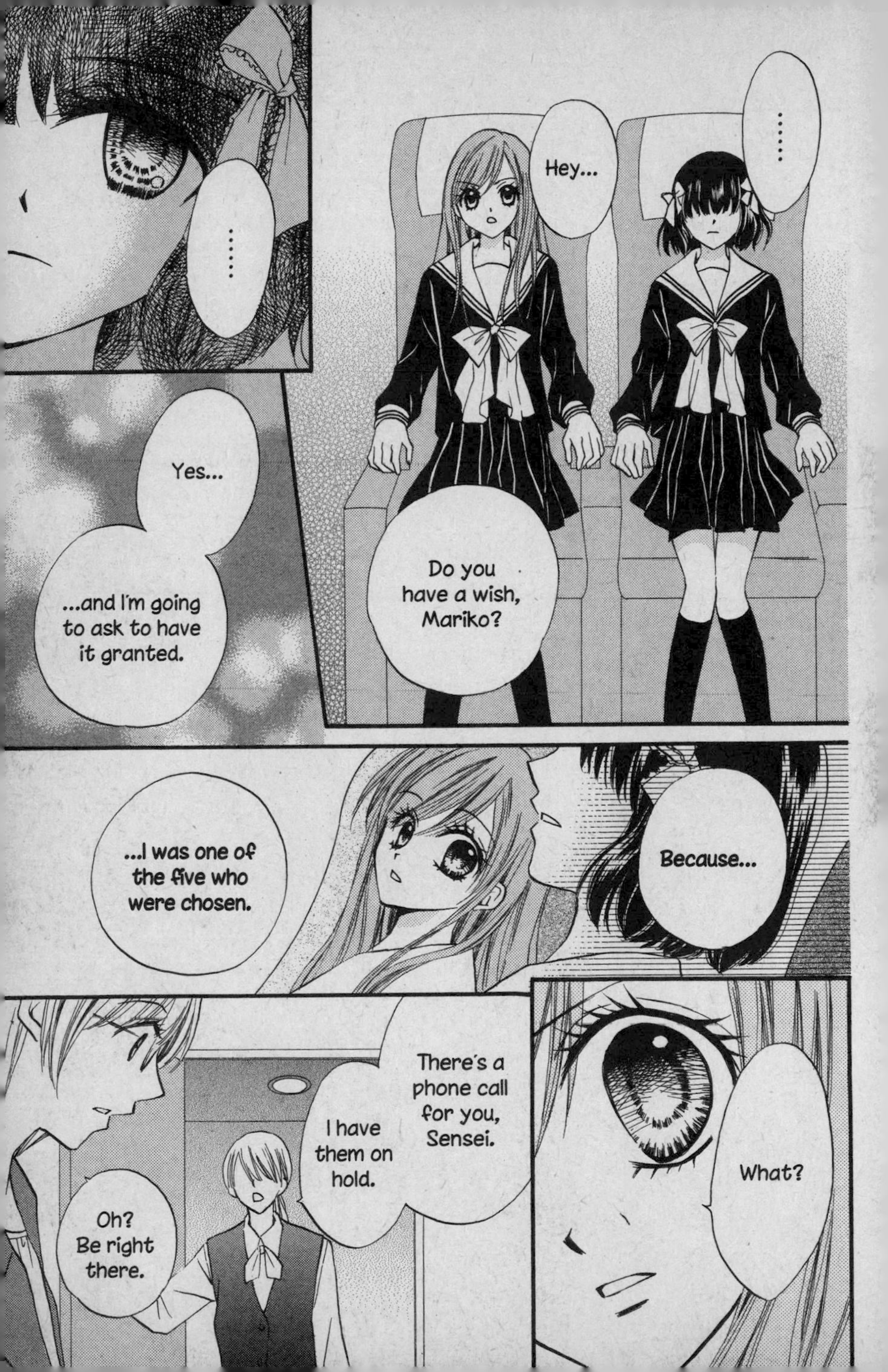
……
Hey...
Do you have a wish, Mariko?
……
Yes...
...and I'm going to ask to have it granted.
Because...
...I was one of the five who were chosen.
What?
There's a phone call for you, Sensei.
I have them on hold.
Oh? Be right there.

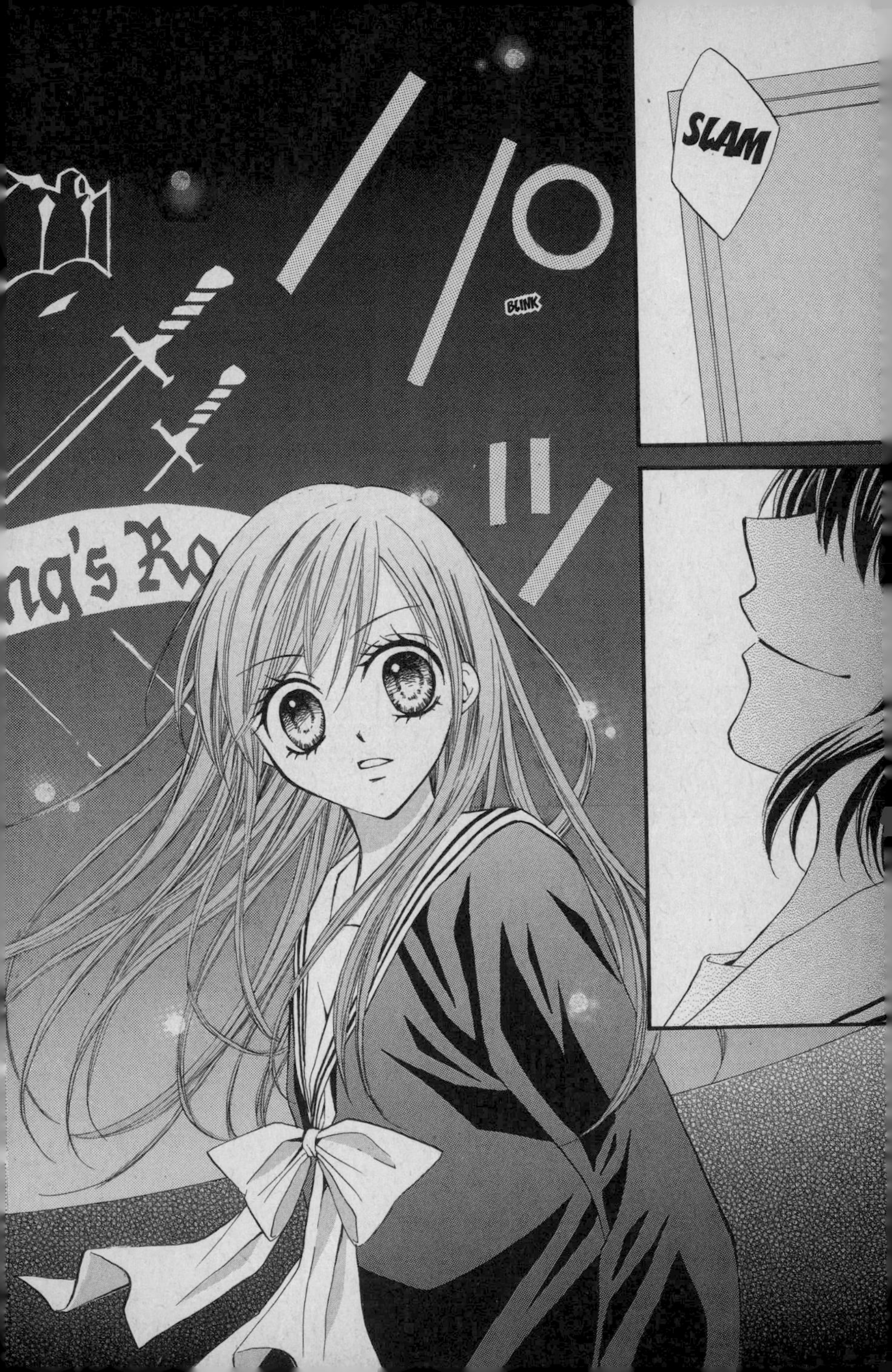
SLAM
BLINK
ng's Ro

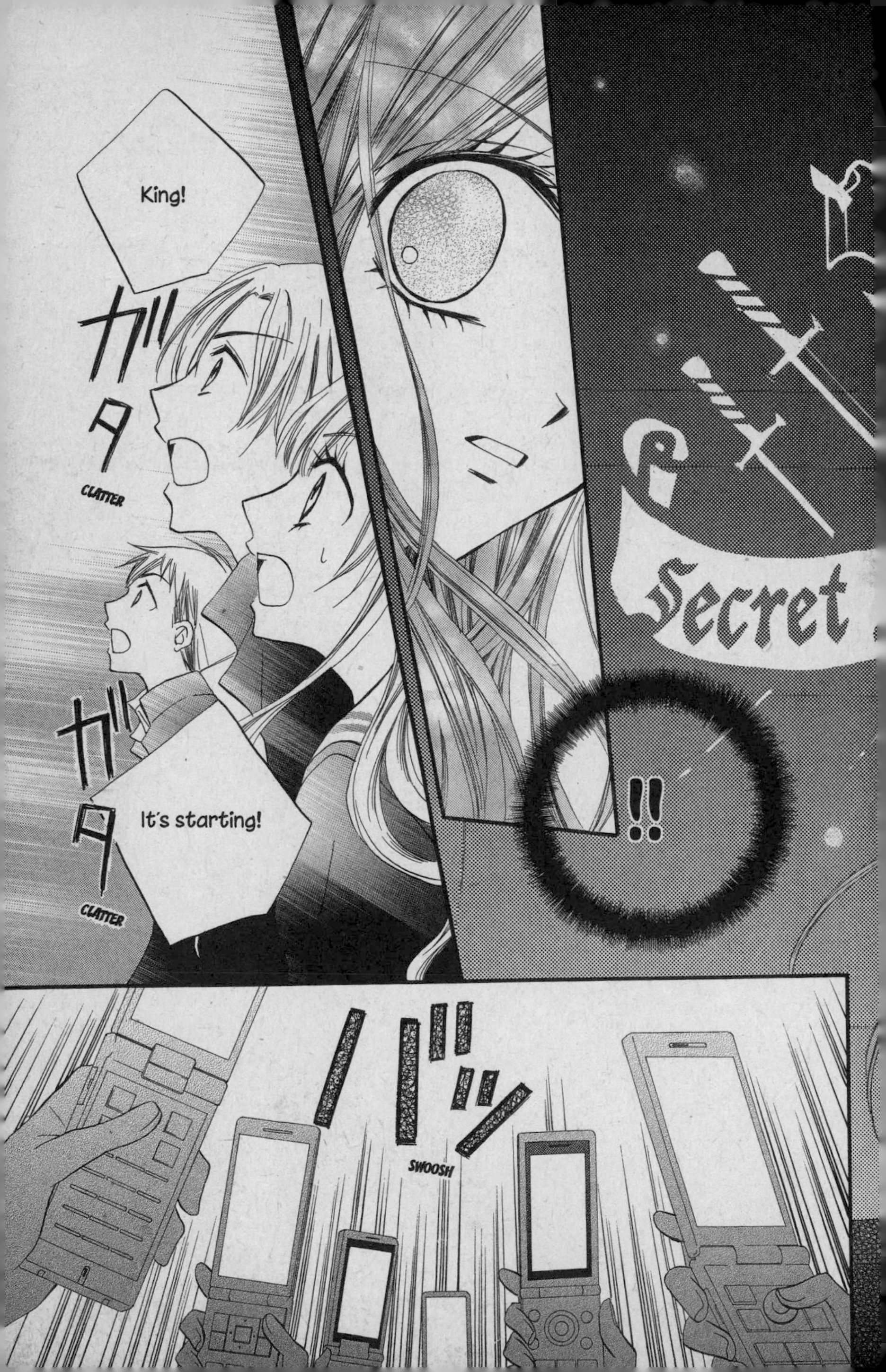
Secret
!!
King!
ガタ
CLATTER
It's starting!
ガタ
CLATTER
バッ
SWOOSH

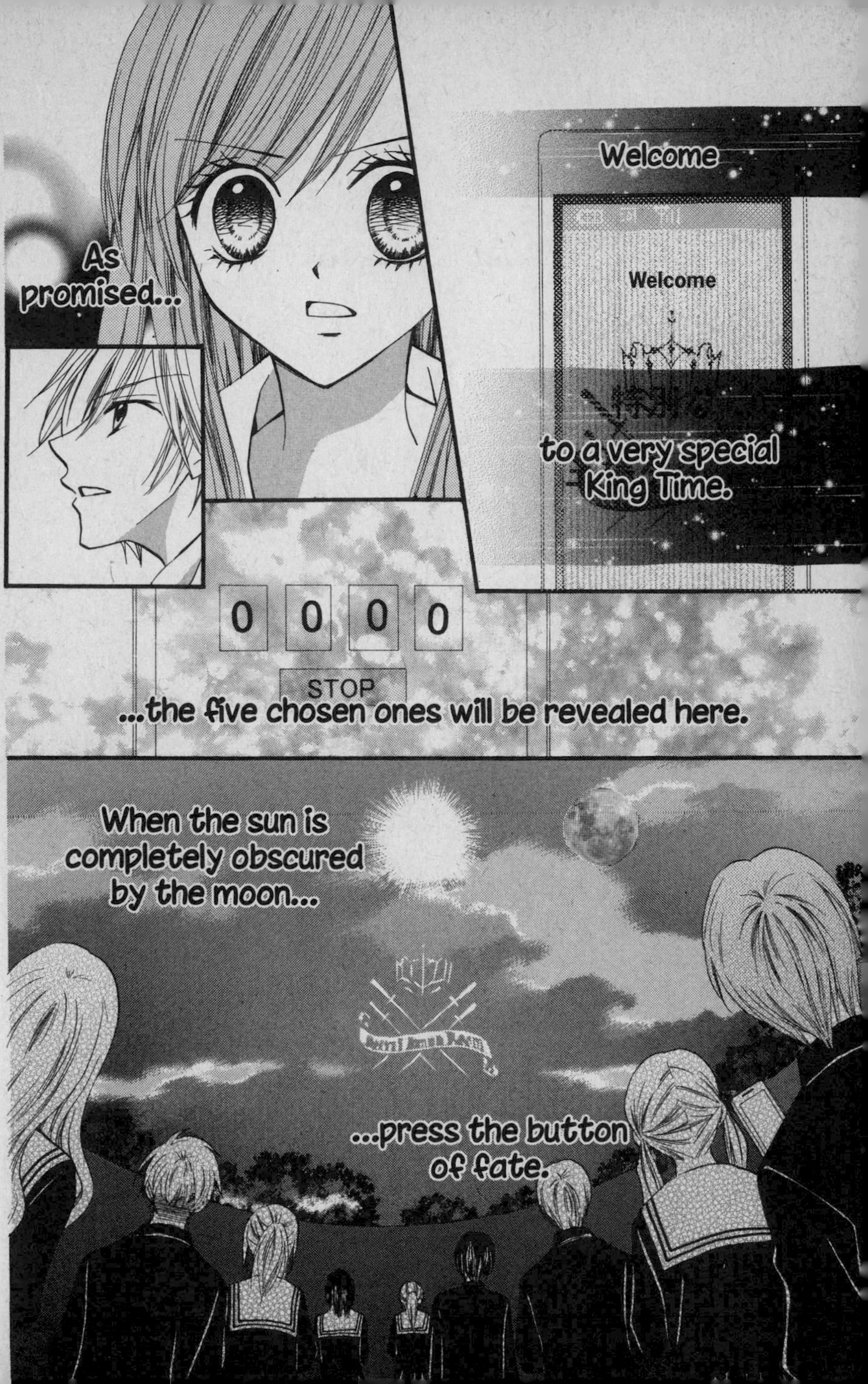

Welcome
Welcome
to a very special King Time.
As promised...
0 0 0 0
STOP
...the five chosen ones will be revealed here.
When the sun is completely obscured by the moon...
...press the button of fate.

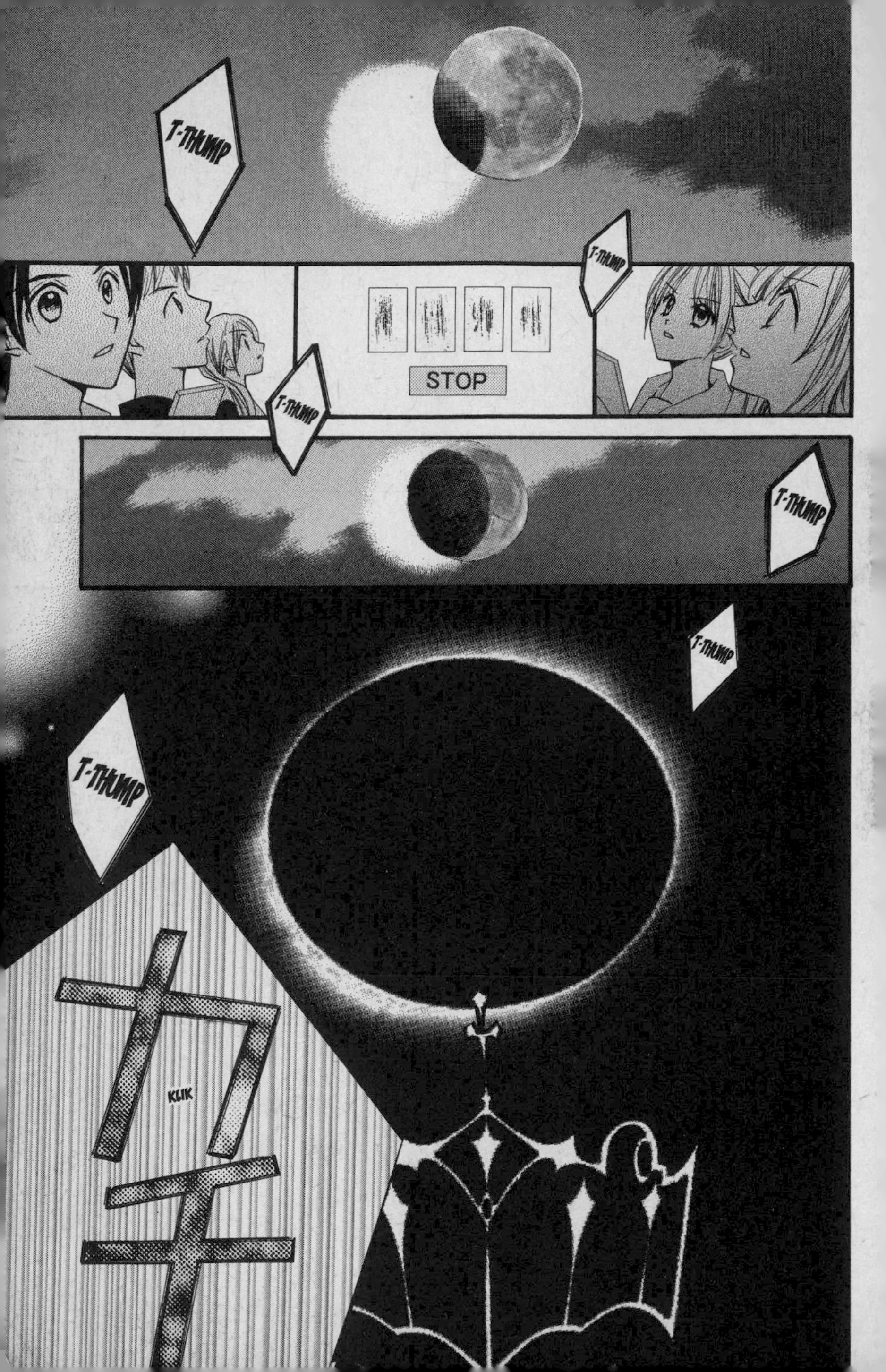
T-THUMP
T-THUMP
STOP
T-THUMP
T-THUMP
T-THUMP
T-THUMP
カチ
KLIK

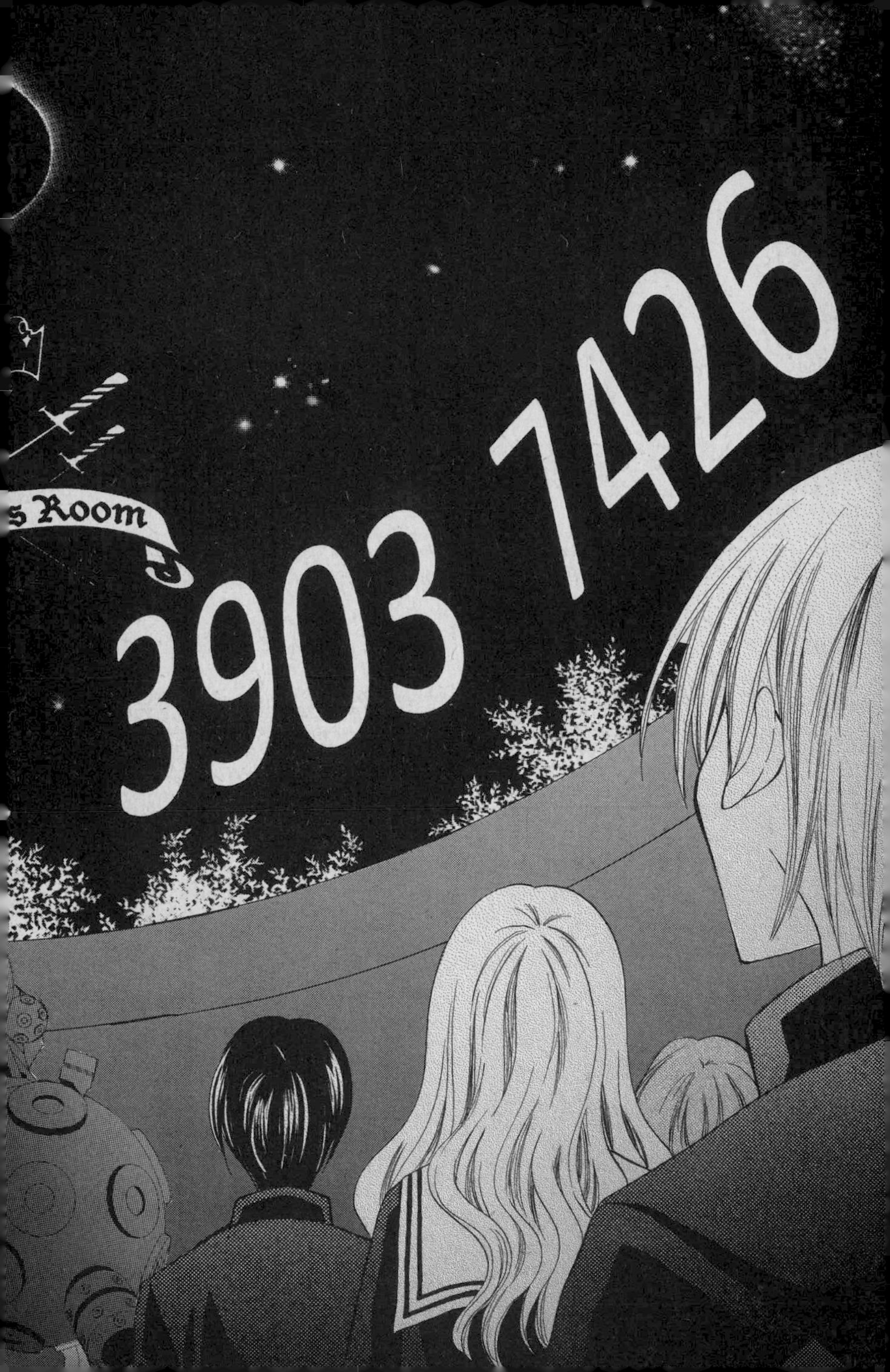
s Room
3903 7426

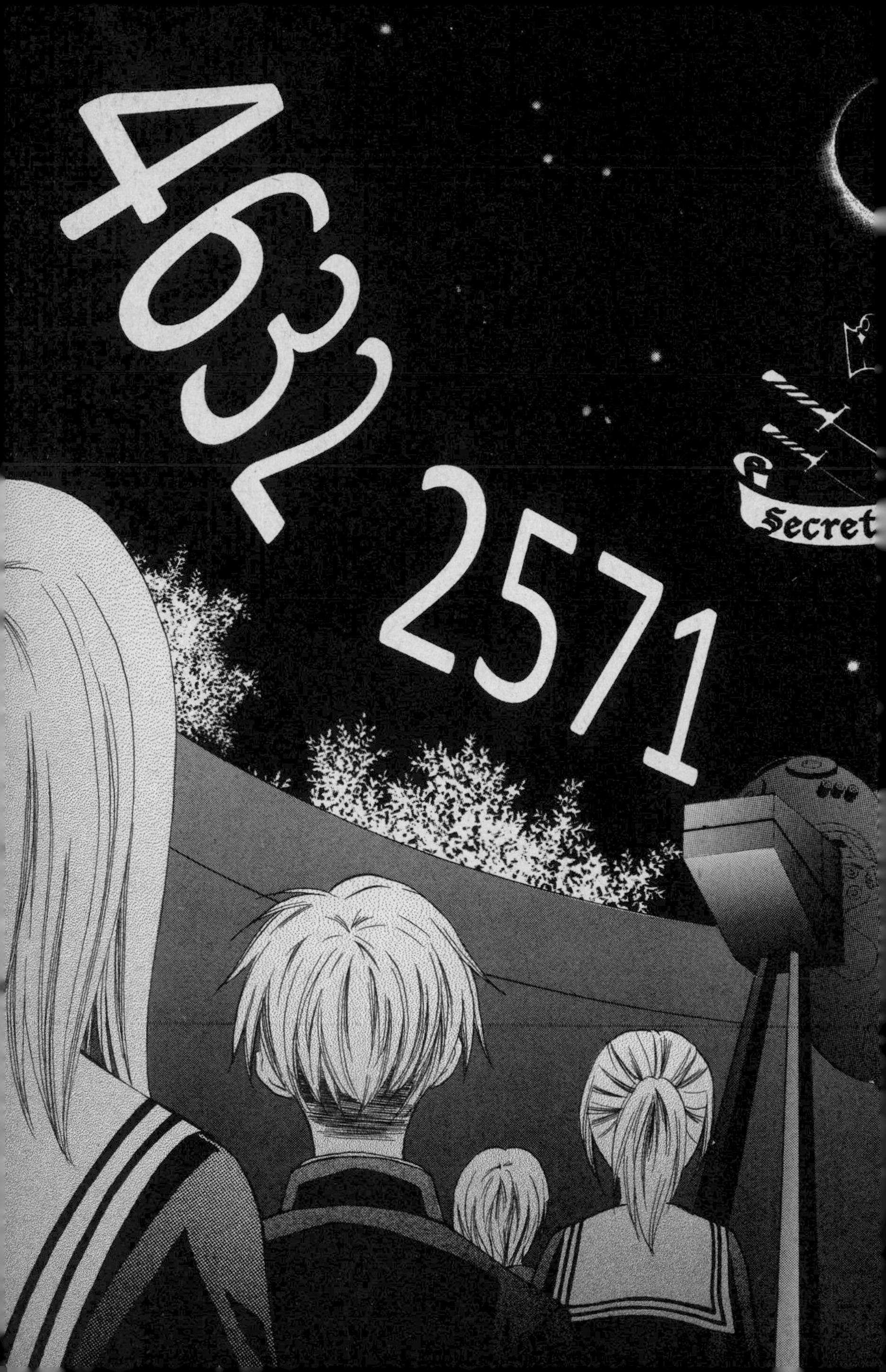
4632
2571
Secret

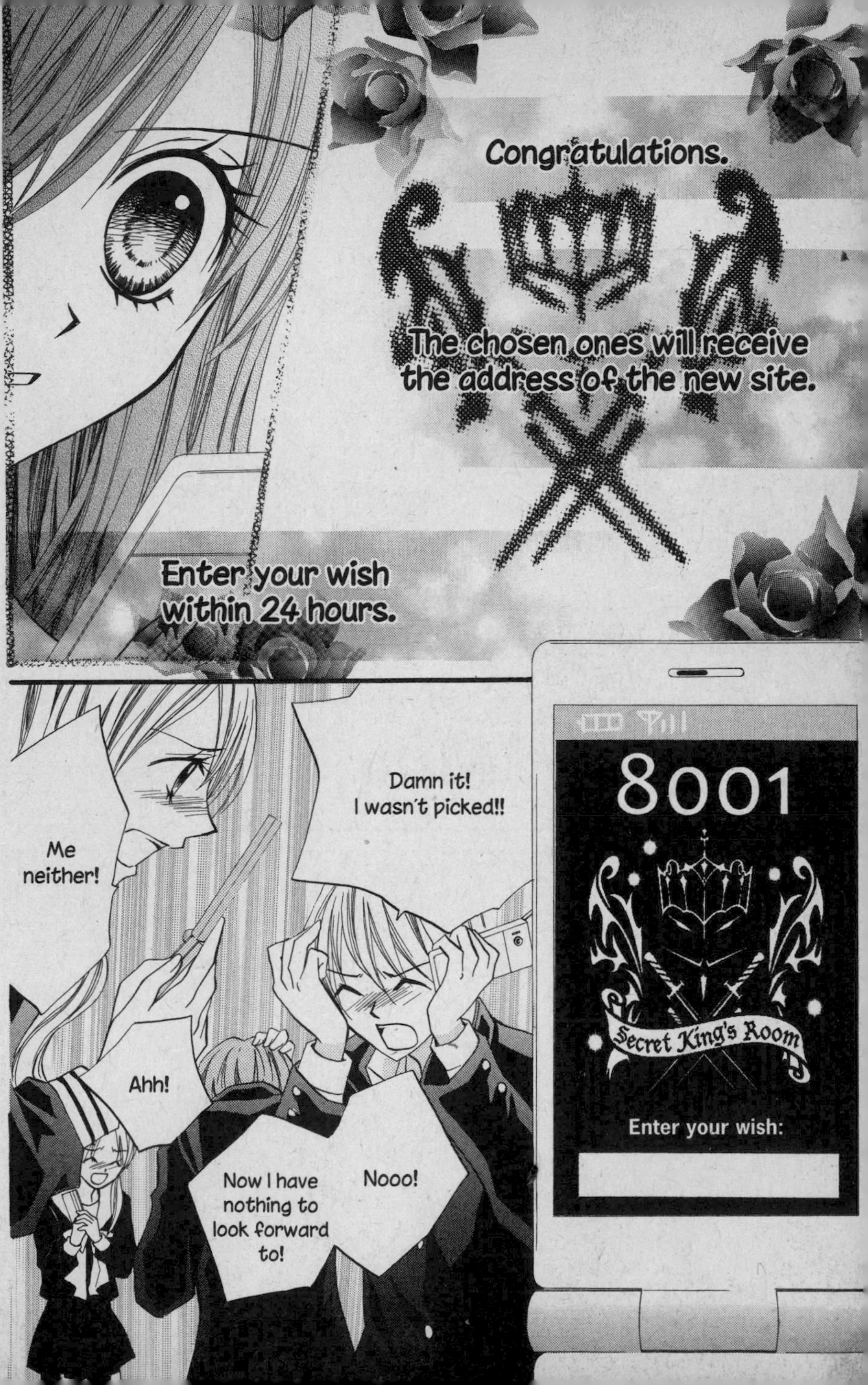
Congratulations.
The chosen ones will receive the address of the new site.
Enter your wish within 24 hours.
8001
Secret King's Room
Enter your wish:
Damn it! I wasn't picked!!
Me neither!
Nooo!
Ahh!
Now I have nothing to look forward to!

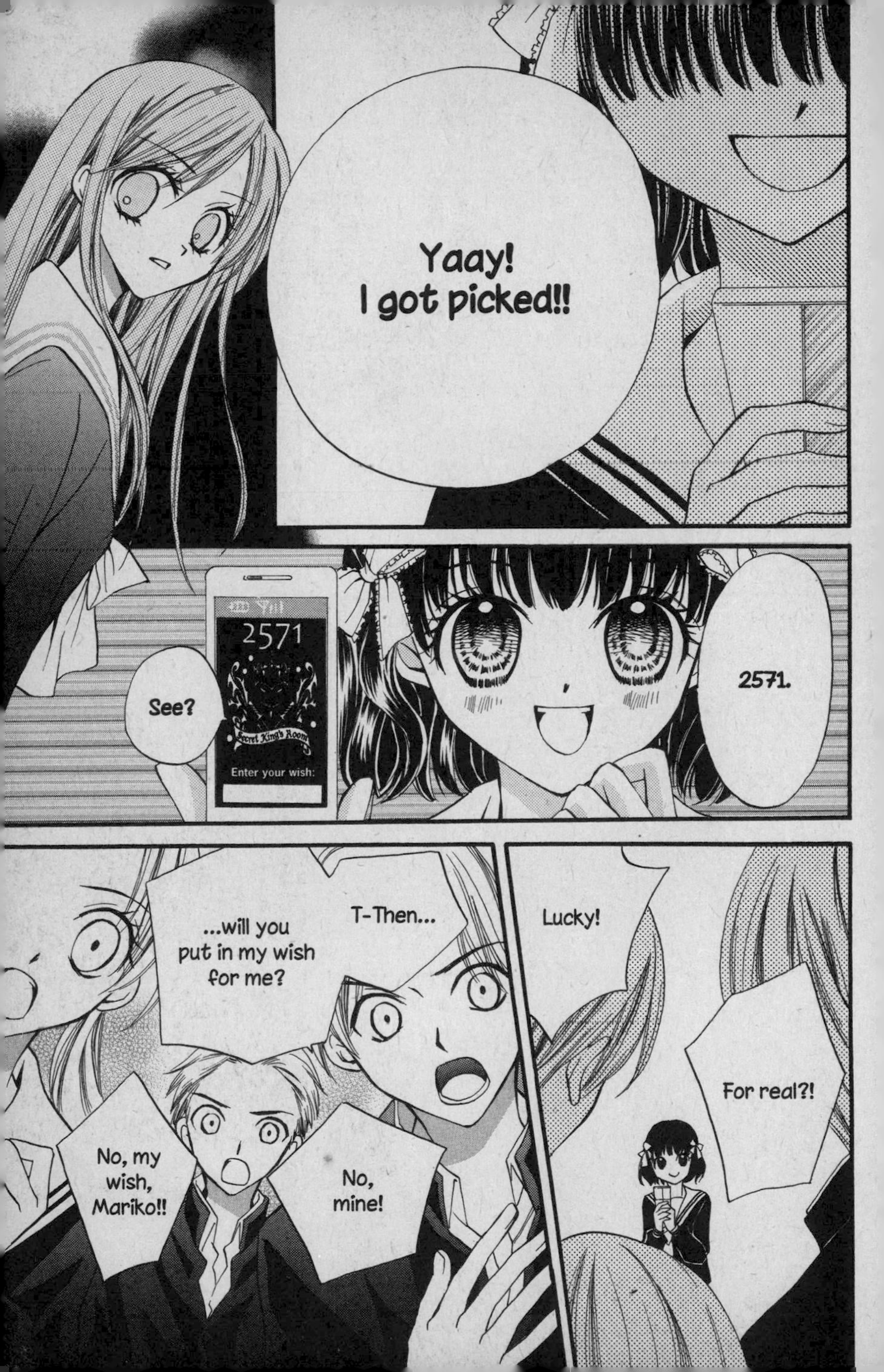
Yaay!
I got picked!!
2571.
2571
Secret King's Room
Enter your wish:
See?
Lucky!
For real?!
T-Then...
...will you put in my wish for me?
No, mine!
No, my wish, Mariko!!

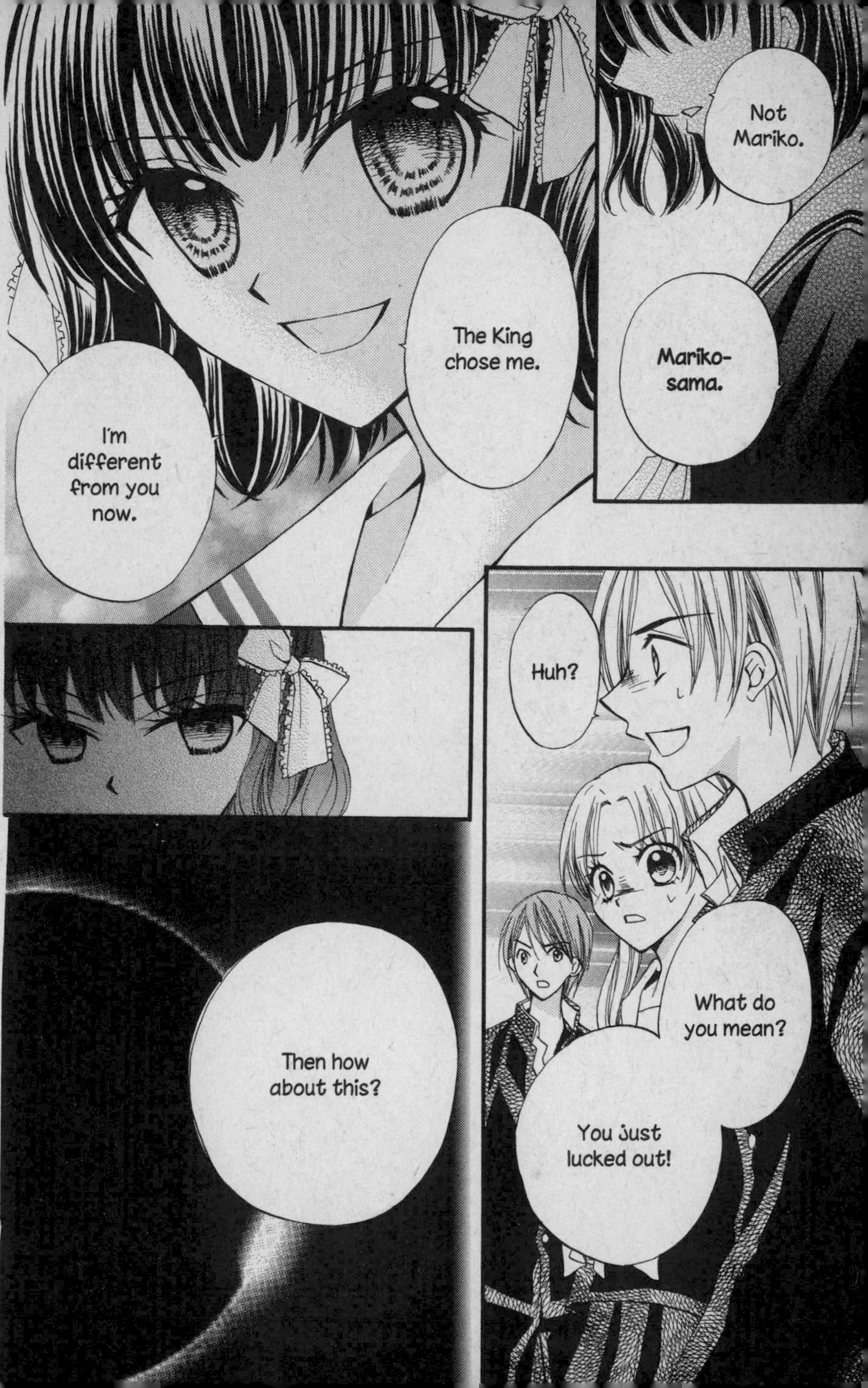
Not Mariko.
Mariko-sama.
The King chose me.
I'm different from you now.
Huh?
What do you mean?
You just lucked out!
Then how about this?

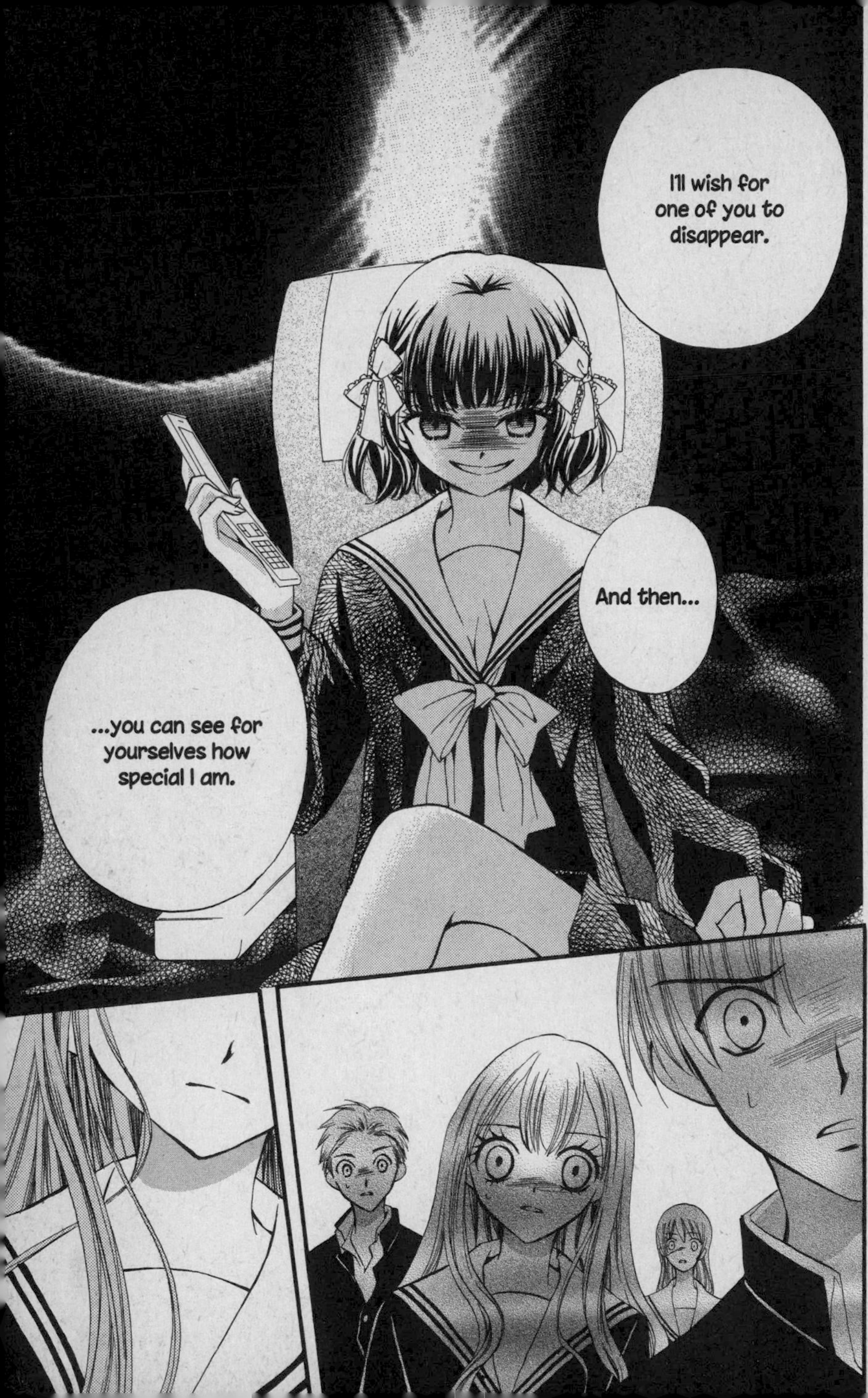
I'll wish for one of you to disappear.
And then...
...you can see for yourselves how special I am.

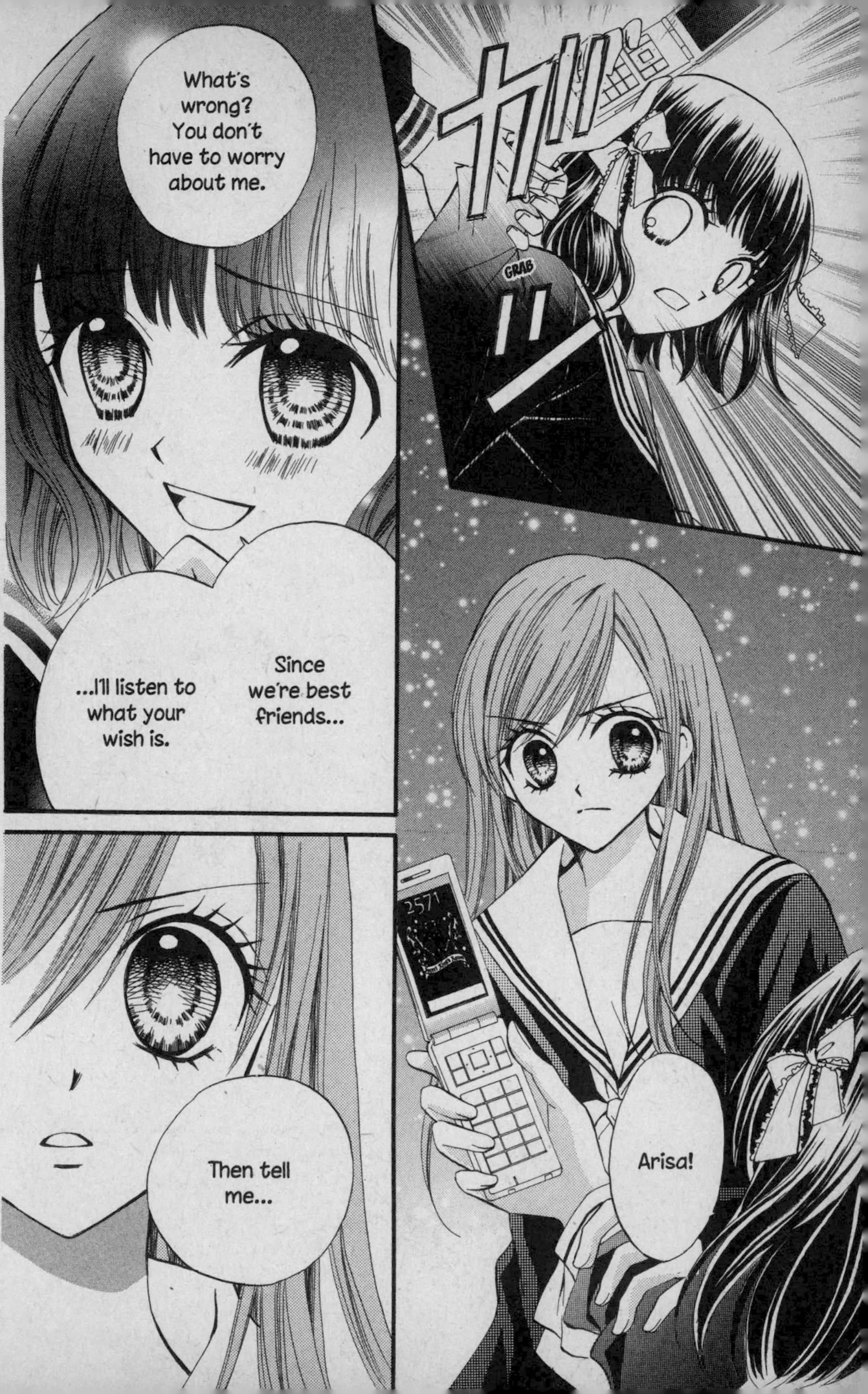

カッ
GRAB
What's wrong? You don't have to worry about me.
Since we're best friends...
...I'll listen to what your wish is.
Arisa!
Then tell me...

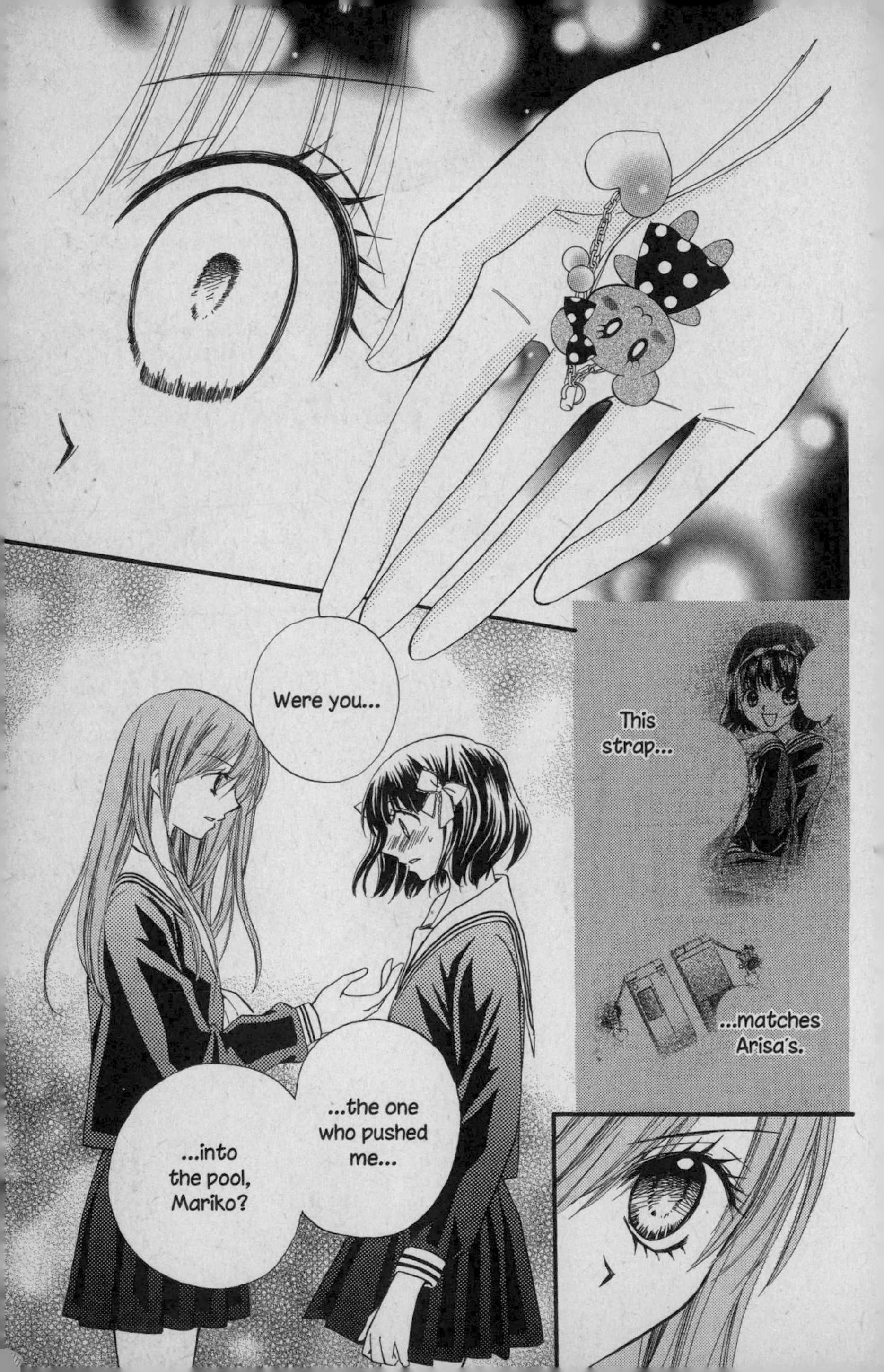
This strap...
...matches Arisa's.
Were you...
...the one who pushed me...
...into the pool, Mariko?

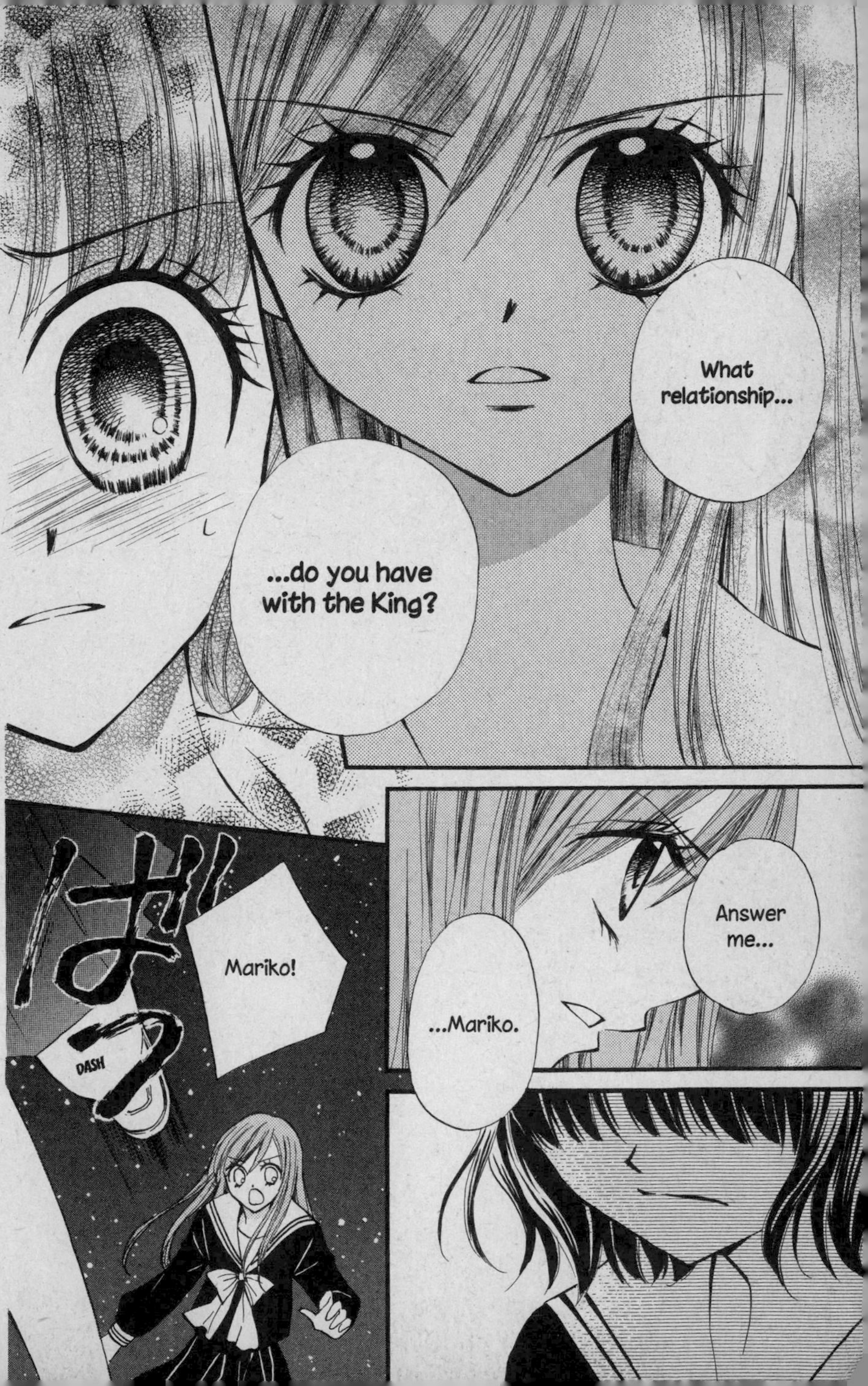
What relationship...
...do you have with the King?
Answer me...
...Mariko.
Mariko!
DASH

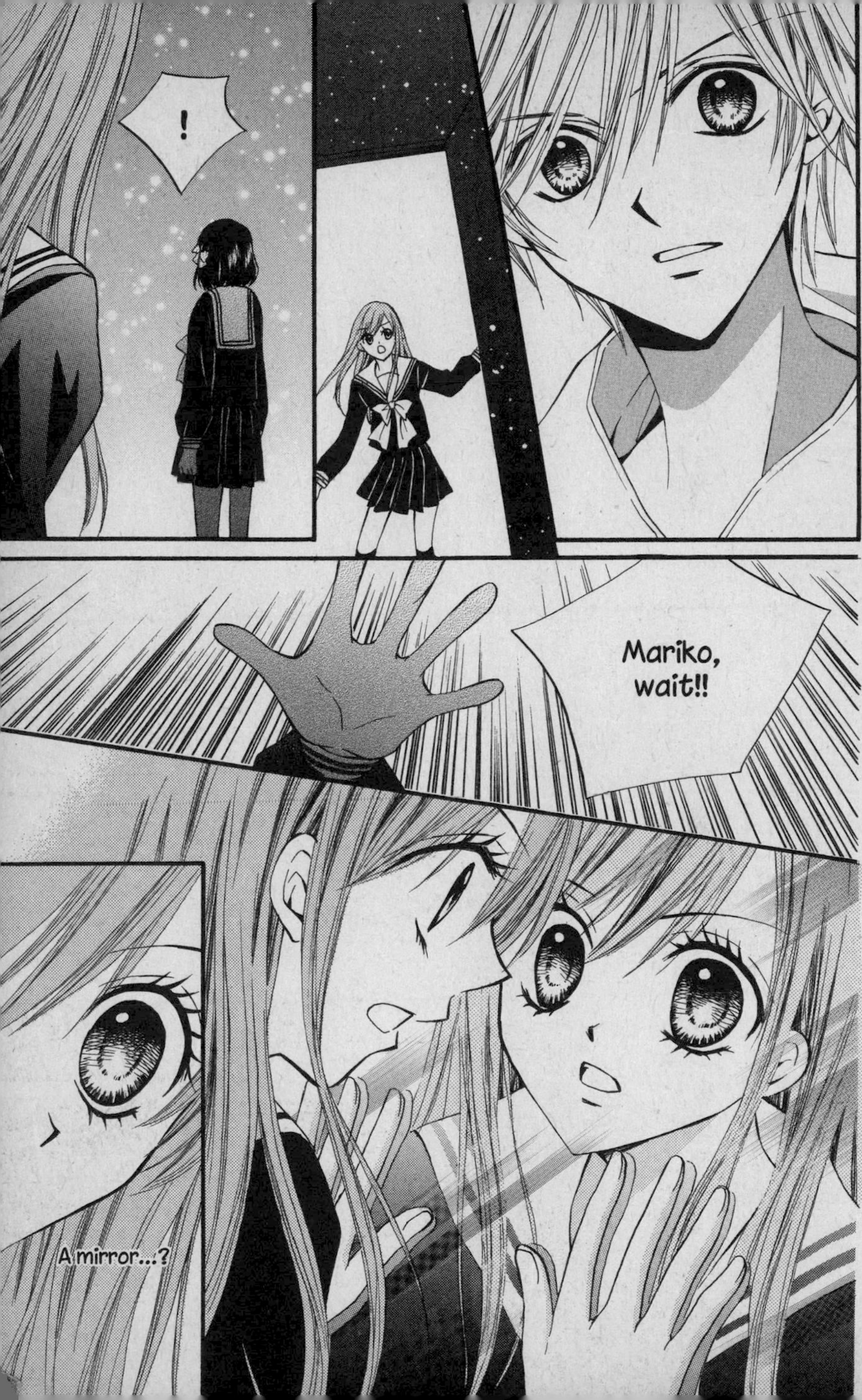
!
Mariko, wait!!
A mirror...?

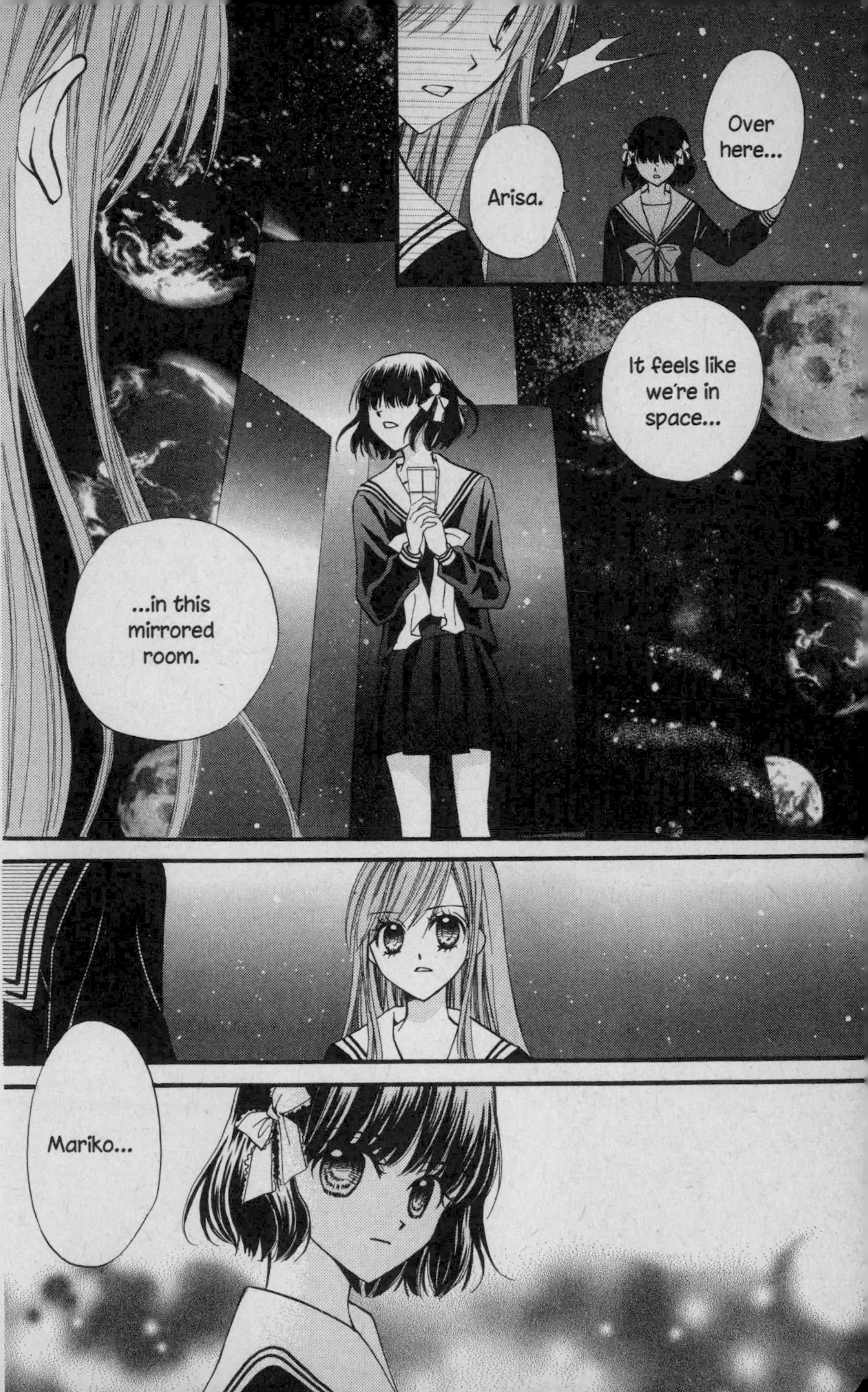
Over here...
Arisa.
It feels like we're in space...
...in this mirrored room.
Mariko...

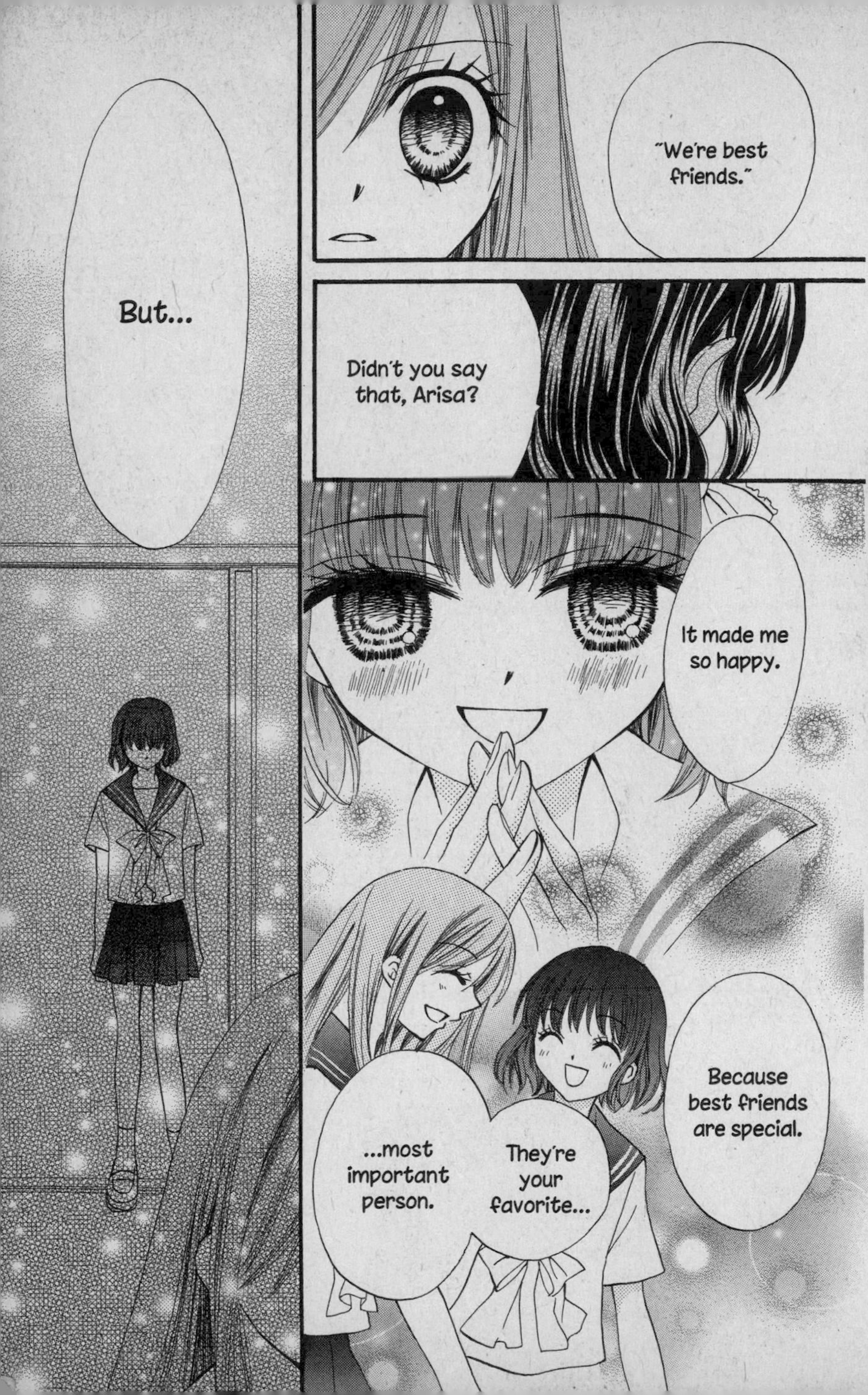
"We're best friends."
Didn't you say that, Arisa?
It made me so happy.
Because best friends are special.
They're your favorite...
...most important person.
But...

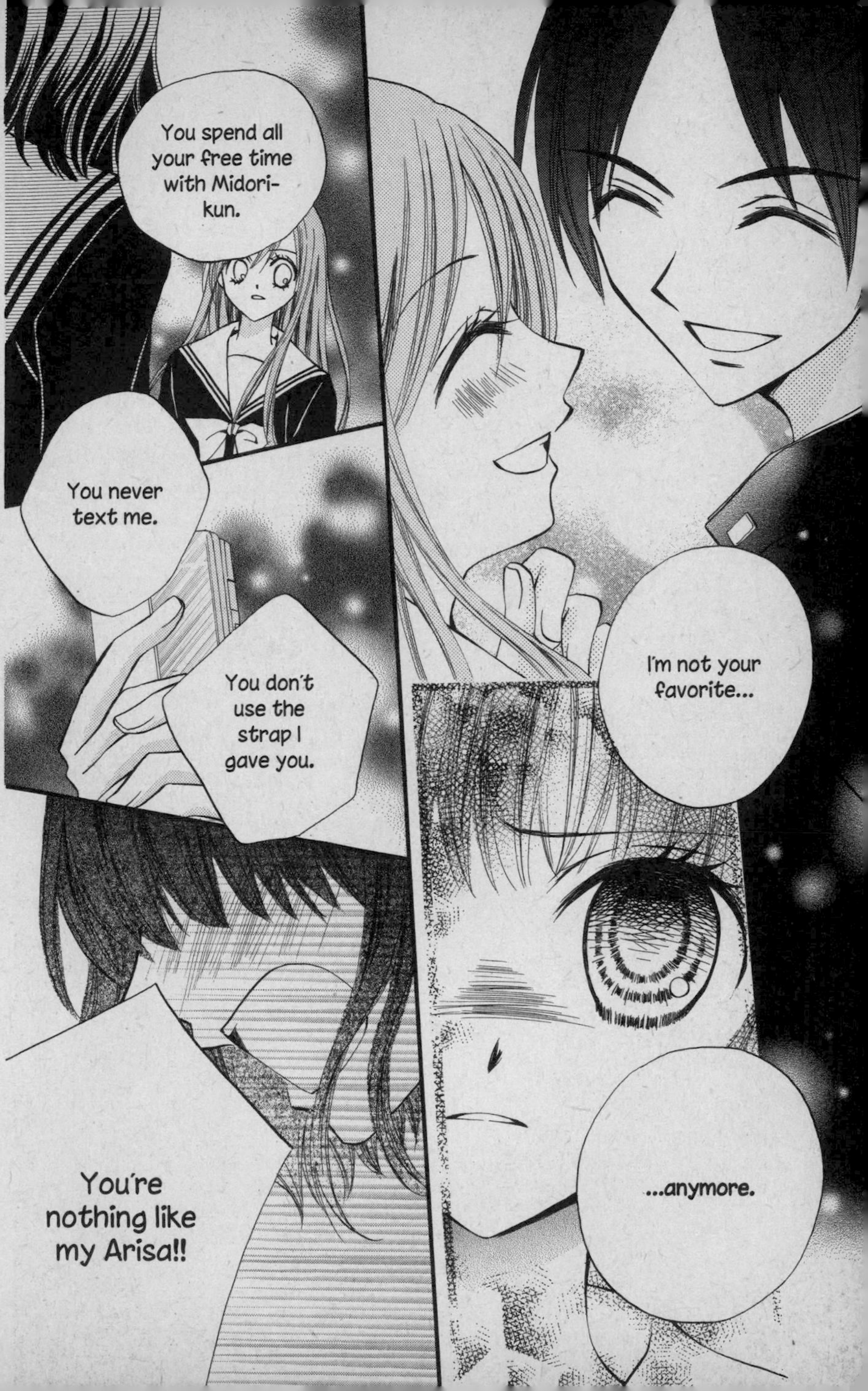
I'm not your favorite...
...anymore.
You spend all your free time with Midori-kun.
You never text me.
You don't use the strap I gave you.
You're nothing like my Arisa!!

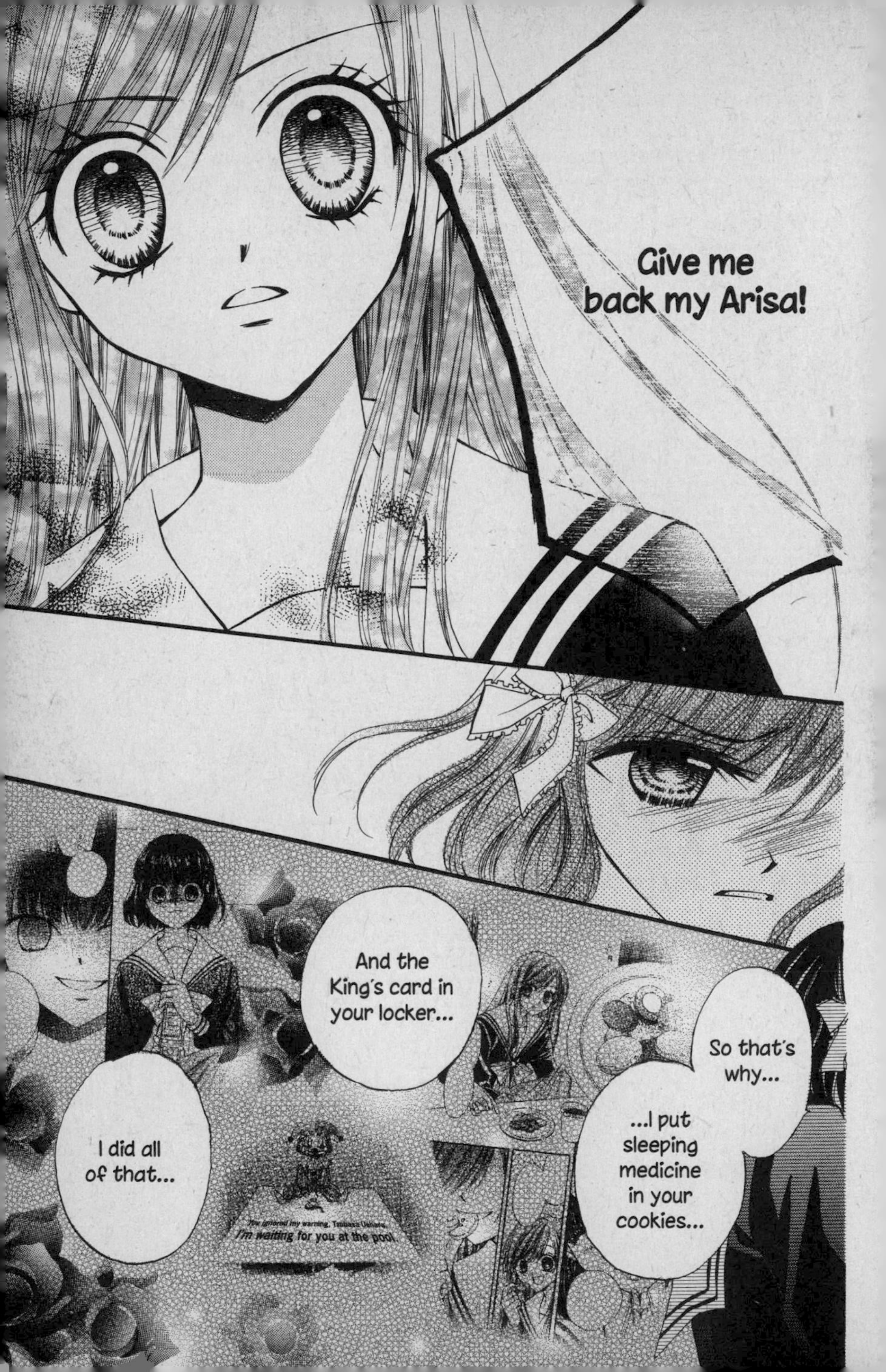
Give me back my Arisa!
So that's why...
...I put sleeping medicine in your cookies...
And the King's card in your locker...
You ignored my warning, Tsubasa Uehara.
I'm waiting for you at the pool.
I did all of that...

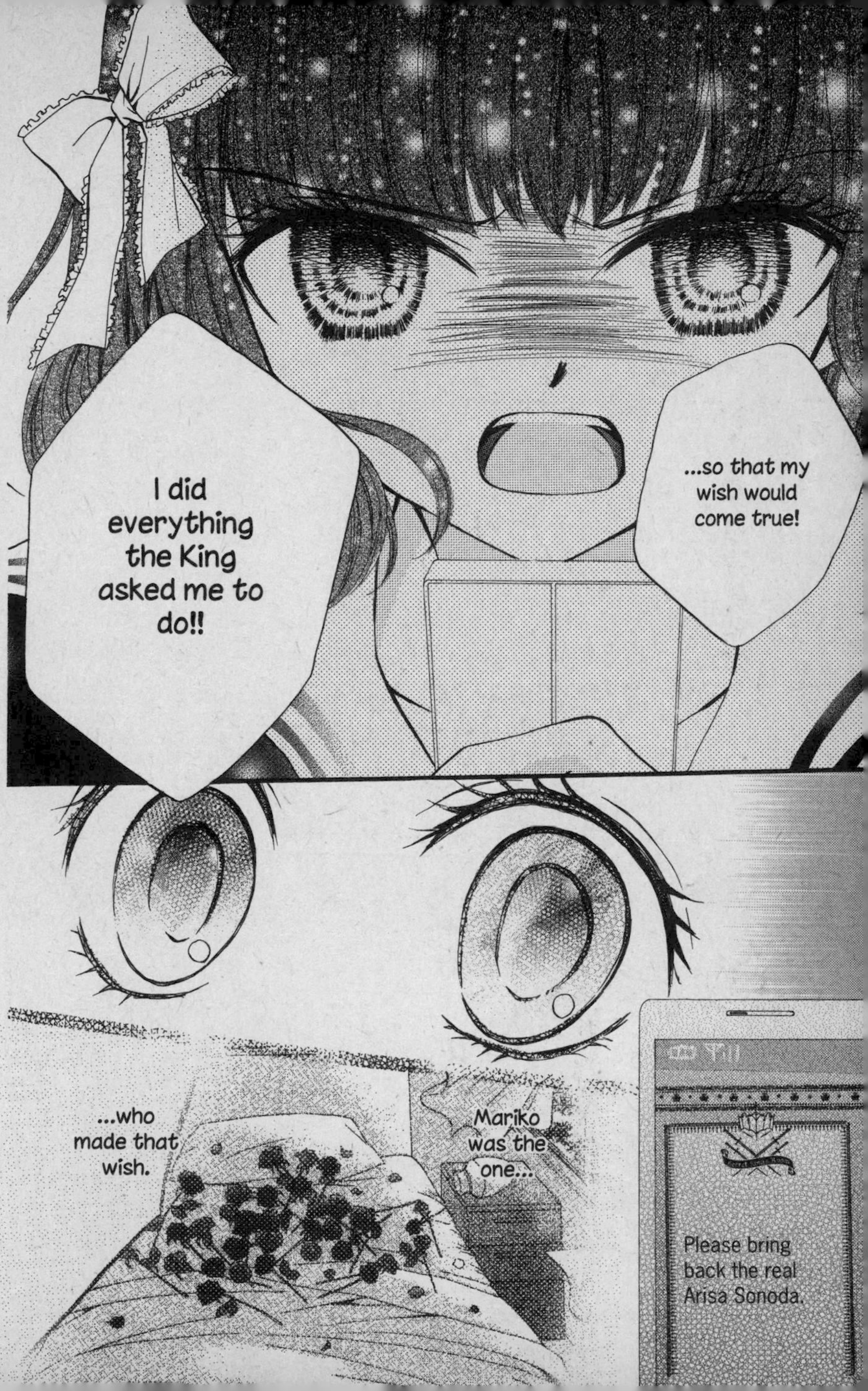
I did everything the King asked me to do!!
...so that my wish would come true!
Please bring back the real Arisa Sonoda.
Mariko was the one...
...who made that wish.

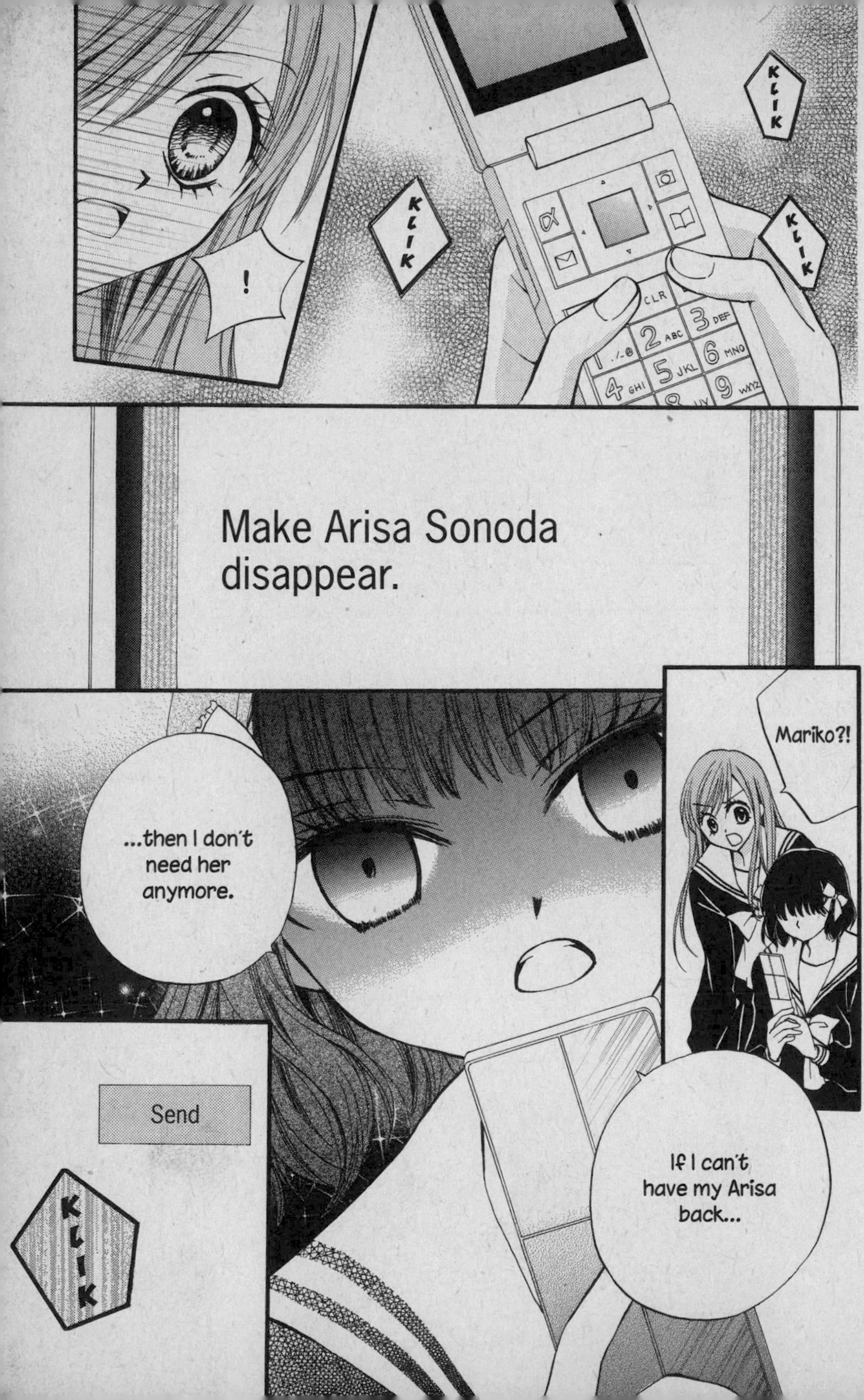
KLIK
KLIK
KLIK
!
Make Arisa Sonoda disappear.
Mariko?!
If I can't have my Arisa back...
...then I don't need her anymore.
Send
KLIK

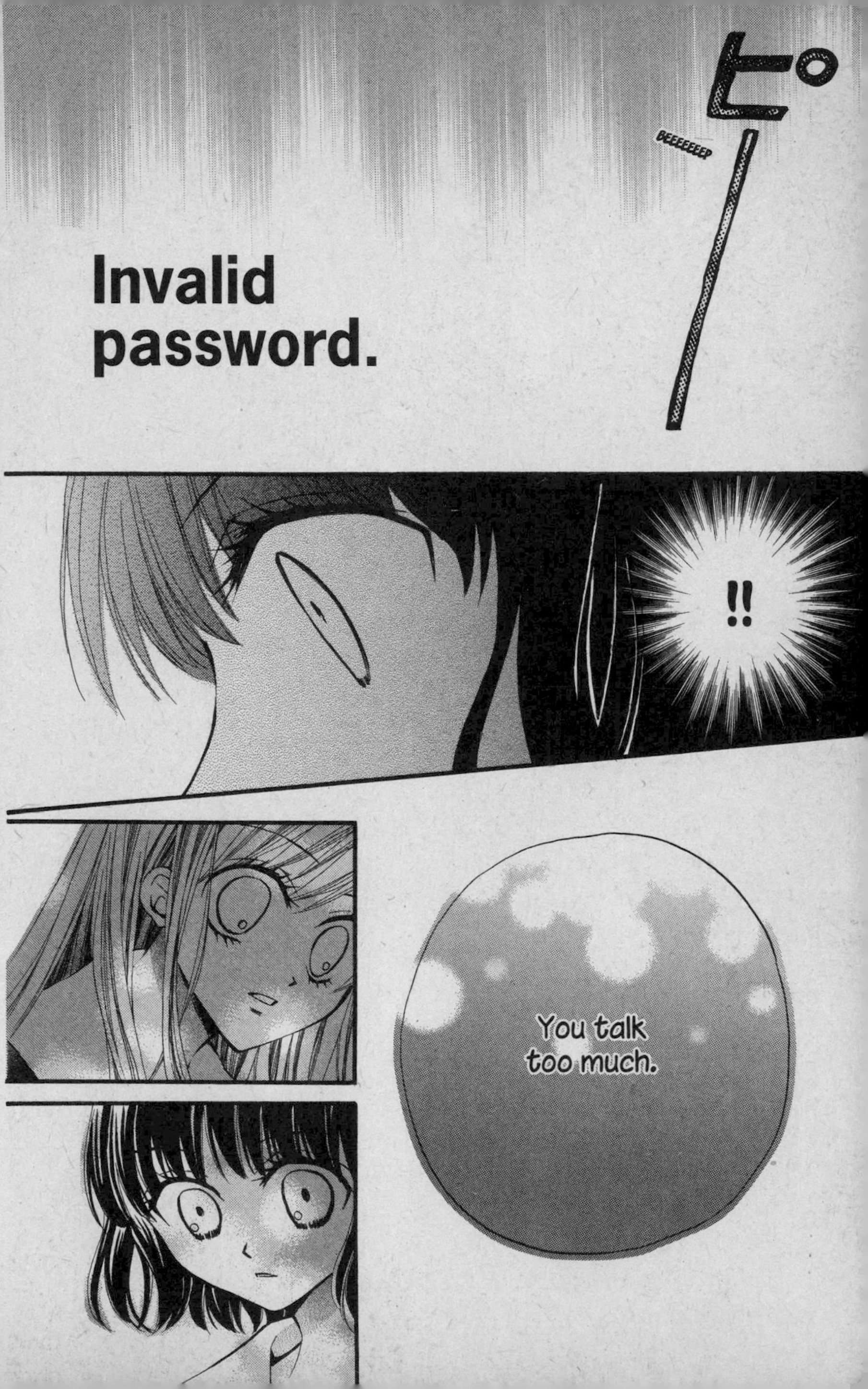
ピ
BEEEEEEEP
Invalid password.
!!
You talk too much.

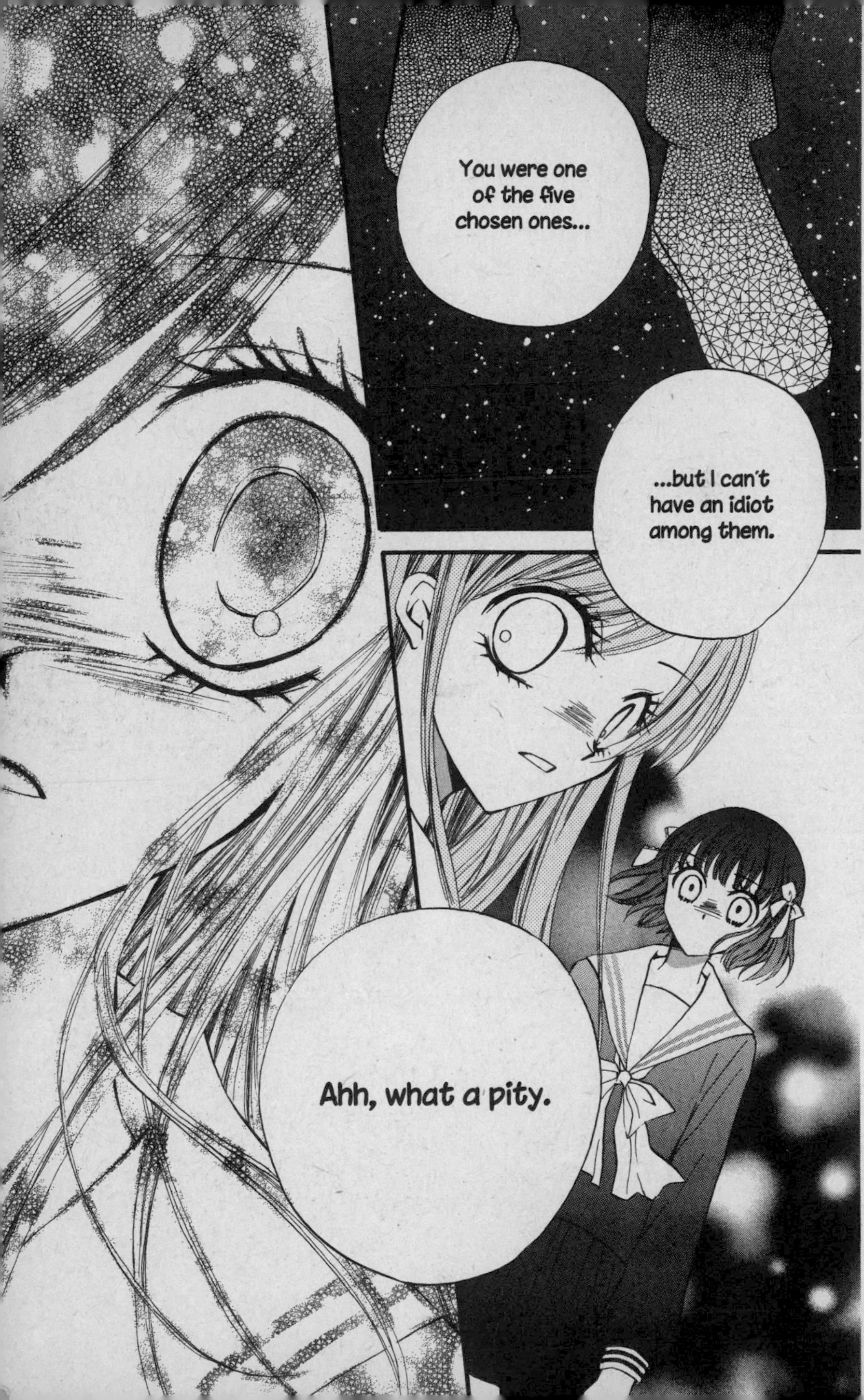
You were one of the five chosen ones...
...but I can't have an idiot among them.
Ahh, what a pity.

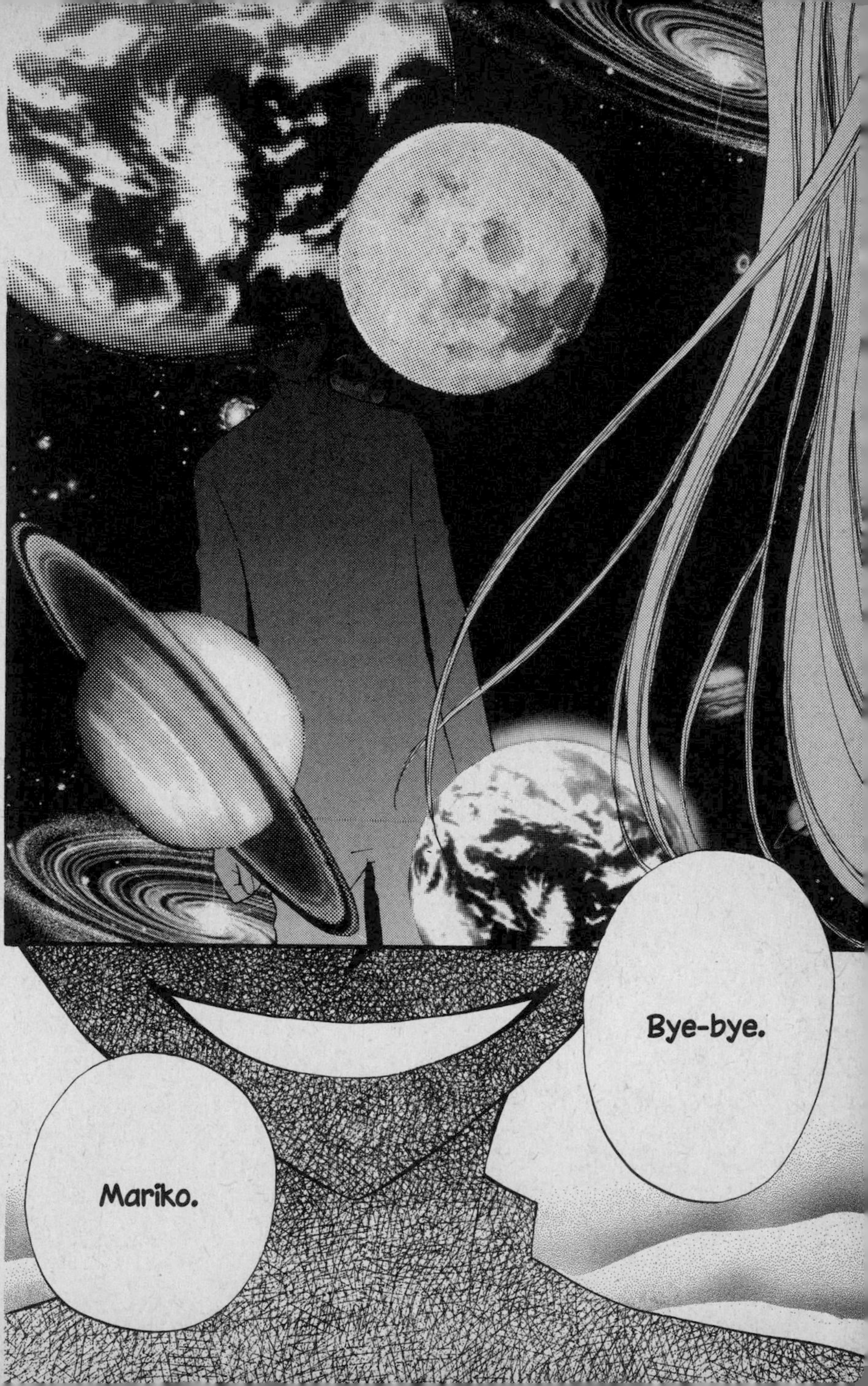
Bye-bye.
Mariko.

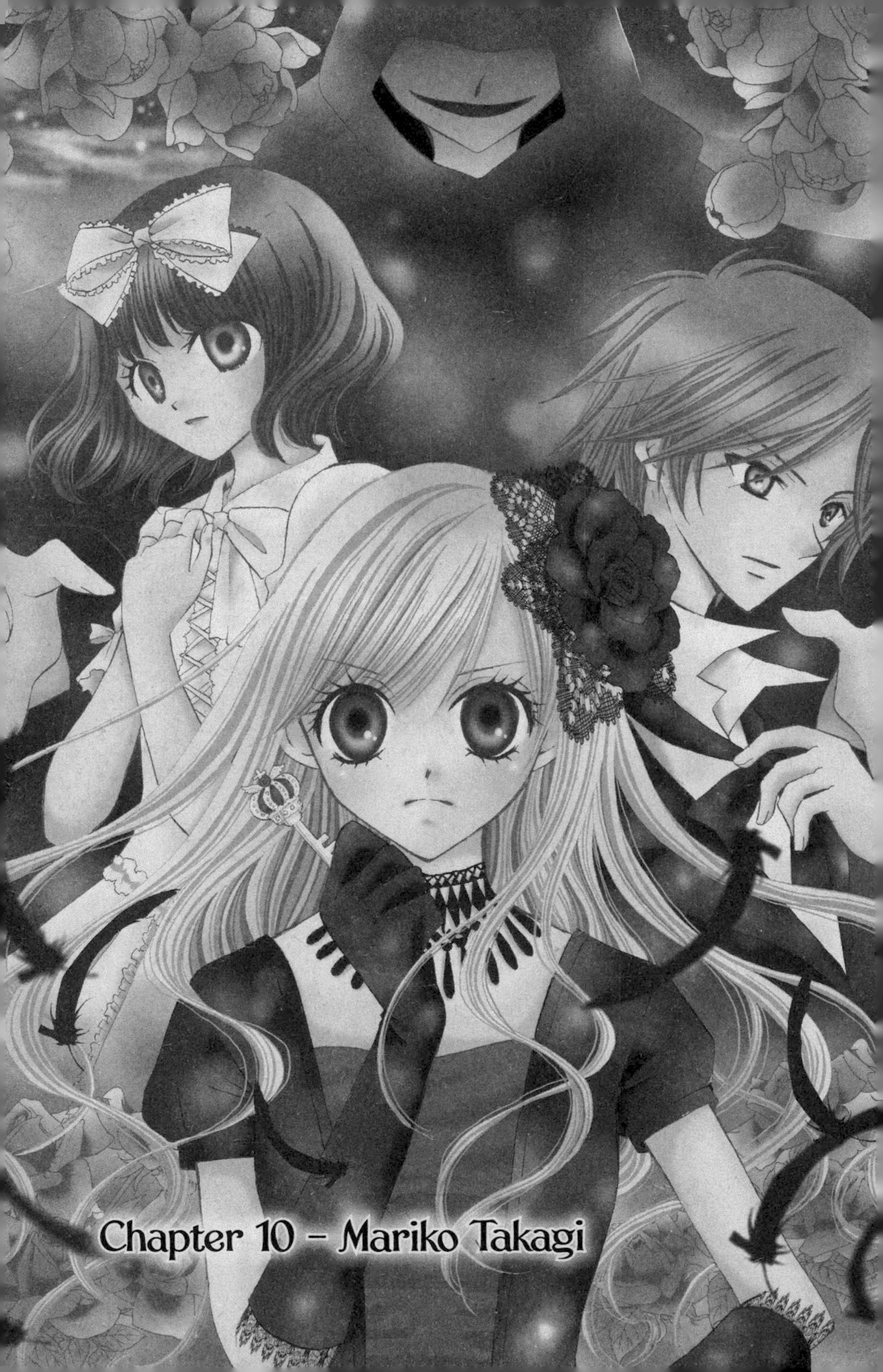
Chapter 10 - Mariko Takagi

ARISA

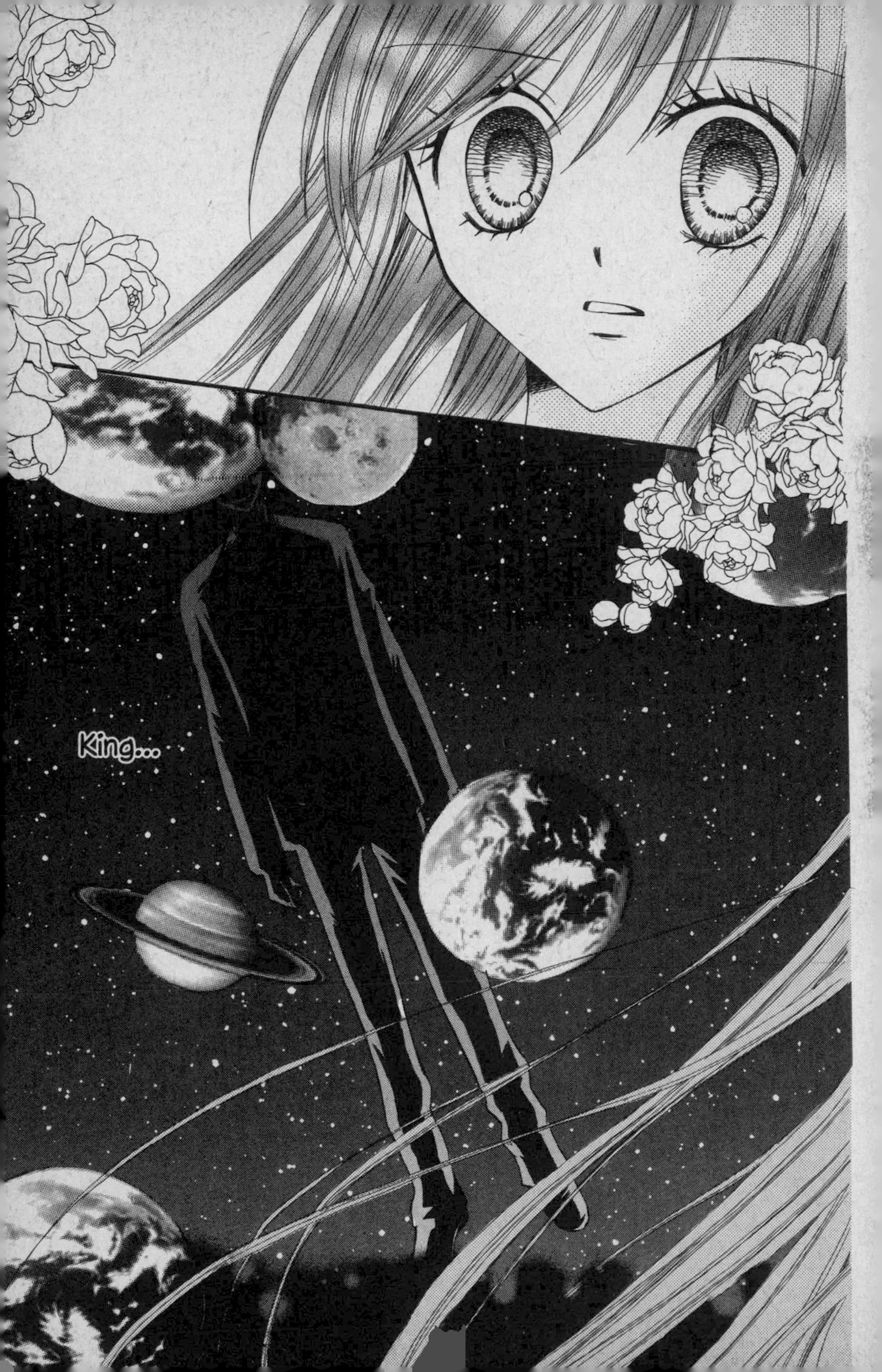
King...

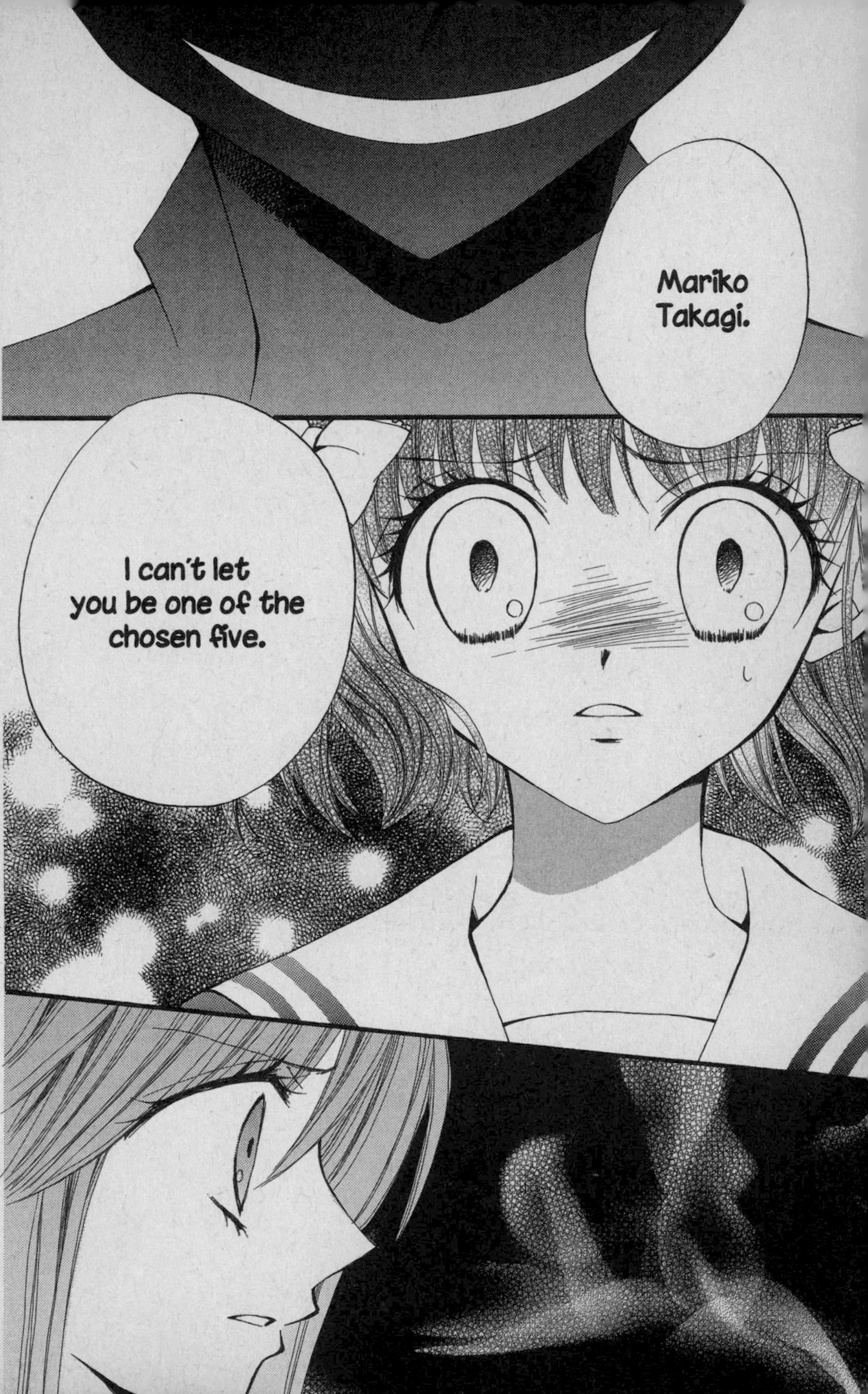
Mariko Takagi.
I can't let you be one of the chosen five.

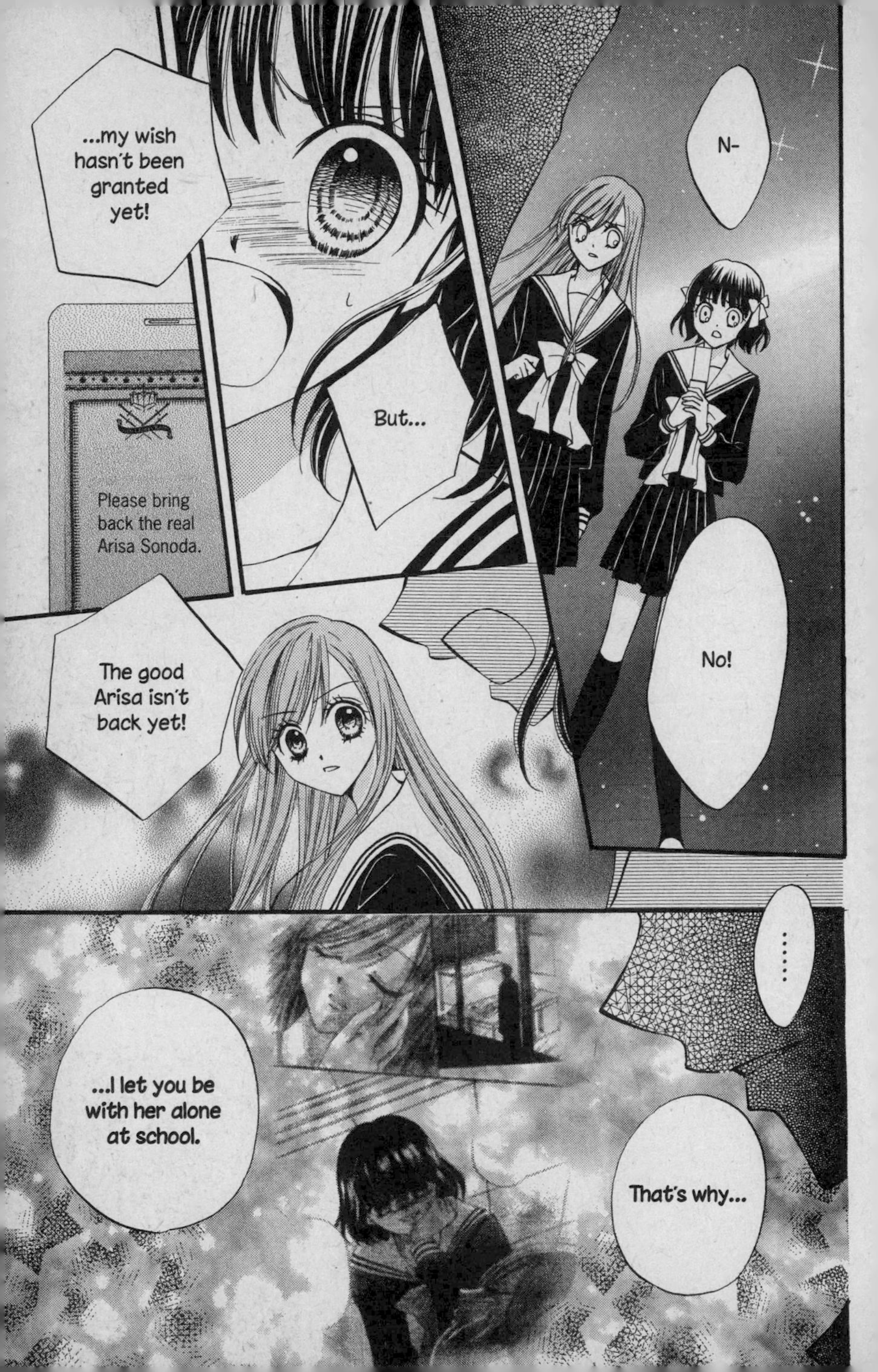
N-
No!
But...
...my wish hasn't been granted yet!
Please bring back the real Arisa Sonoda.
The good Arisa isn't back yet!
......
That's why...
...I let you be with her alone at school.

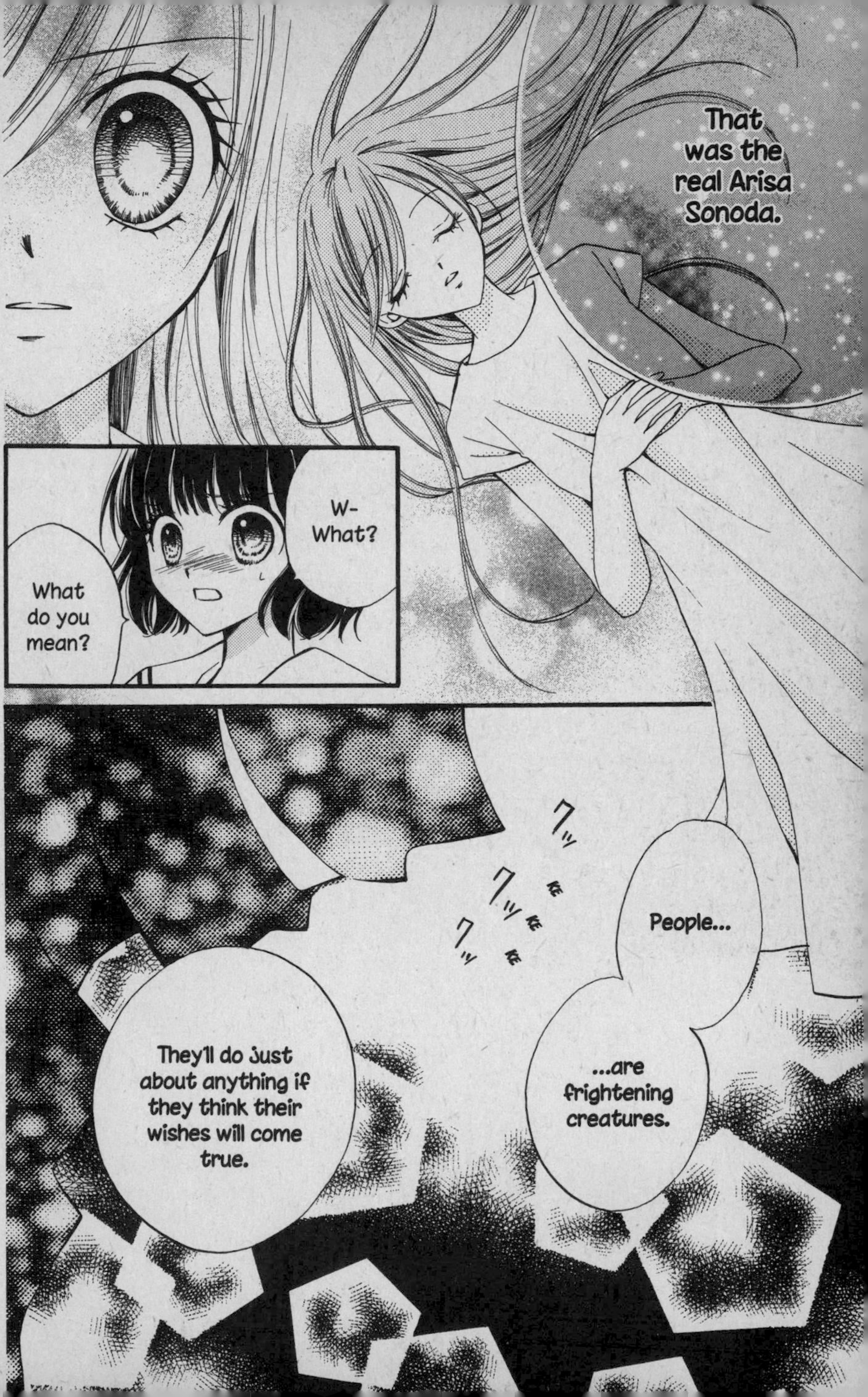
That was the real Arisa Sonoda.
W- What?
What do you mean?
People...
...are frightening creatures.
They'll do just about anything if they think their wishes will come true.

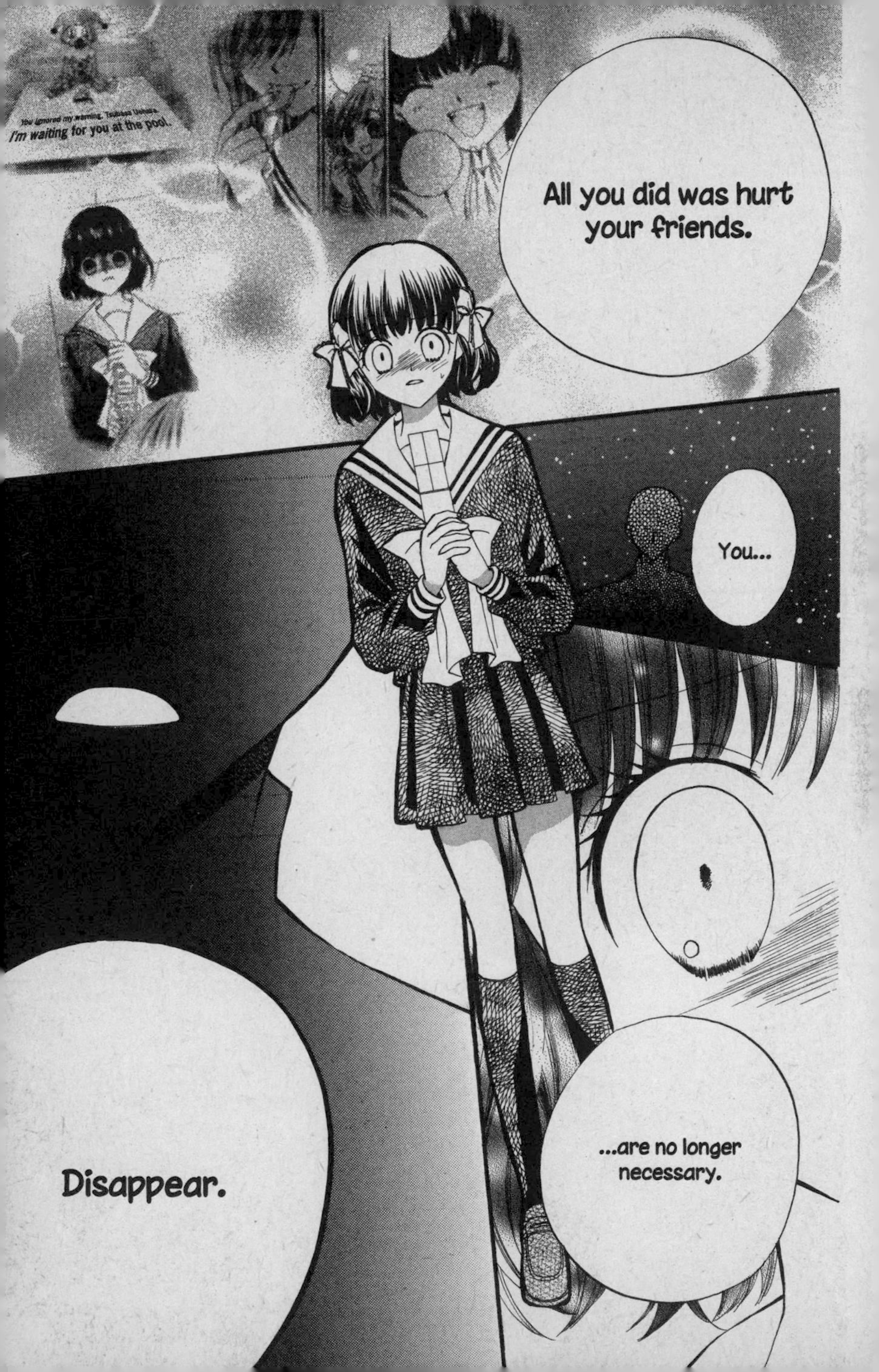
All you did was hurt your friends.
You ignored my warning, Tsubasa Uehara.
I'm waiting for you at the pool.
You...
...are no longer necessary.
Disappear.

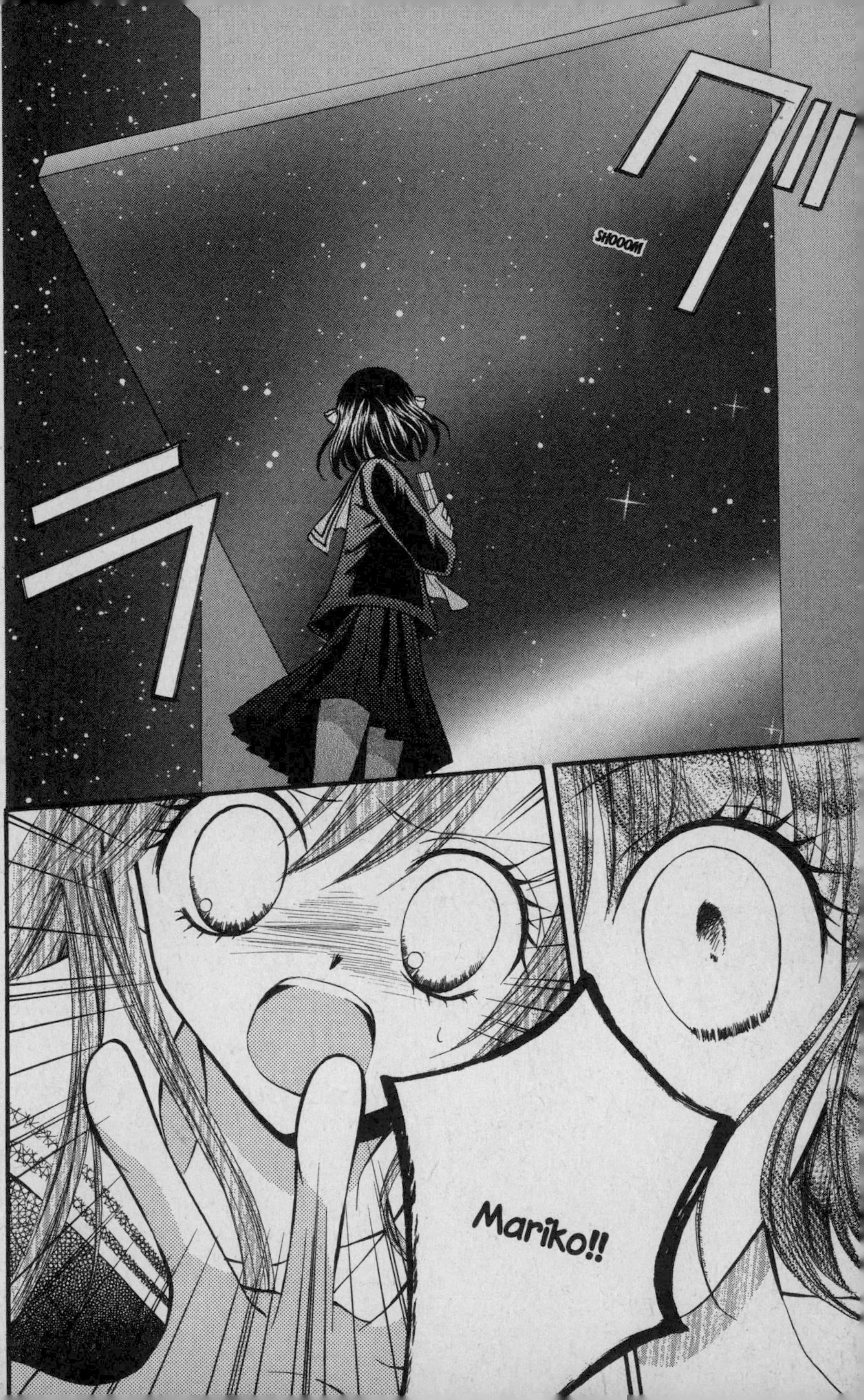
SHOOOM
Mariko!!

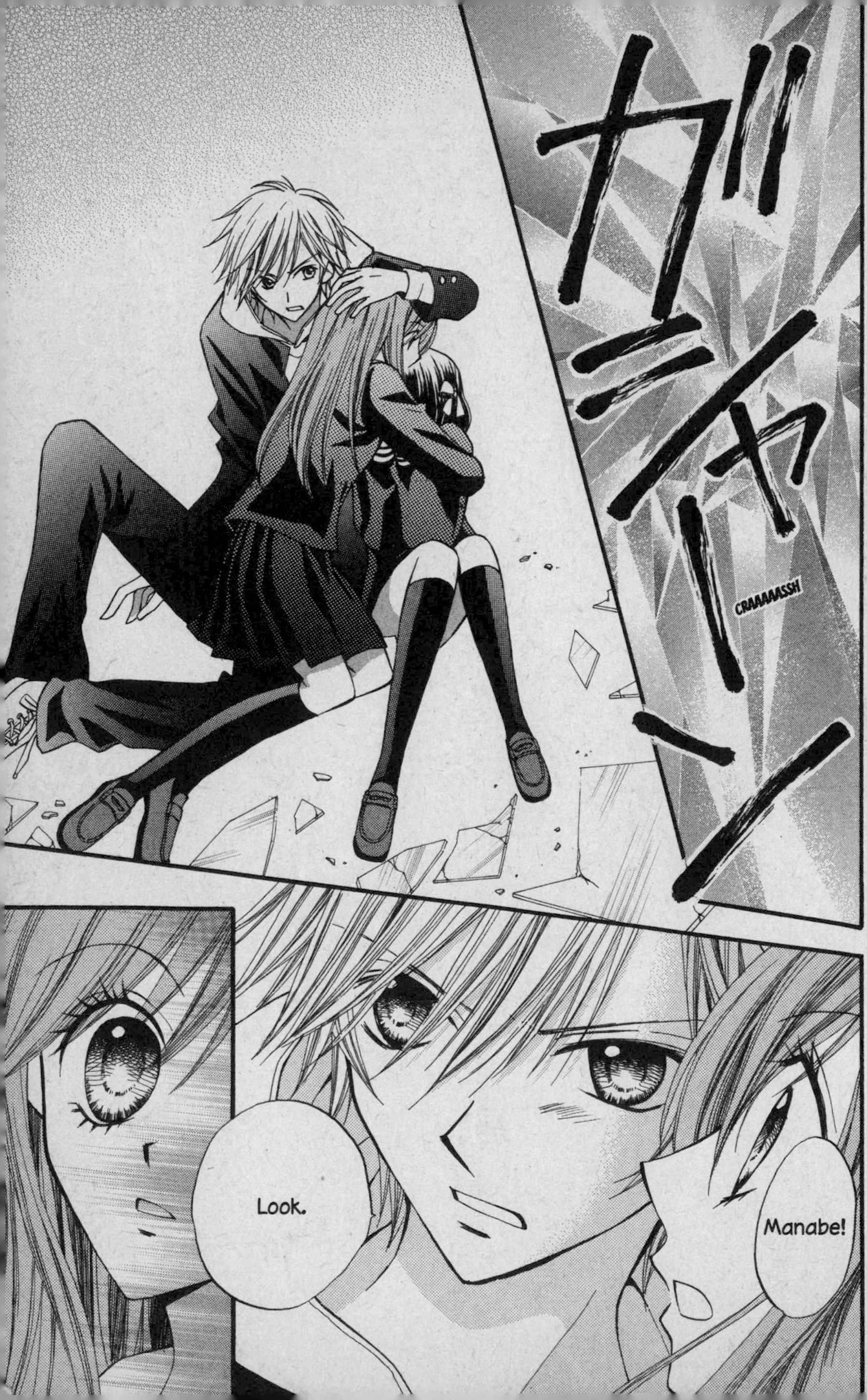
ガシャーン
CRAAAAASSH
Manabe!
Look.

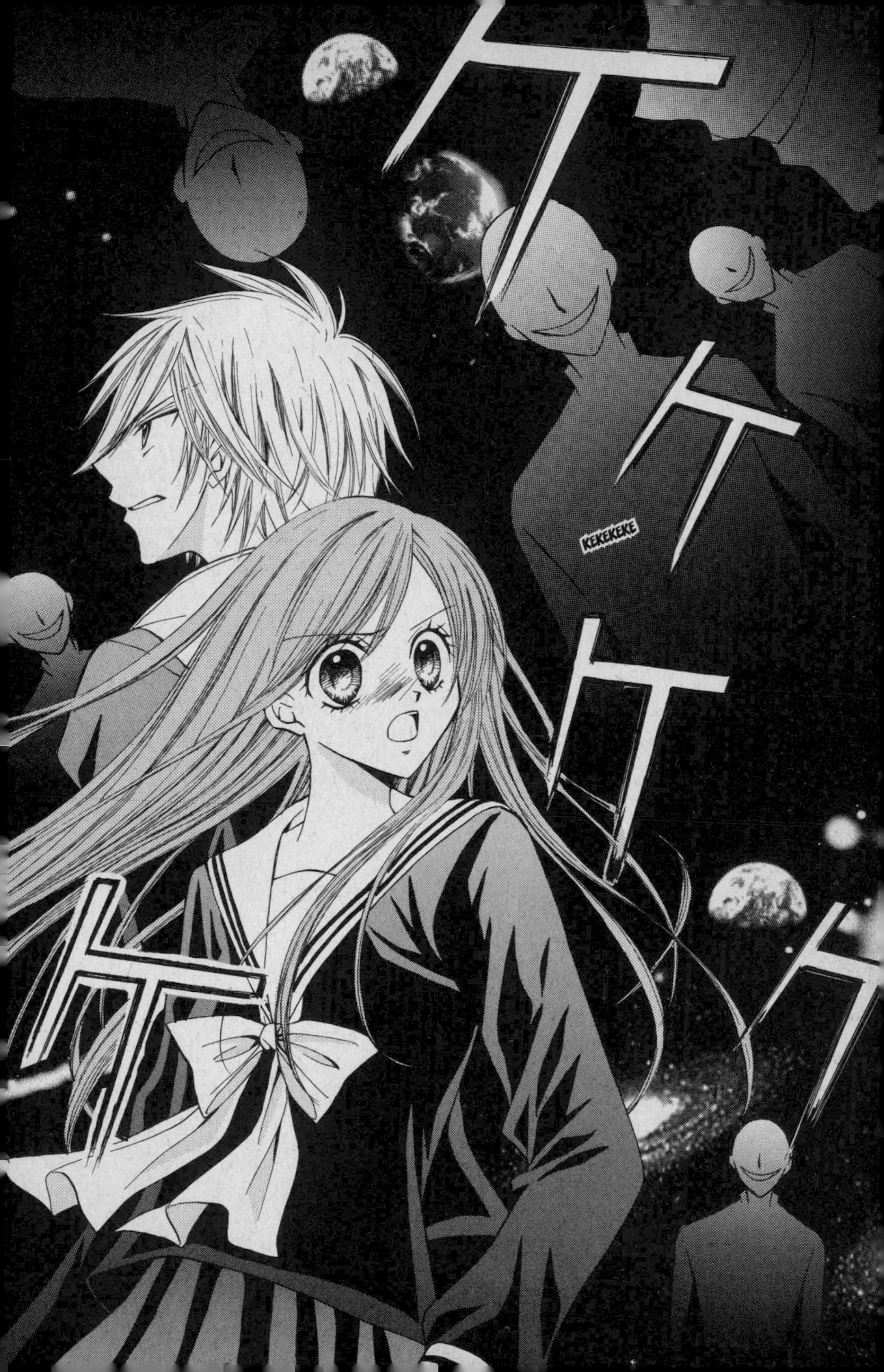
ケ
ケ
ケ
ケ
ケ
KEKEKEKE

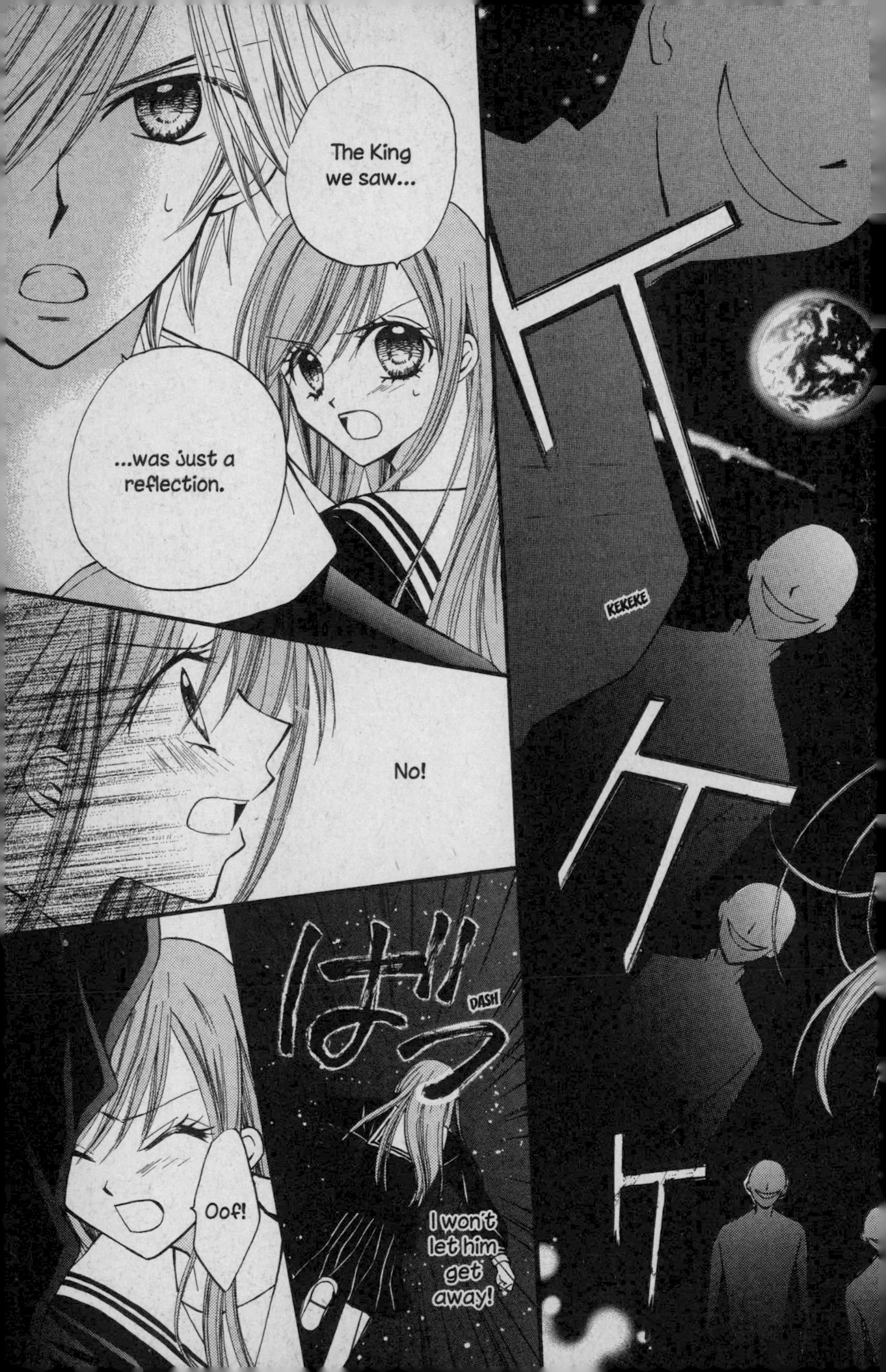
KEKEKE
The King we saw...
...was just a reflection.
No!
はっ
DASH
I won't let him get away!
Oof!

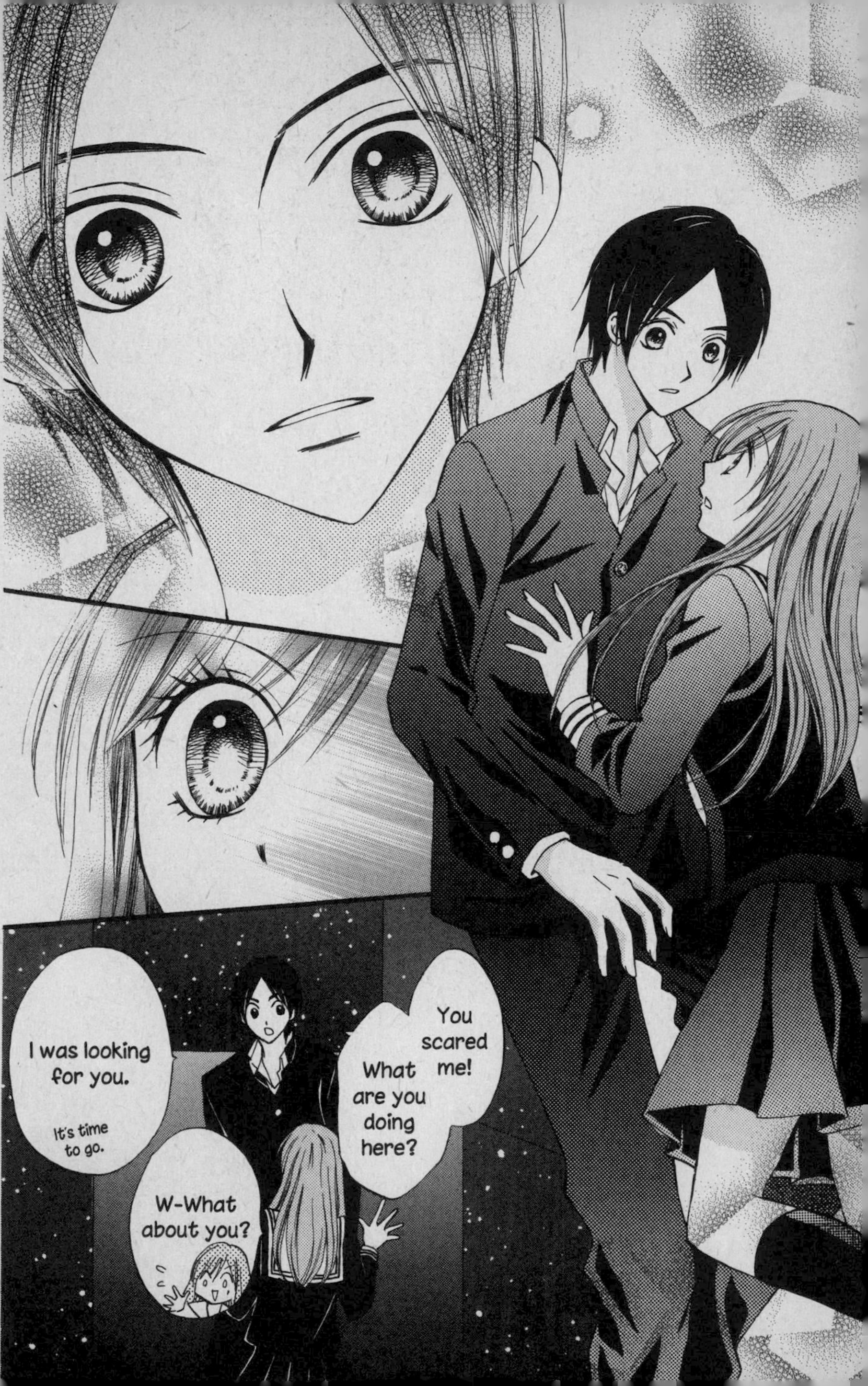

You scared me!
What are you doing here?
I was looking for you.
It's time to go.
W-What about you?

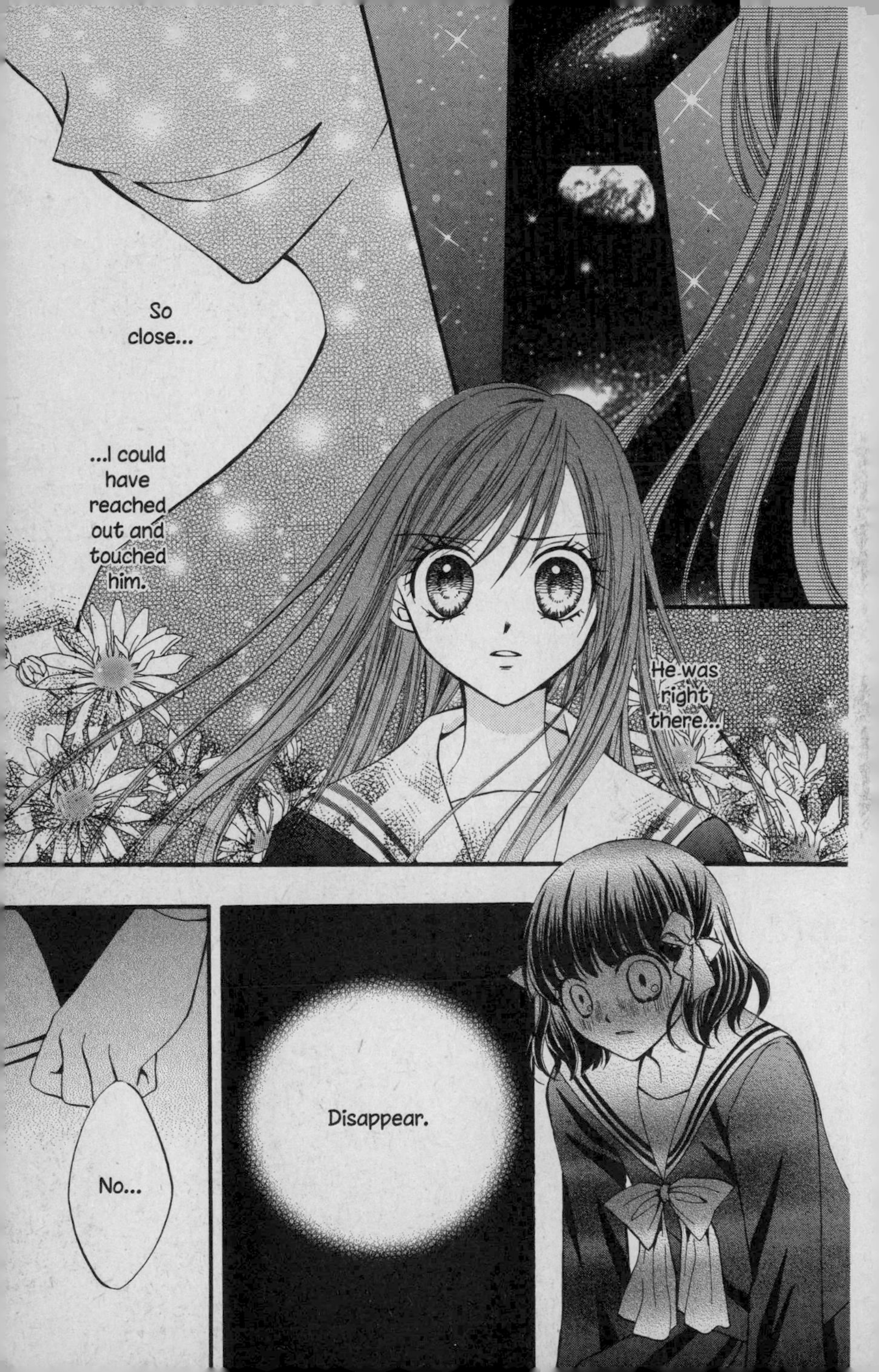
So close...
...I could have reached out and touched him.
He was right there...
Disappear.
No...

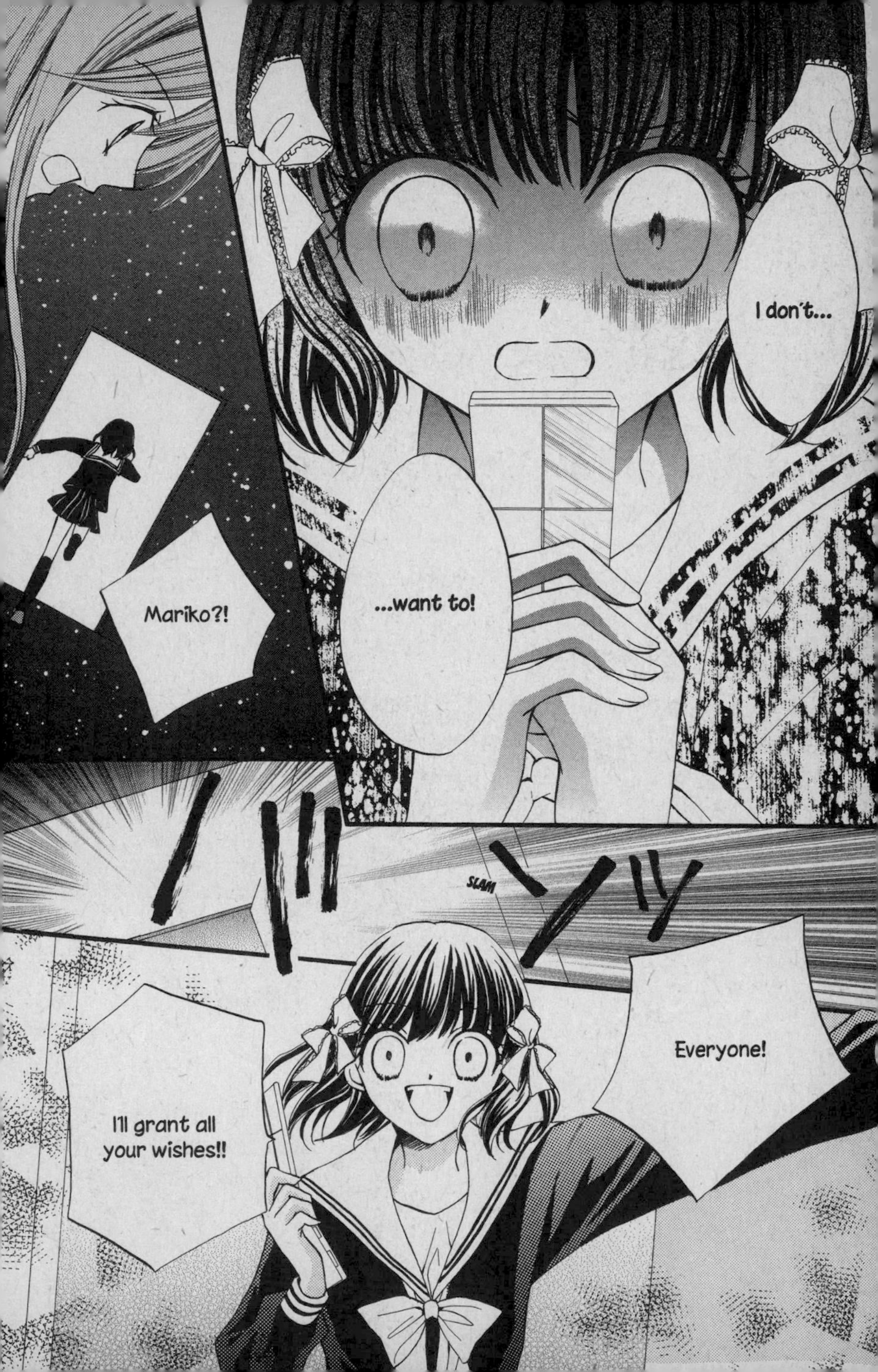
I don't...
...want to!
Mariko?!
SLAM
Everyone!
I'll grant all your wishes!!

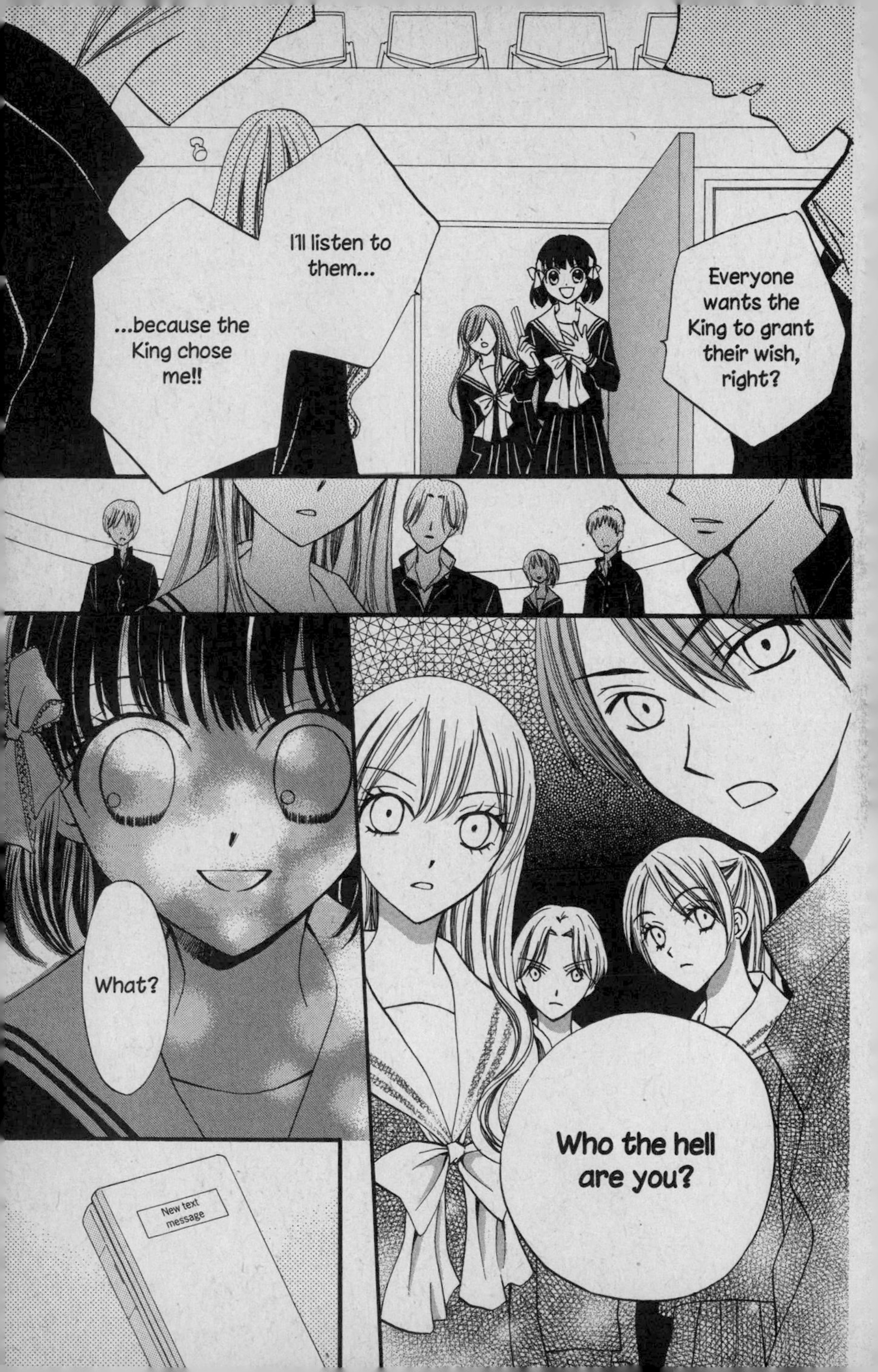
Everyone wants the King to grant their wish, right?
I'll listen to them...
...because the King chose me!!
Who the hell are you?
What?
New text message

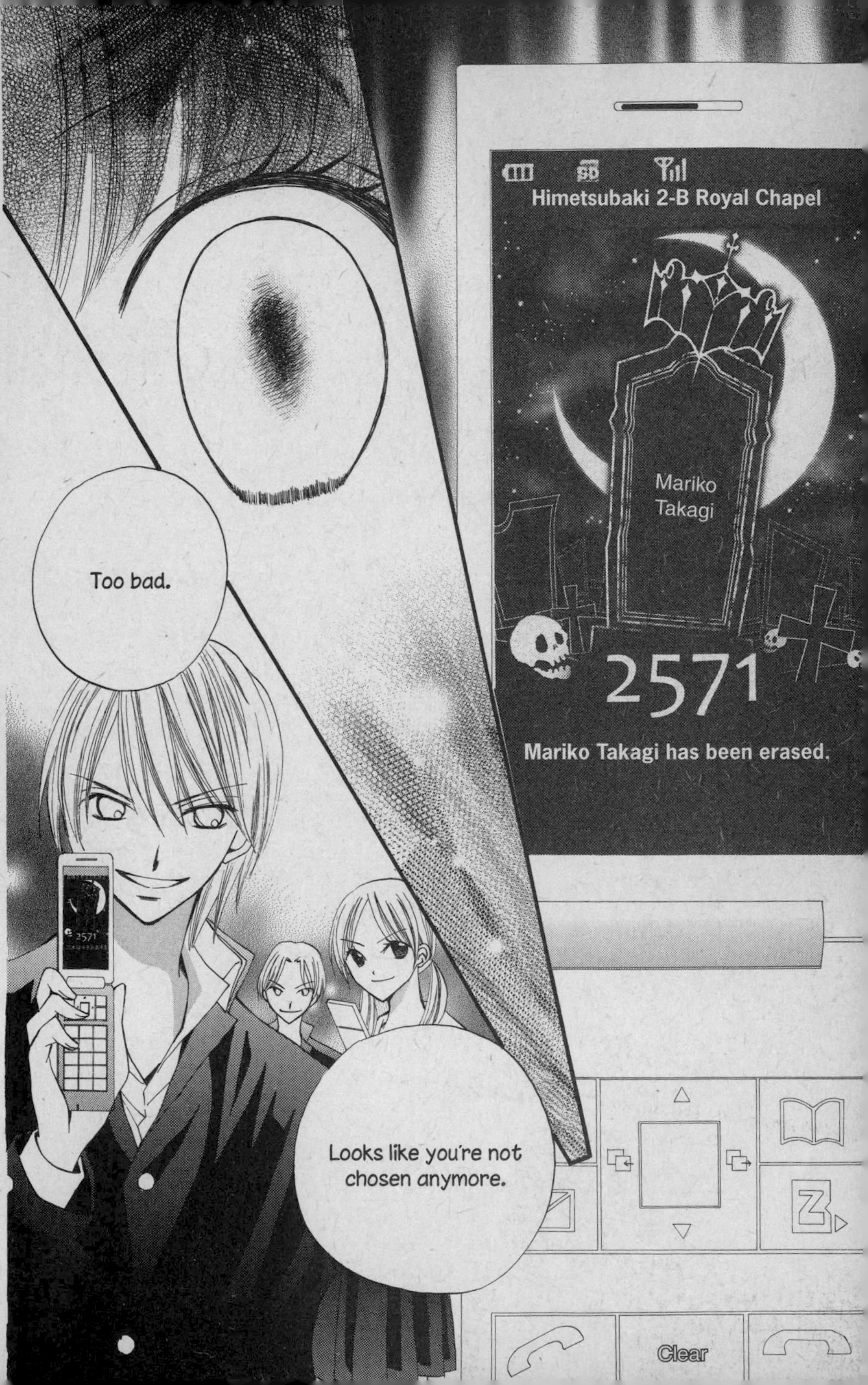
Himetsubaki 2-B Royal Chapel
Mariko Takagi
2571
Mariko Takagi has been erased.
Clear
Too bad.
Looks like you're not chosen anymore.

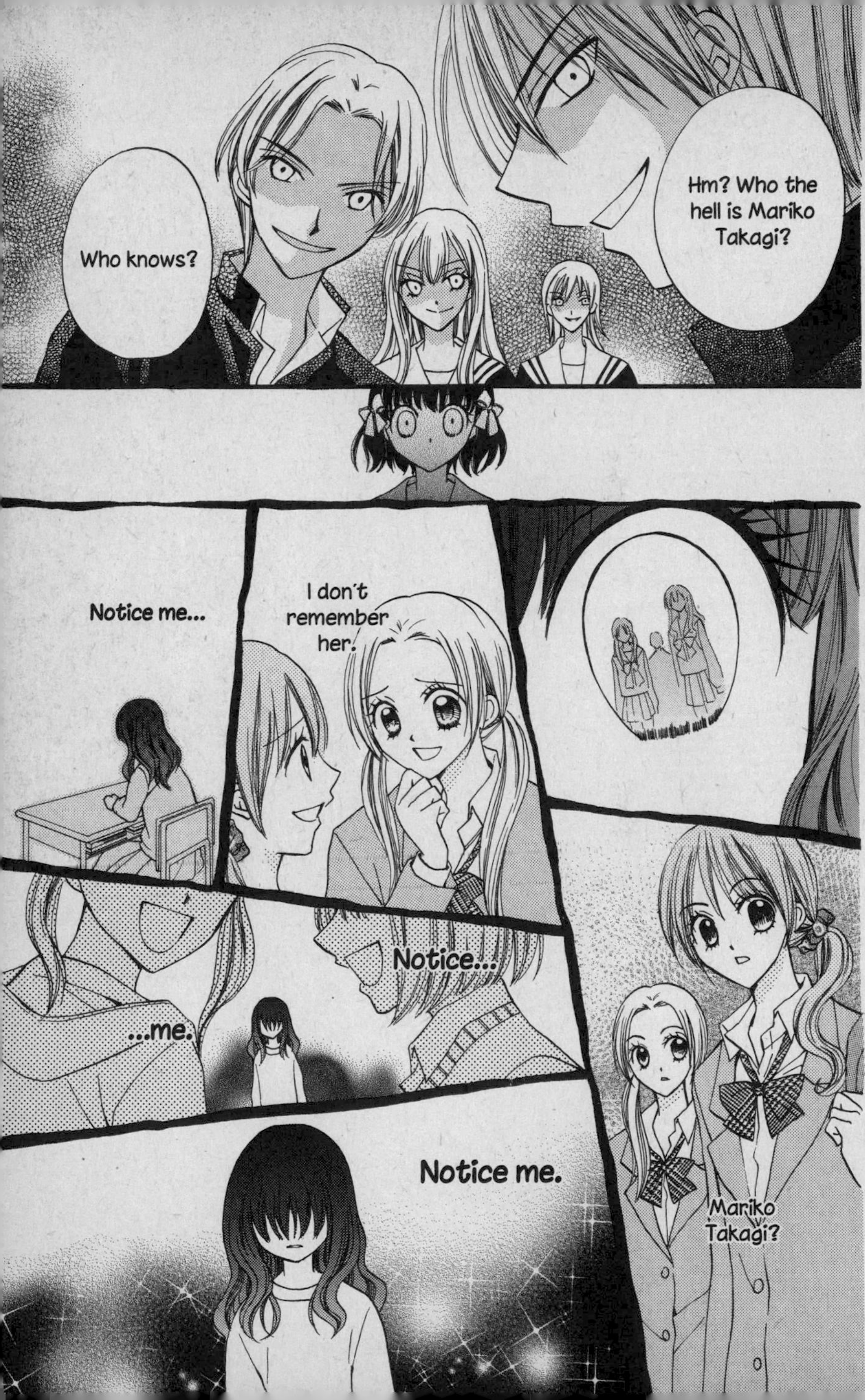
Hm? Who the hell is Mariko Takagi?
Who knows?
I don't remember her.
Notice me...
Mariko Takagi?
Notice...
...me.
Notice me.

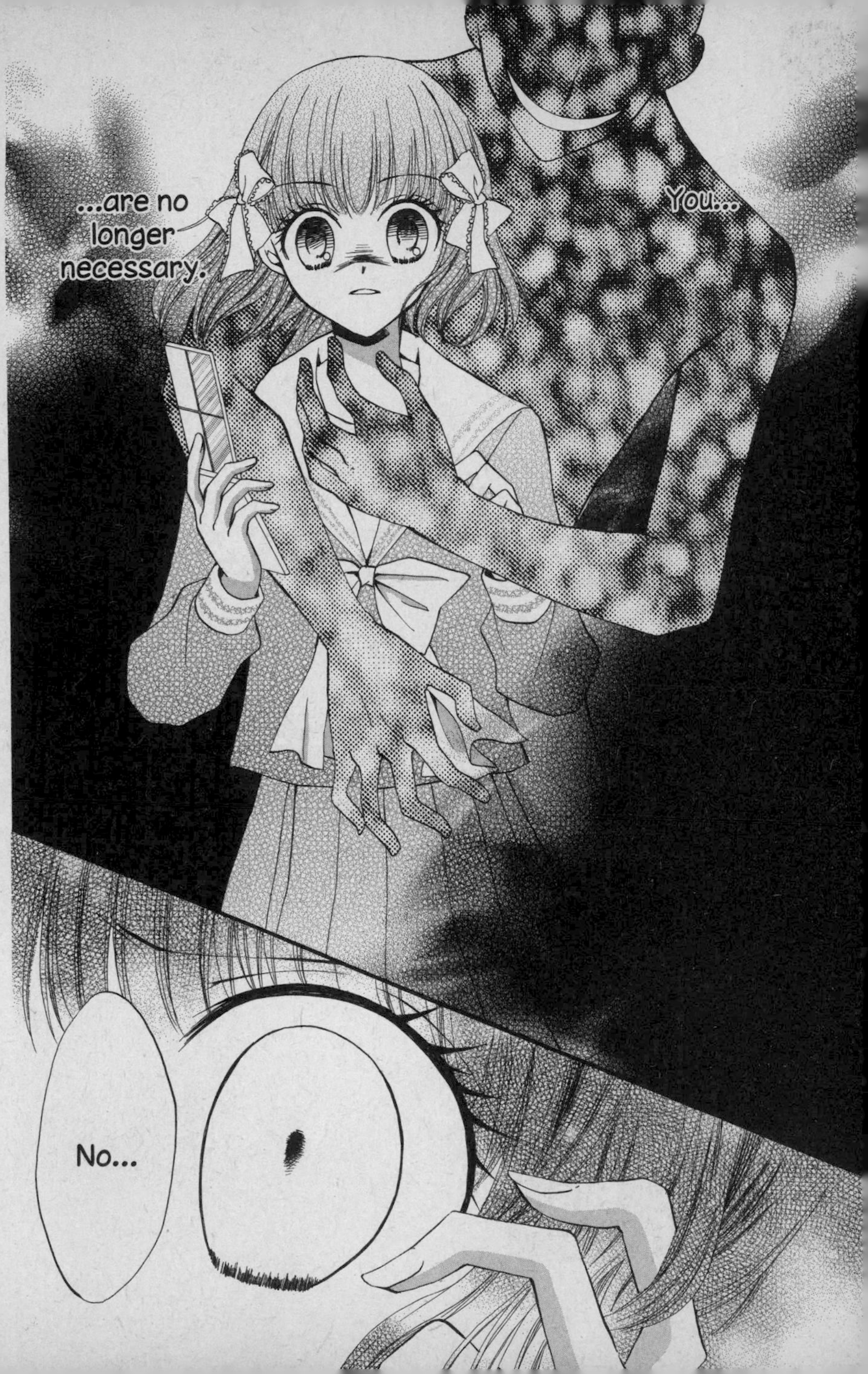
You...
...are no longer necessary.
No...

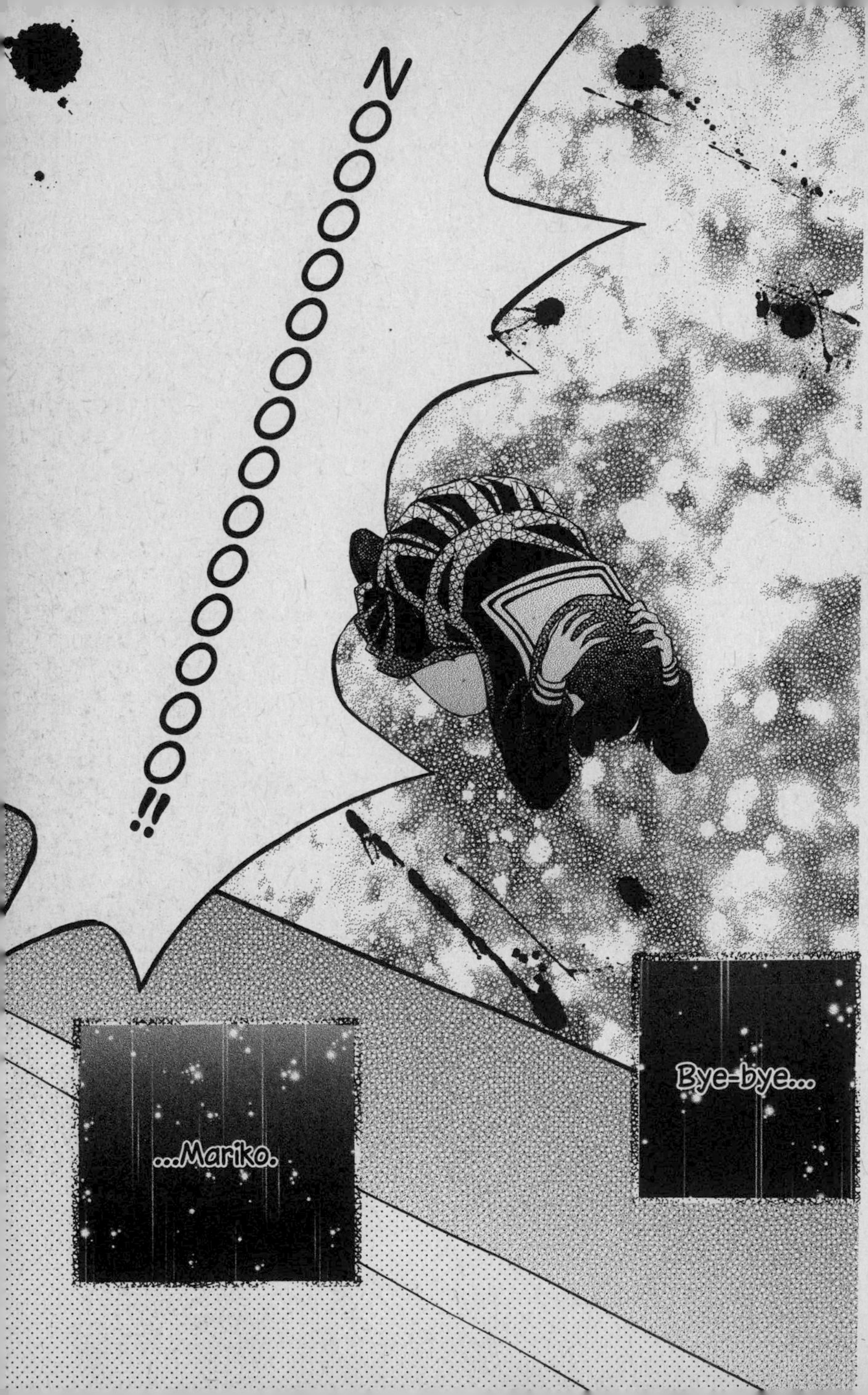
NOOOOOOOOOOOOOO!!
Bye-bye...
...Mariko.

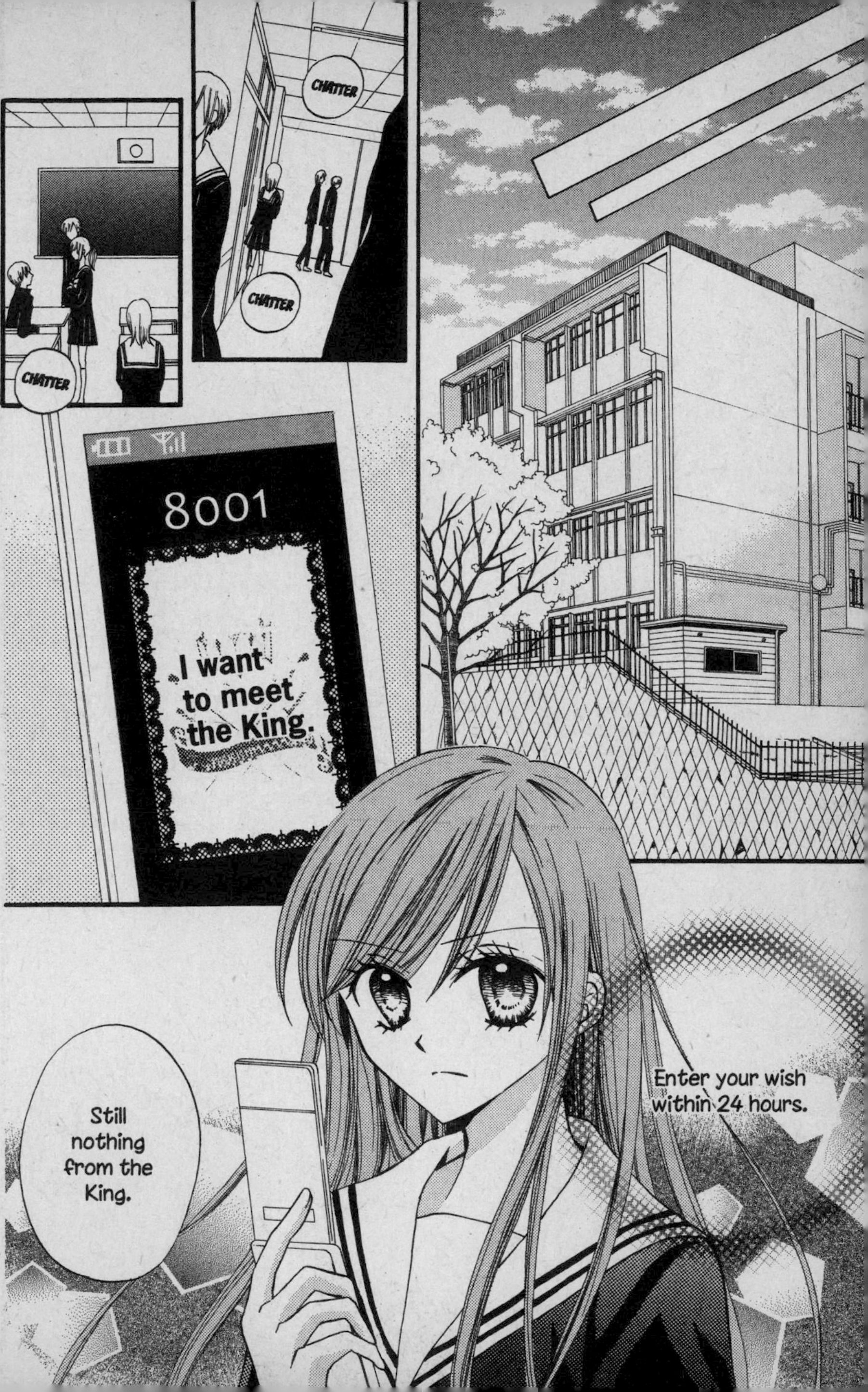
CHATTER
CHATTER
CHATTER
8001
I want to meet the King.
Enter your wish within 24 hours.
Still nothing from the King.

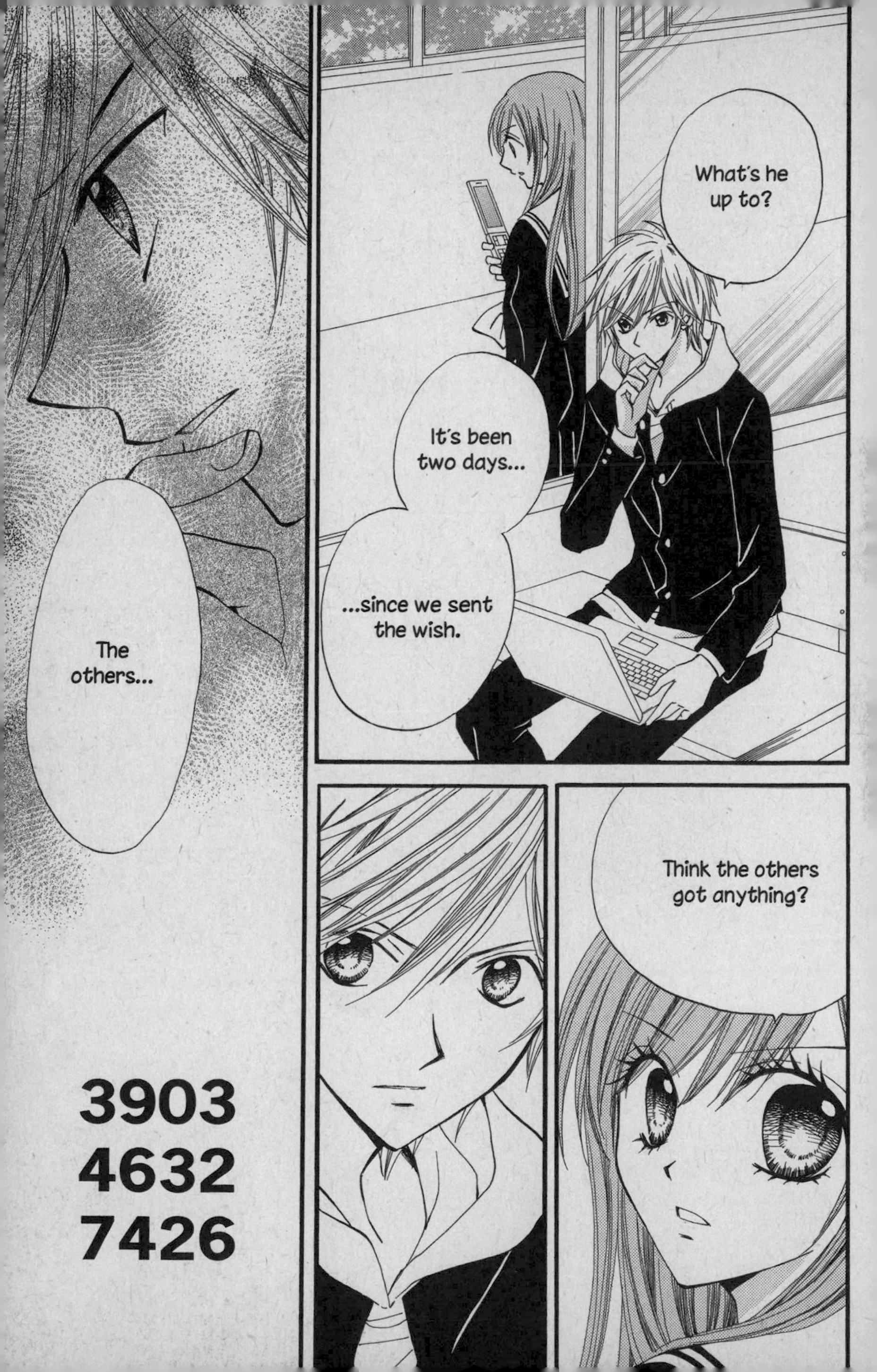
What's he up to?
It's been two days...
...since we sent the wish.
Think the others got anything?
The others...
3903 4632 7426

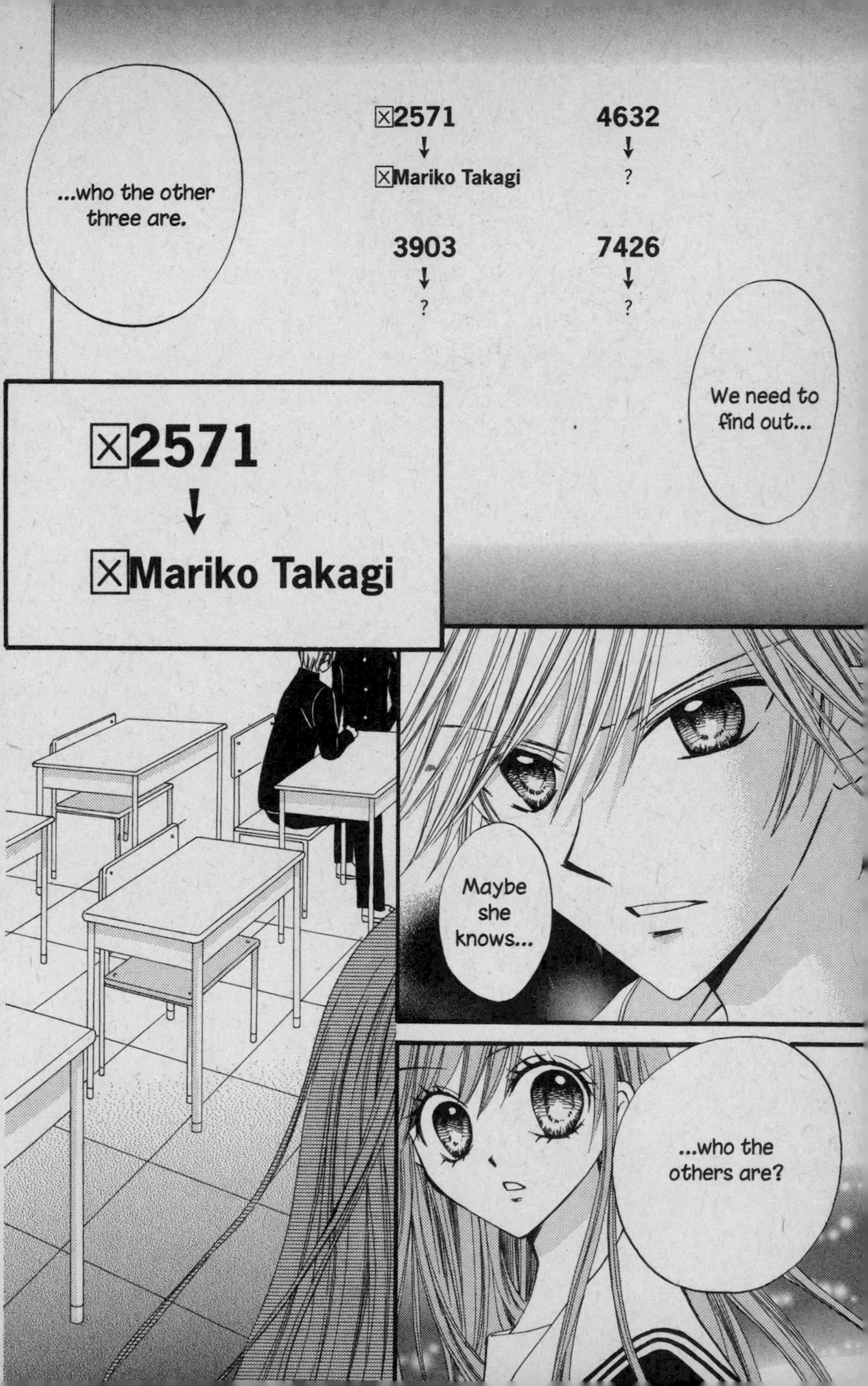
We need to find out...
☒2571 ↓ ☒Mariko Takagi
4632 ↓ ?
3903 ↓ ?
7426 ↓ ?
...who the other three are.
Maybe she knows...
...who the others are?
☒2571 ↓ ☒Mariko Takagi

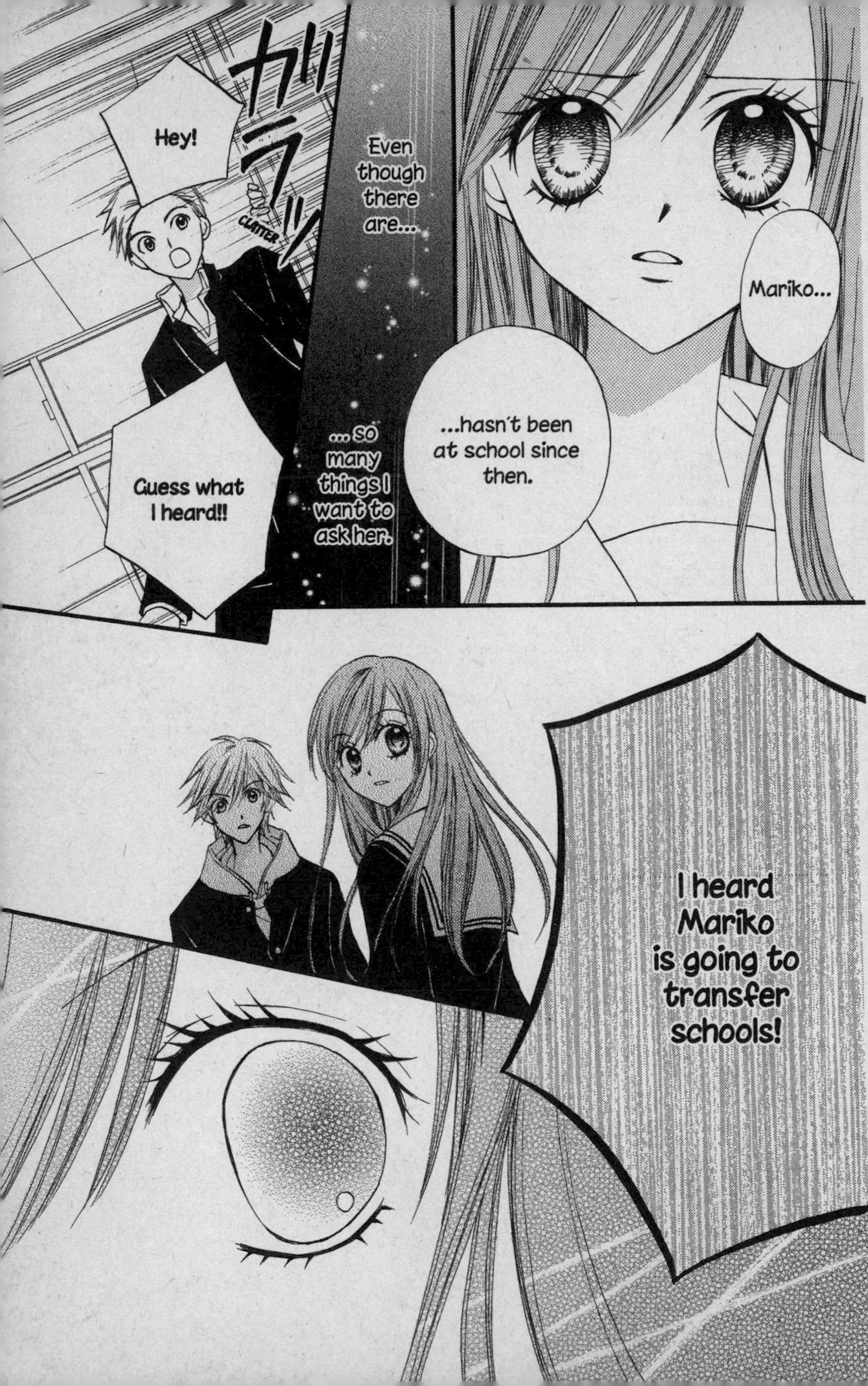
Mariko...
...hasn't been at school since then.
Even though there are...
...so many things I want to ask her.
ガラッ
CLATTER
Hey!
Guess what I heard!!
I heard Mariko is going to transfer schools!

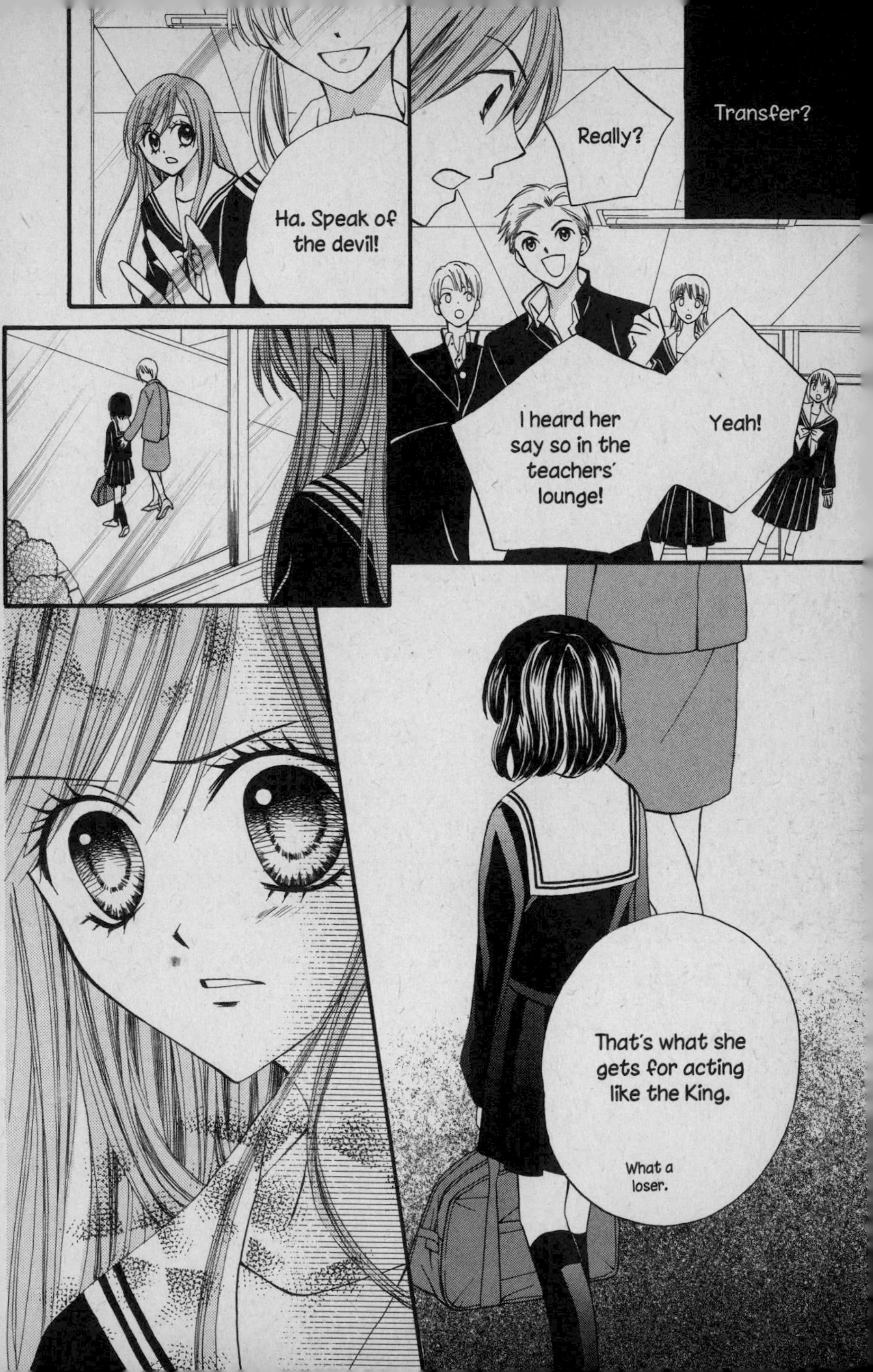
Transfer?
Really?
I heard her say so in the teachers' lounge!
Yeah!
Ha. Speak of the devil!
That's what she gets for acting like the King.
What a loser.

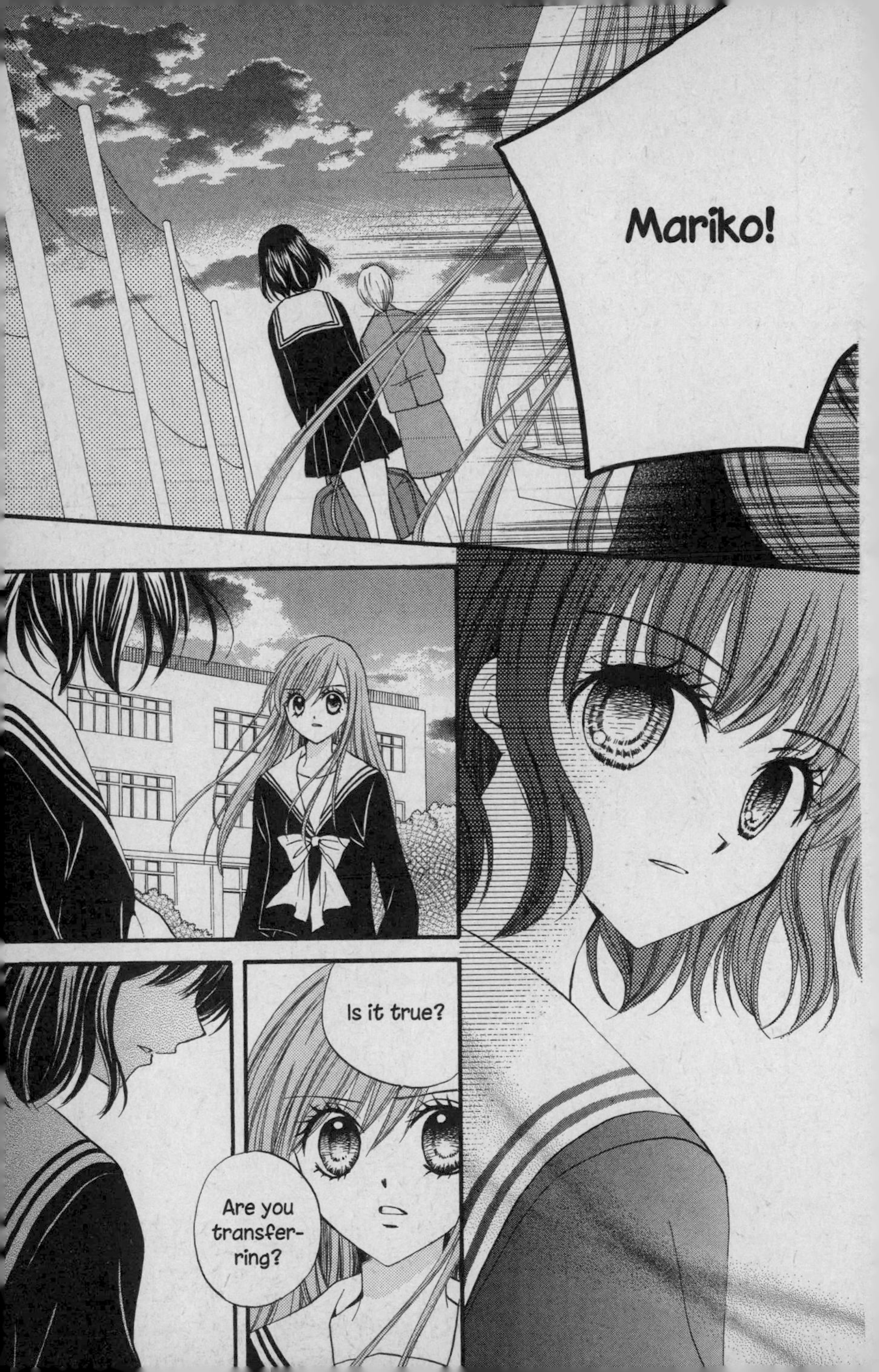
Mariko!
Is it true?
Are you transfer-ring?

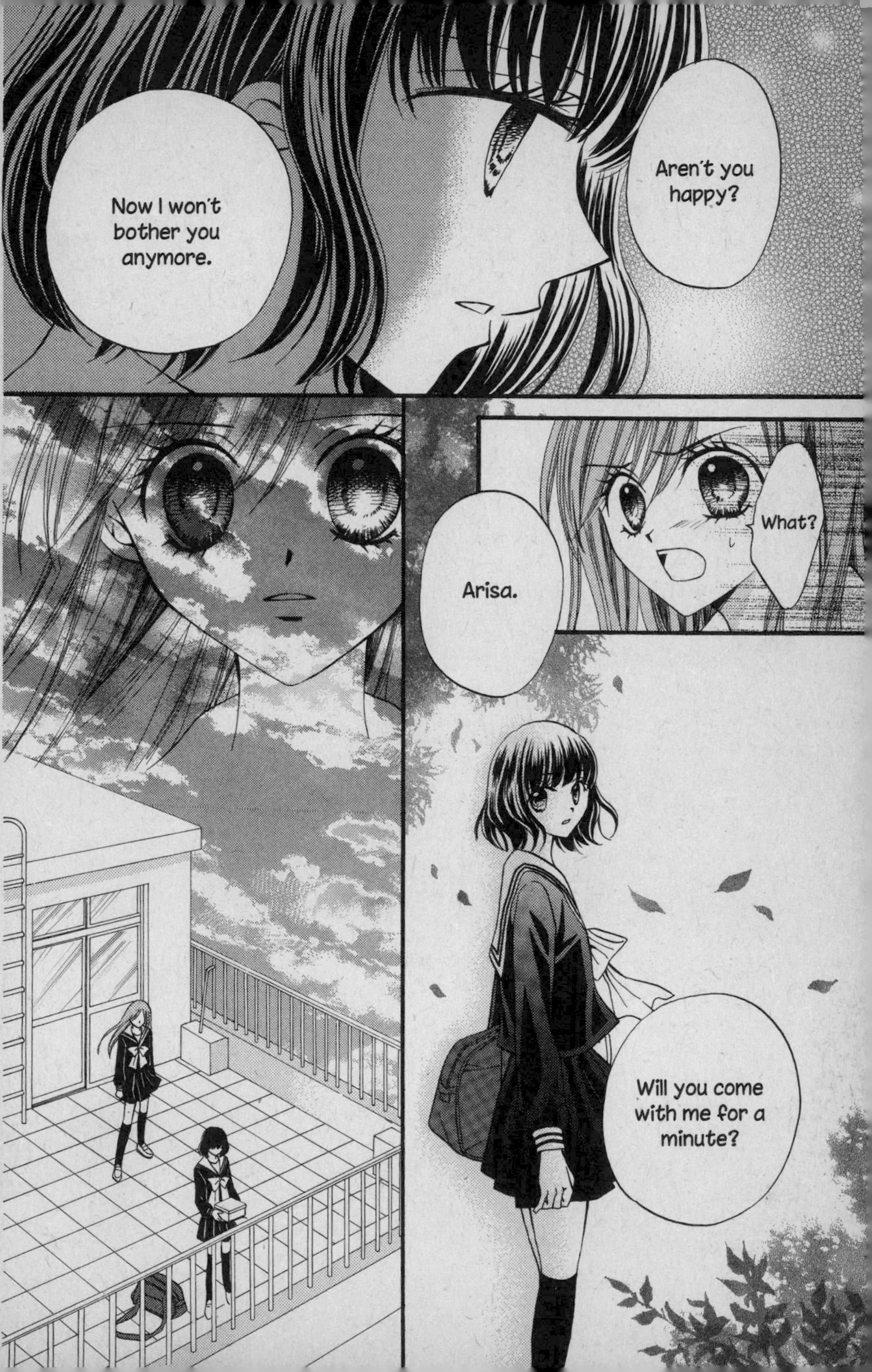
Aren't you happy?
Now I won't bother you anymore.
What?
Arisa.
Will you come with me for a minute?

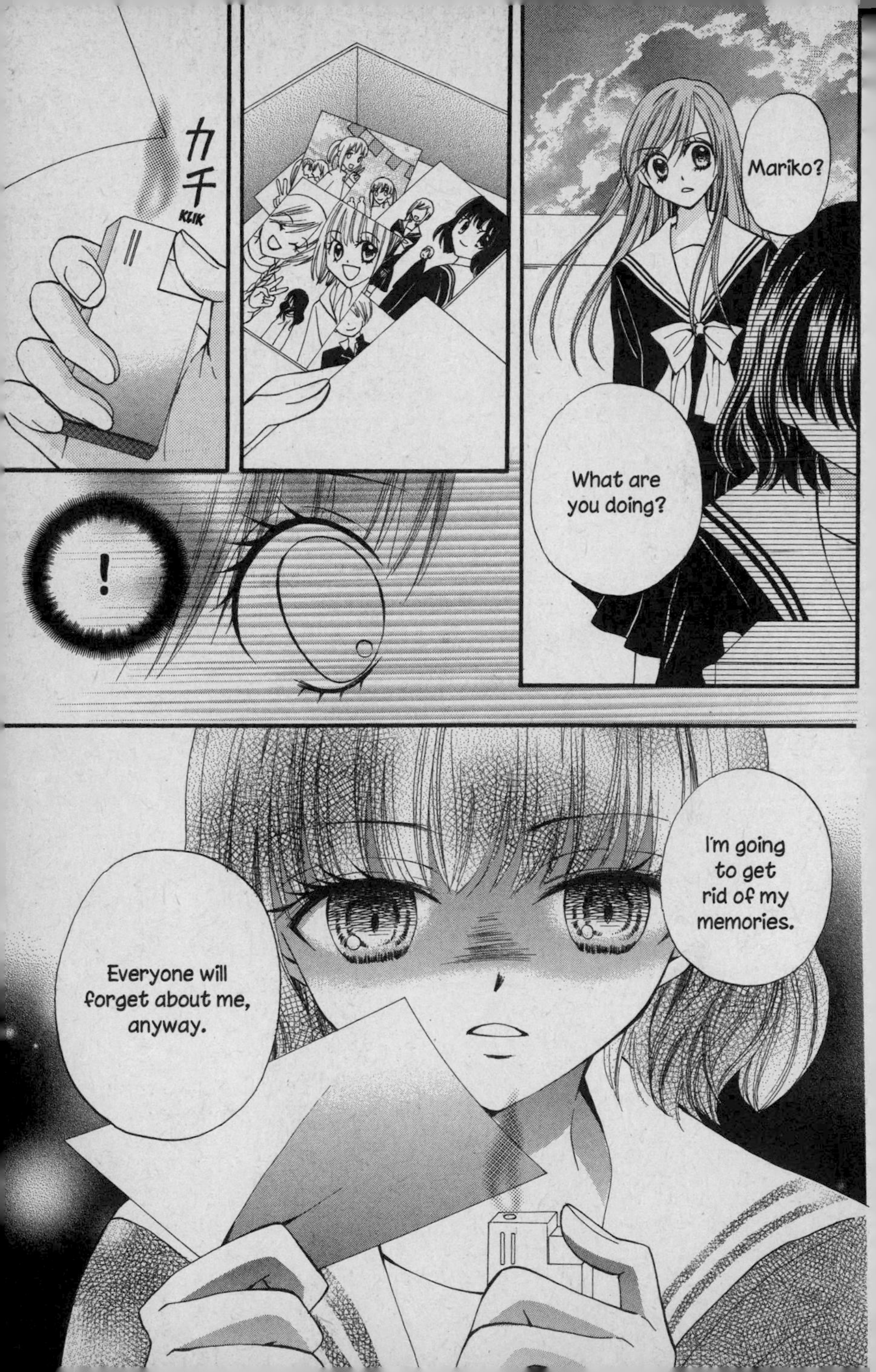
Mariko?
What are you doing?
カチ
KLIK
!
I'm going to get rid of my memories.
Everyone will forget about me, anyway.

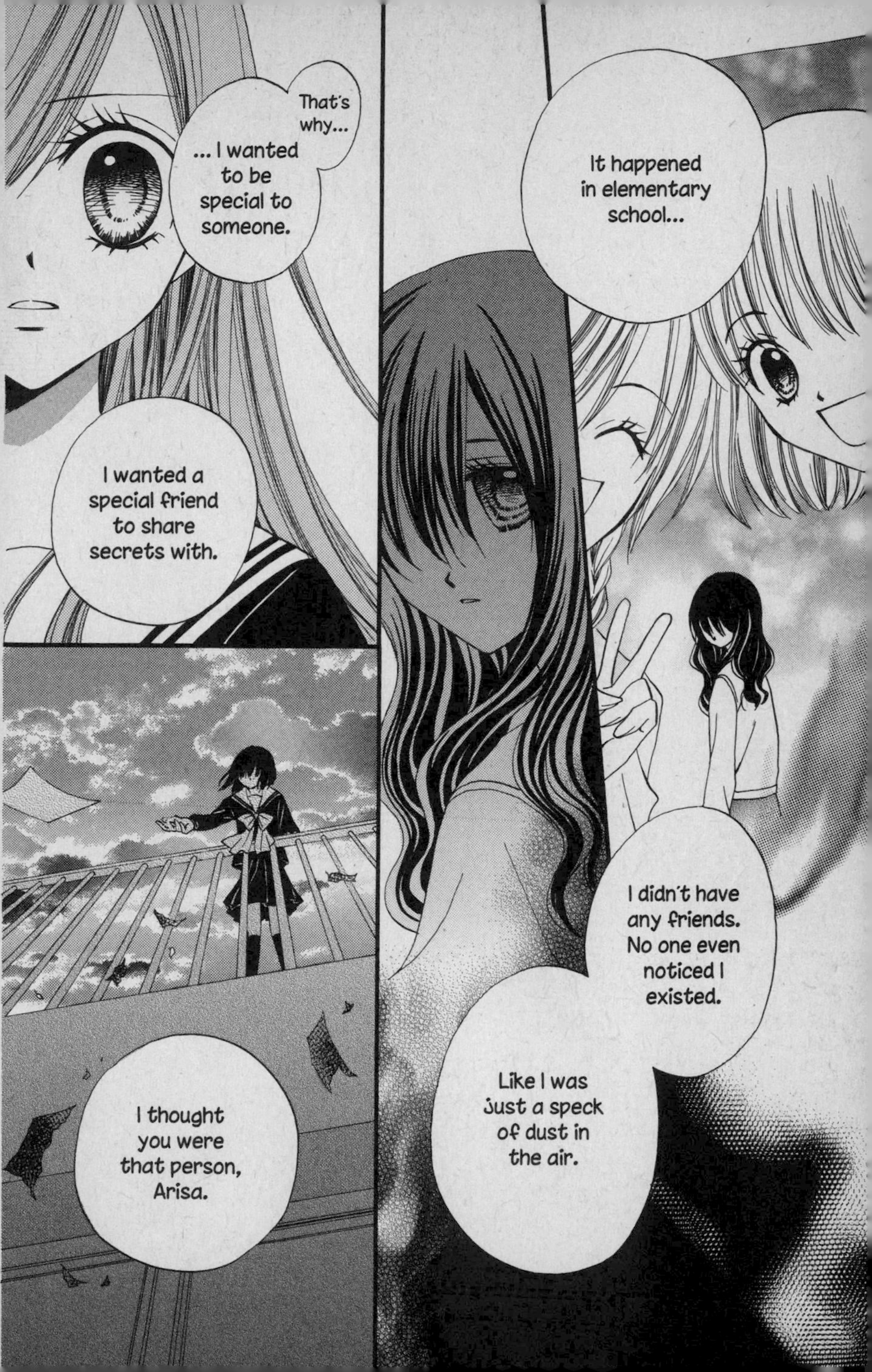
It happened in elementary school...
I didn't have any friends. No one even noticed I existed.
Like I was just a speck of dust in the air.
That's why...
...I wanted to be special to someone.
I wanted a special friend to share secrets with.
I thought you were that person, Arisa.

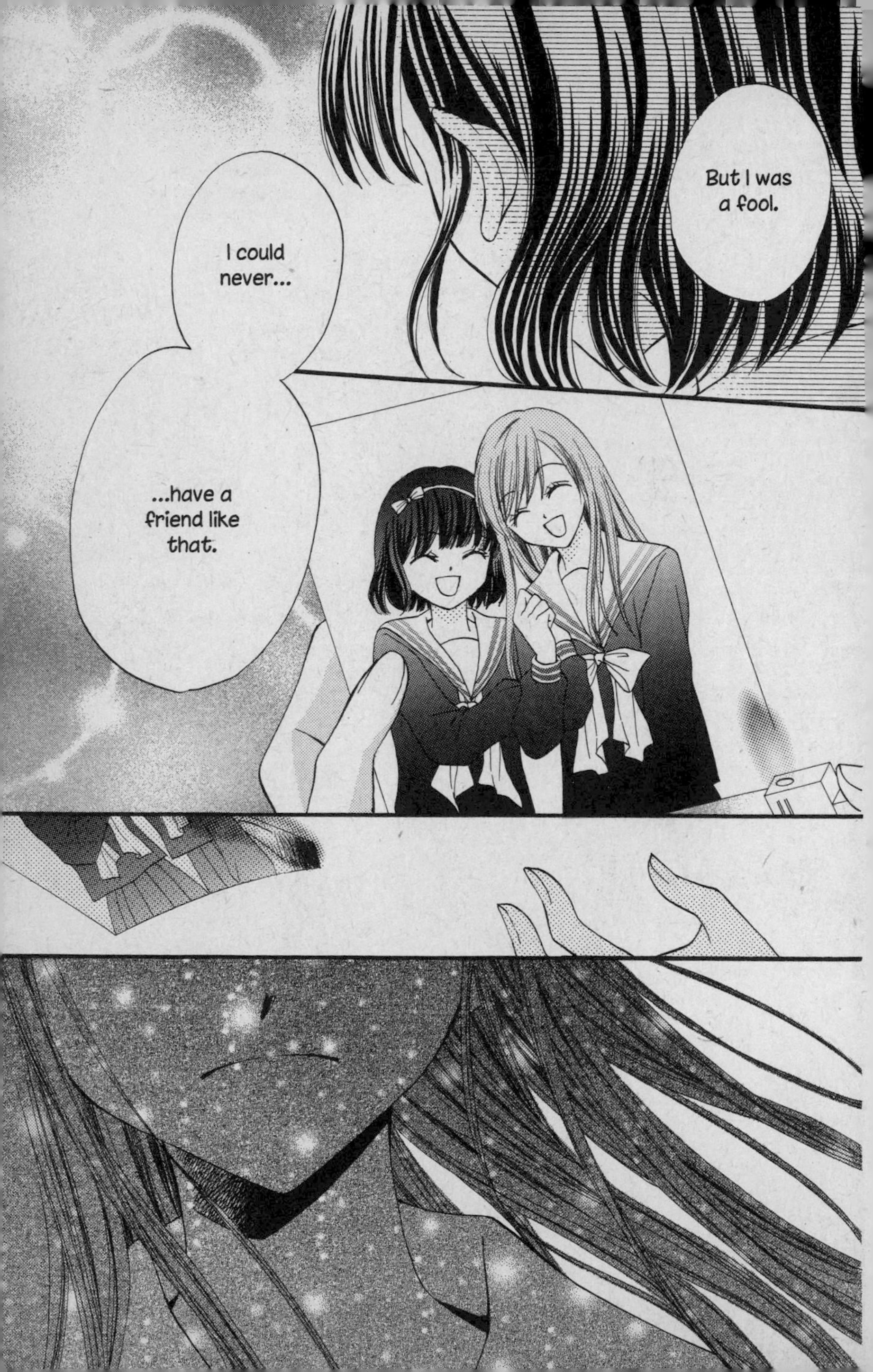
But I was a fool.
I could never...
...have a friend like that.

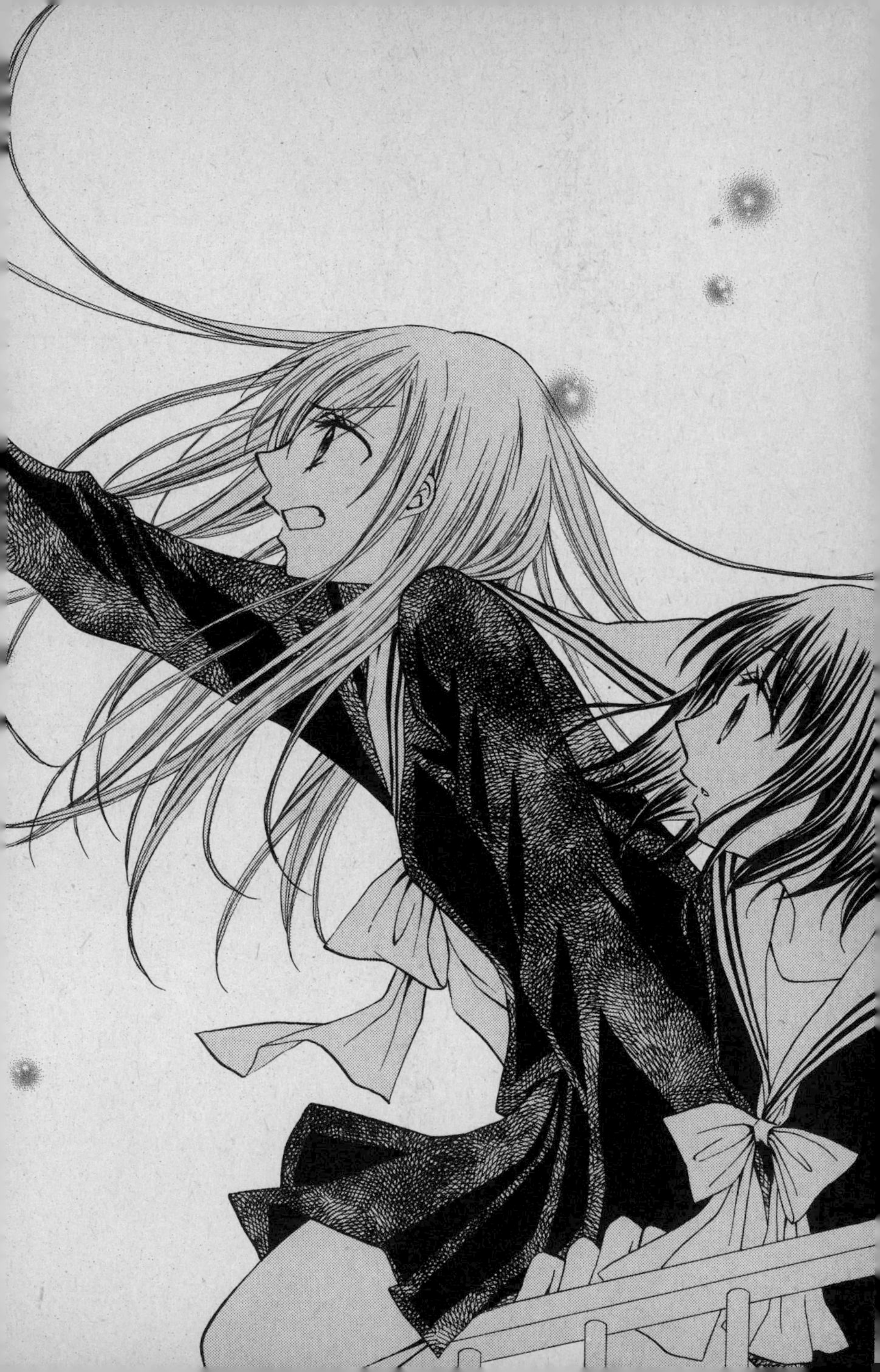

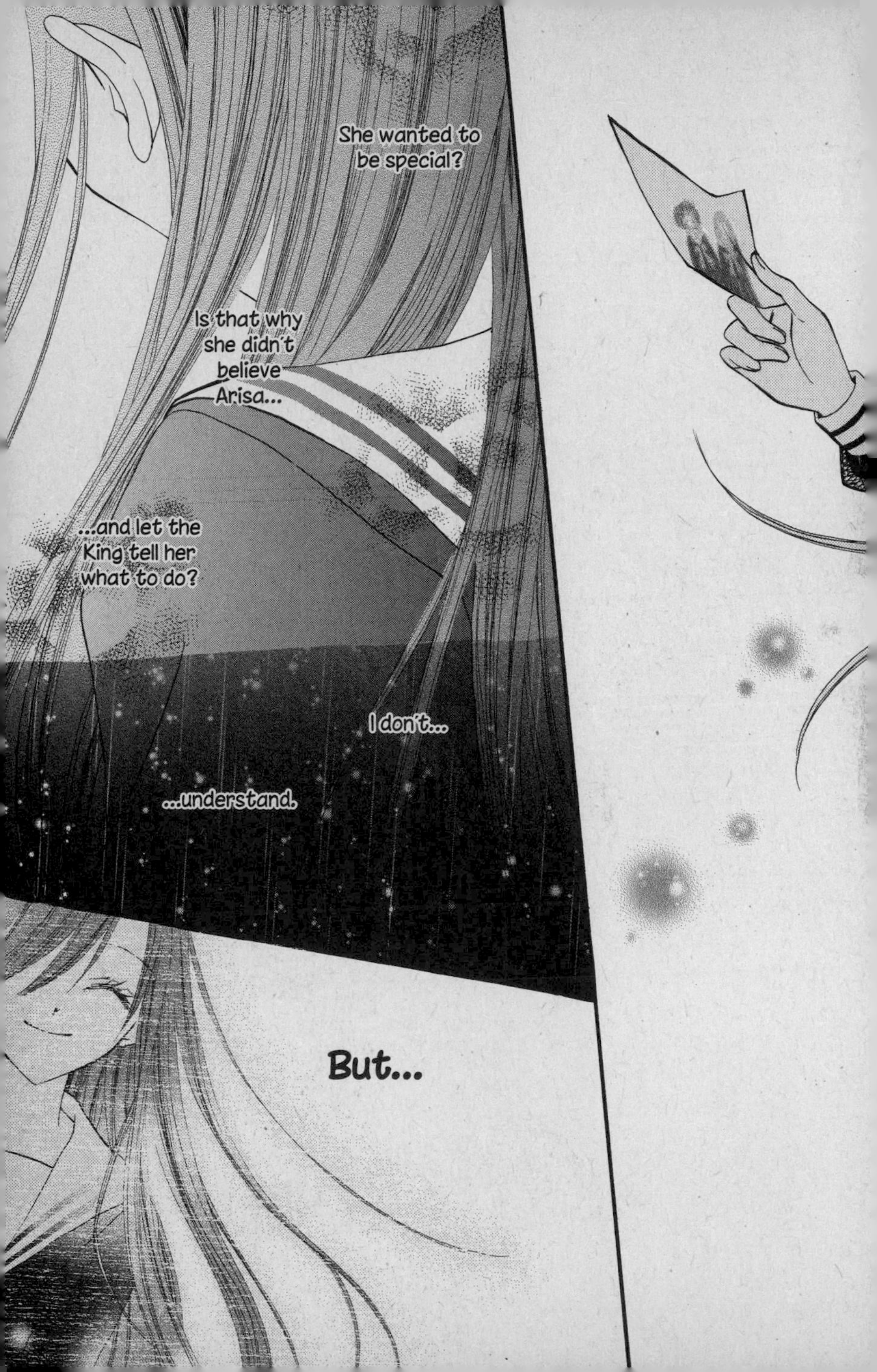
She wanted to be special?
Is that why she didn´t believe Arisa...
...and let the King tell her what to do?
I don´t...
...understand.
But...

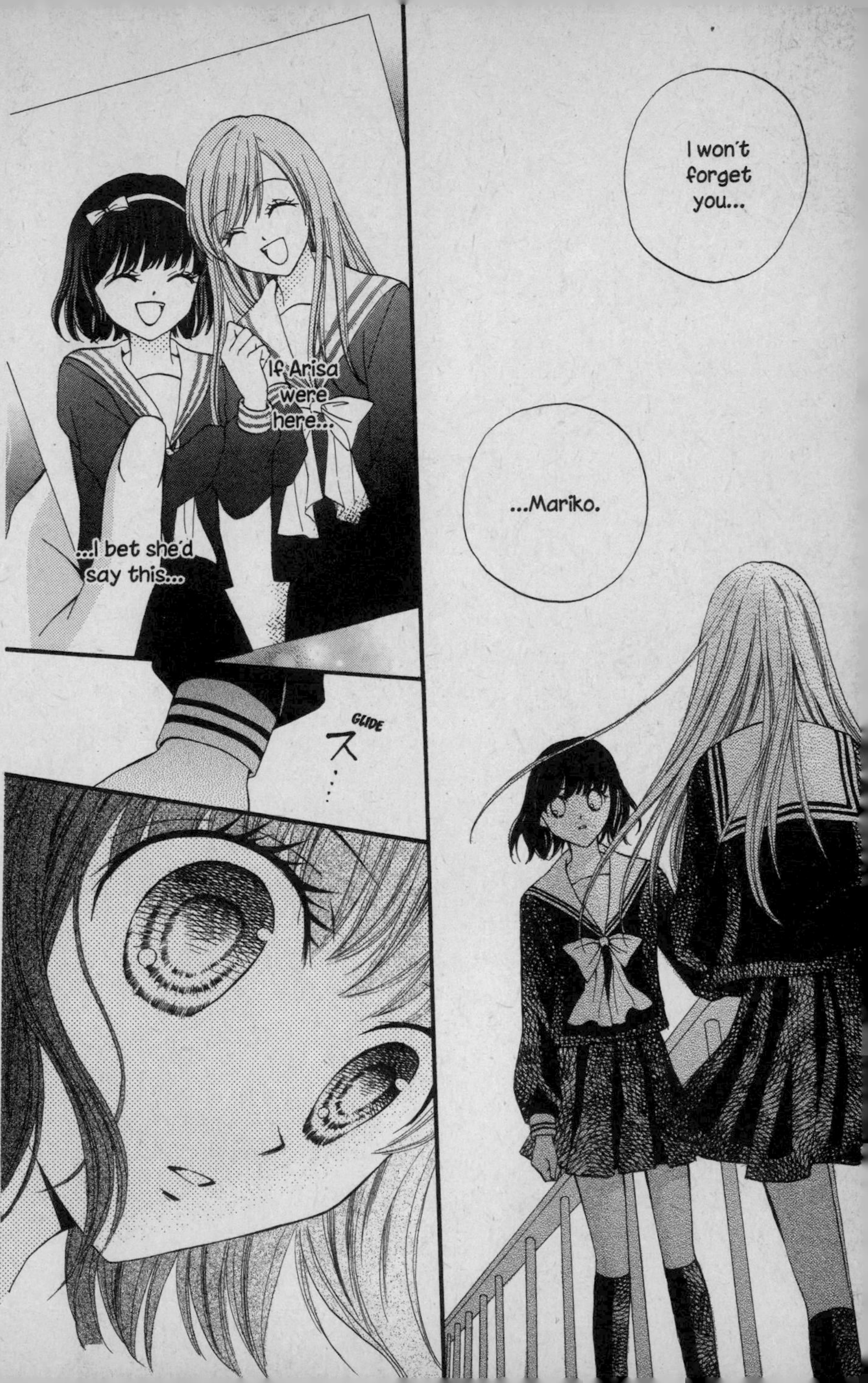
I won't forget you...
...Mariko.
If Arisa were here...
...I bet she'd say this...
GLIDE
ス...

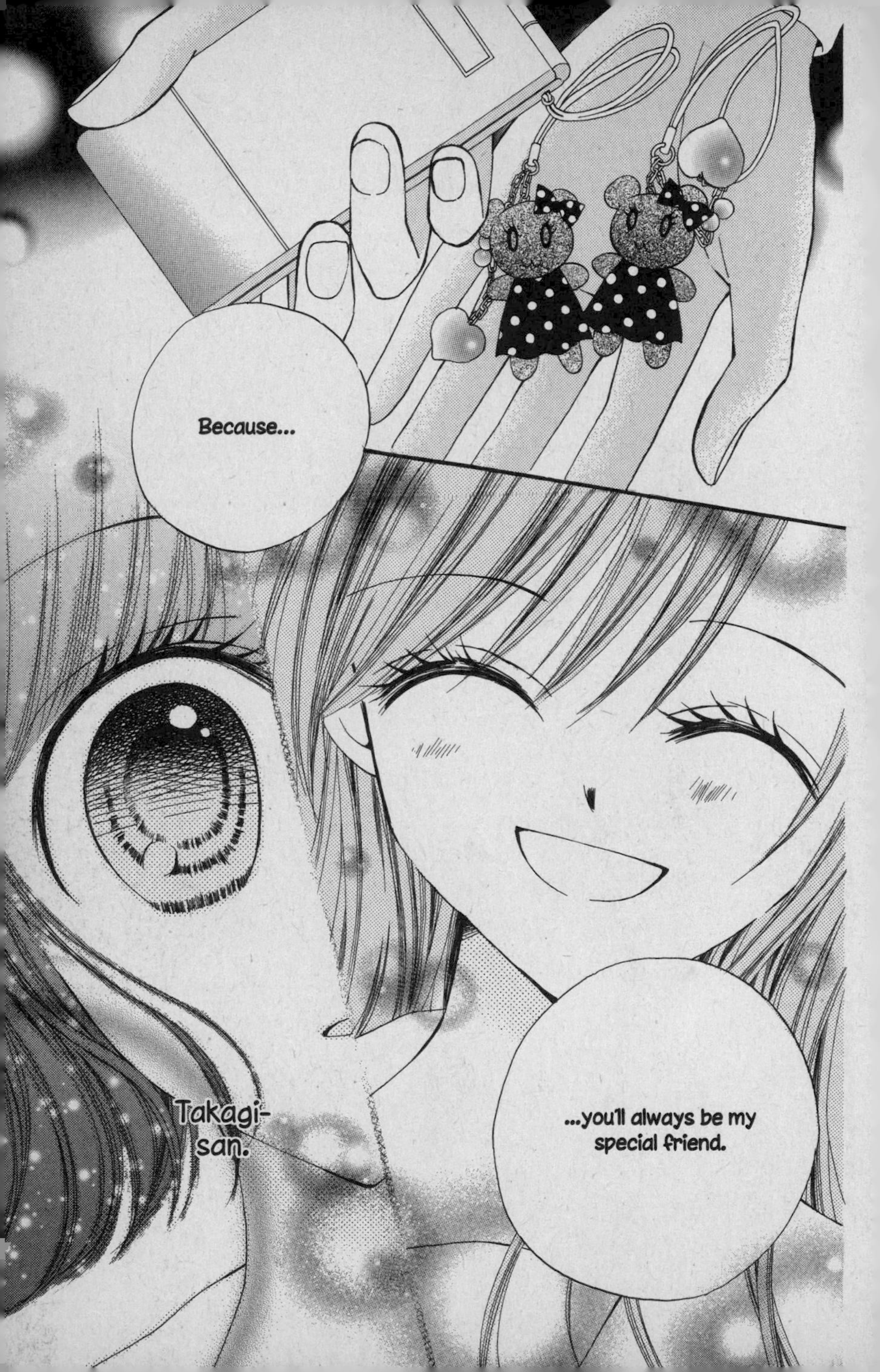
Because...
...you'll always be my special friend.
Takagi-san.

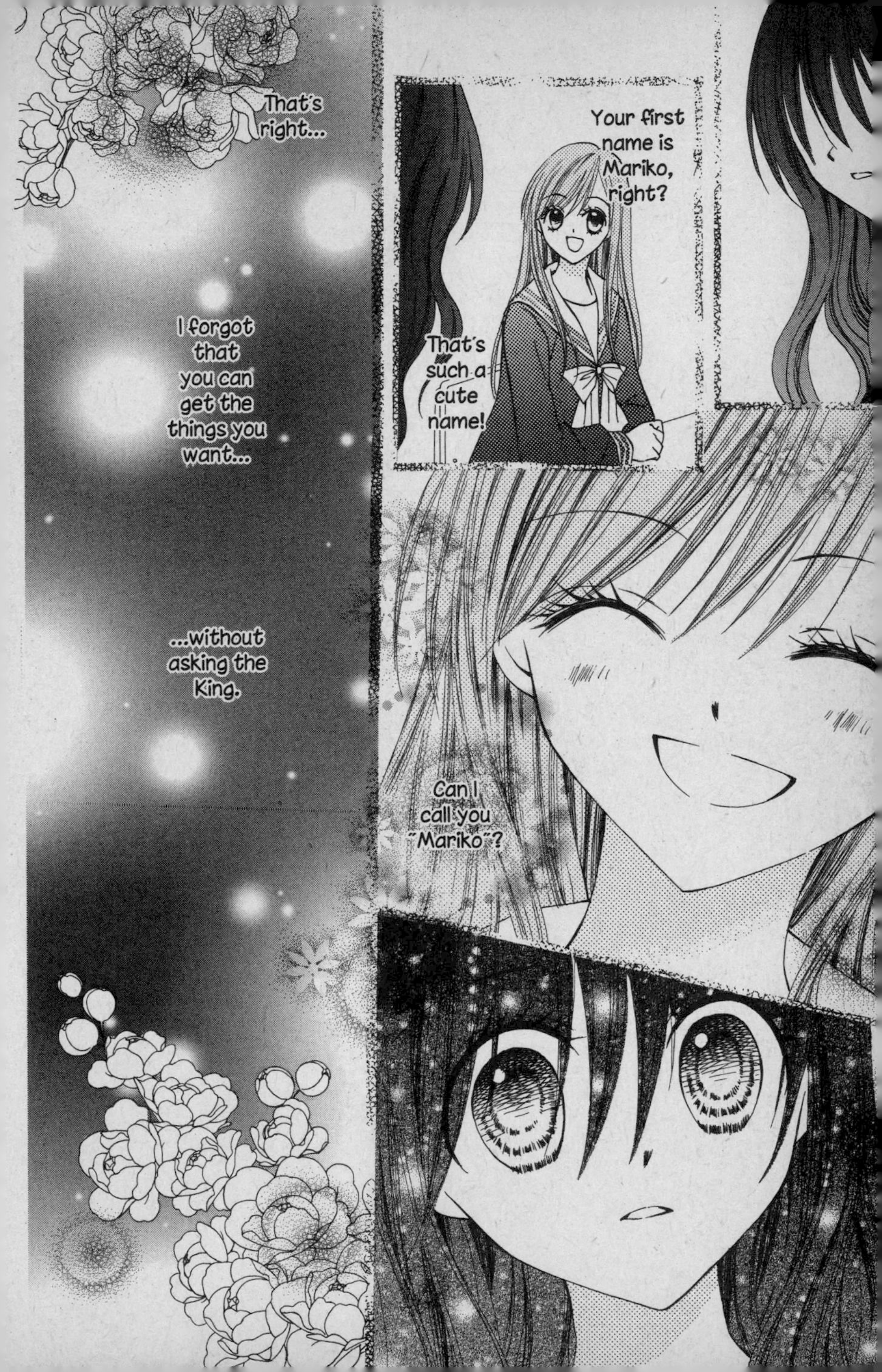
Your first name is Mariko, right?
That's such a cute name!
Can I call you "Mariko"?
That's right...
I forgot that you can get the things you want...
...without asking the King.

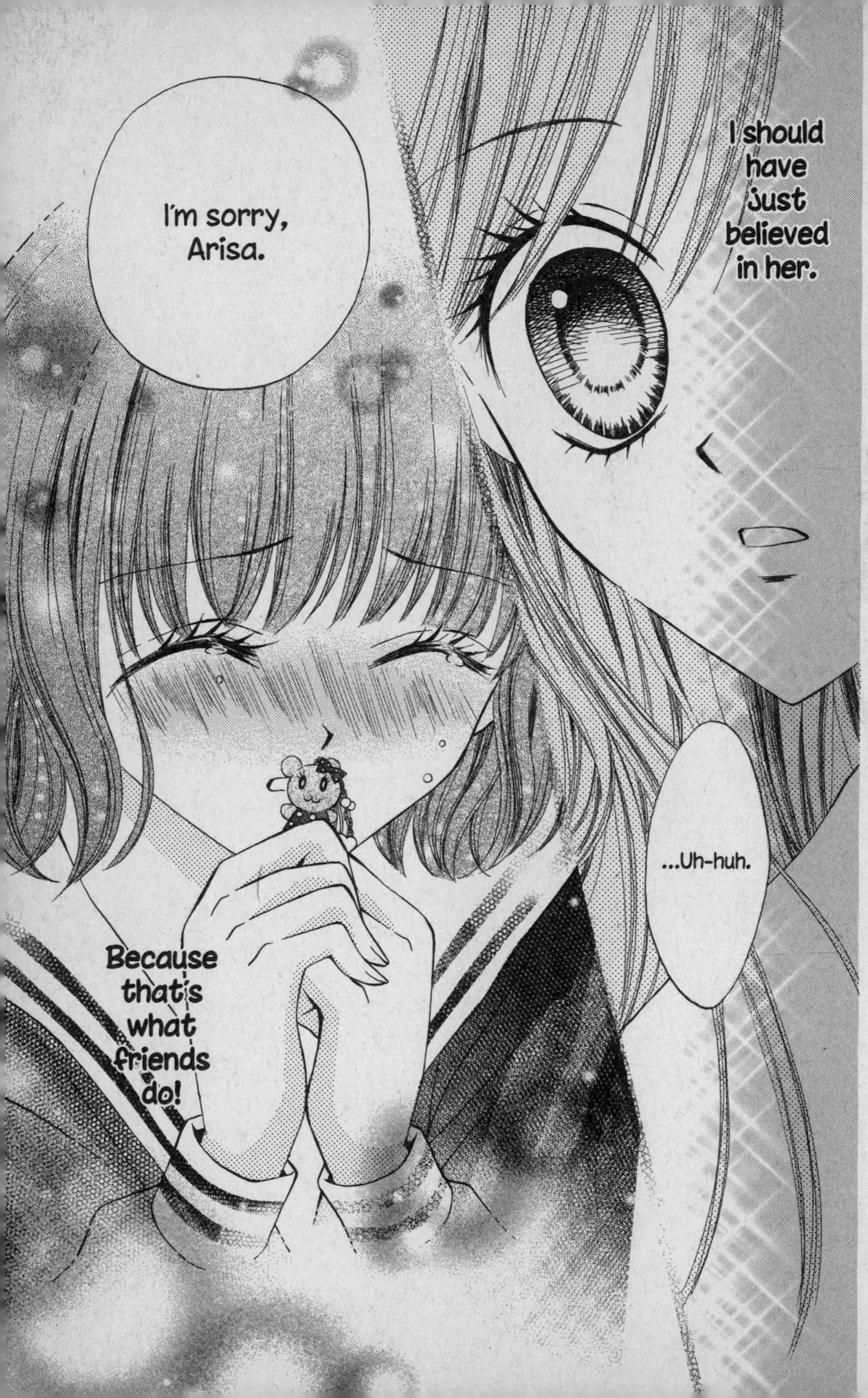
I should have just believed in her.
I'm sorry, Arisa.
...Uh-huh.
Because that's what friends do!

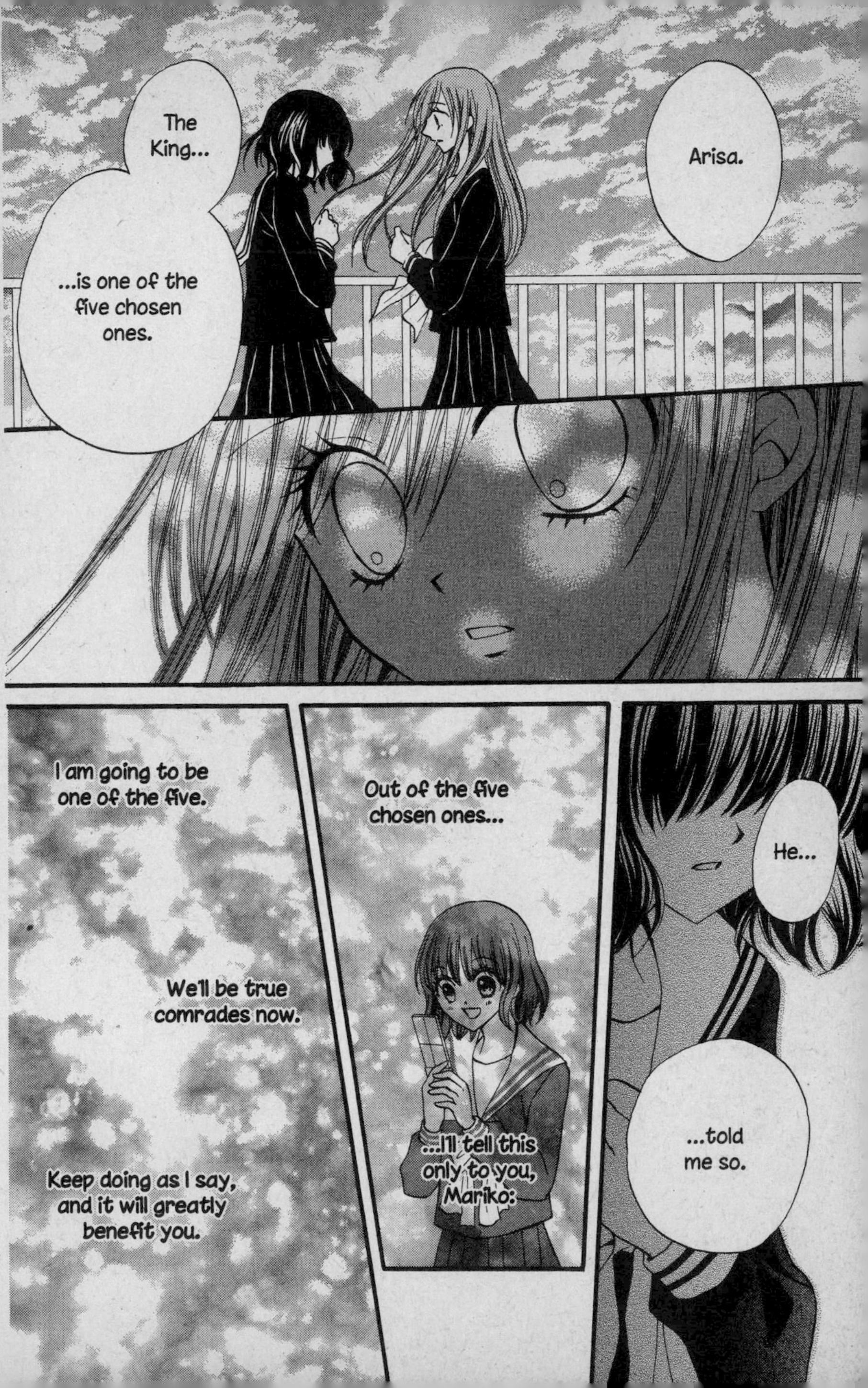
Arisa.
The King...
...is one of the five chosen ones.
He...
...told me so.
Out of the five chosen ones...
...I'll tell this only to you, Mariko.
I am going to be one of the five.
We'll be true comrades now.
Keep doing as I say, and it will greatly benefit you.

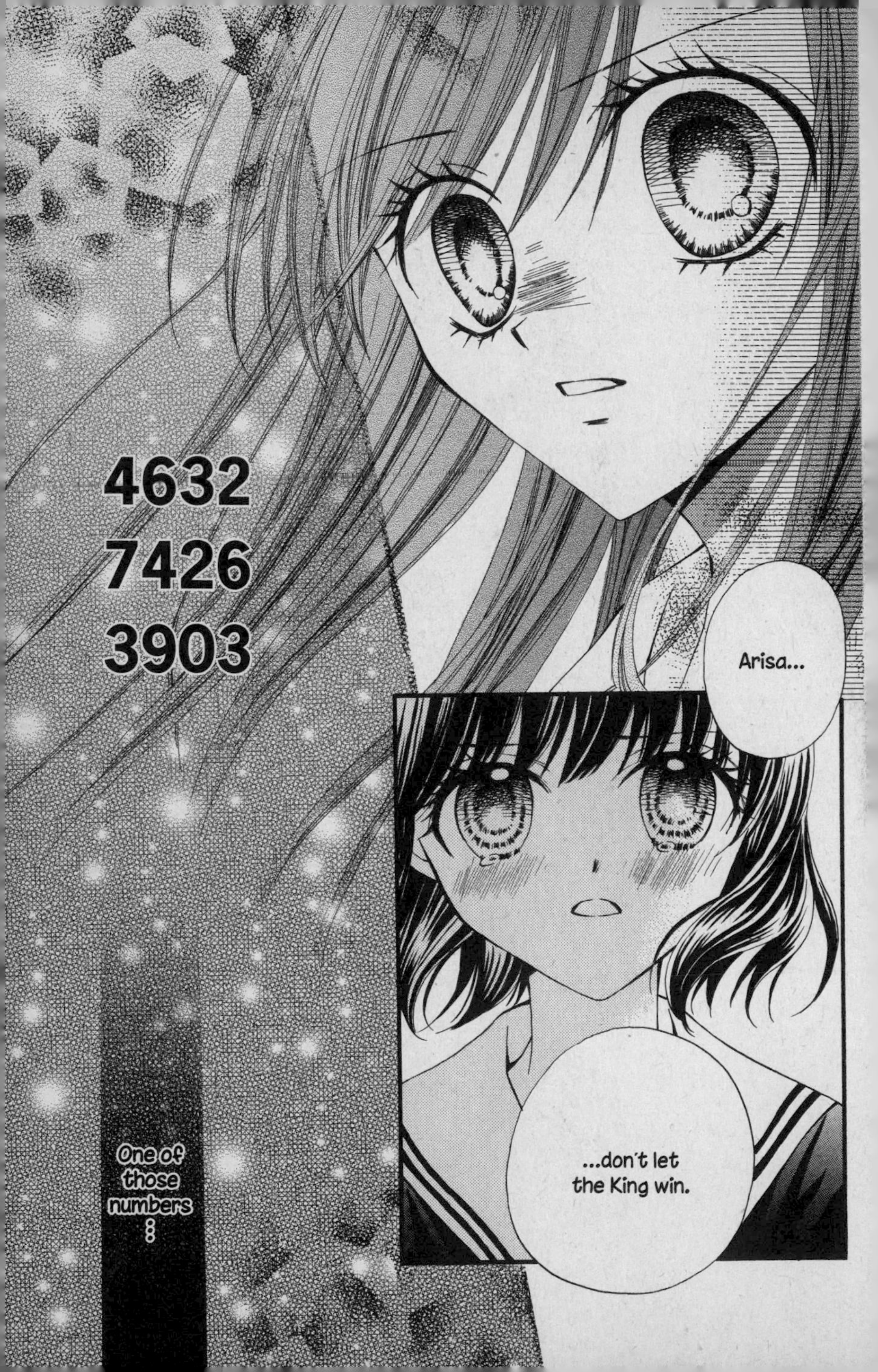
Arisa...
...don't let the King win.
4632 7426 3903
One of those numbers...

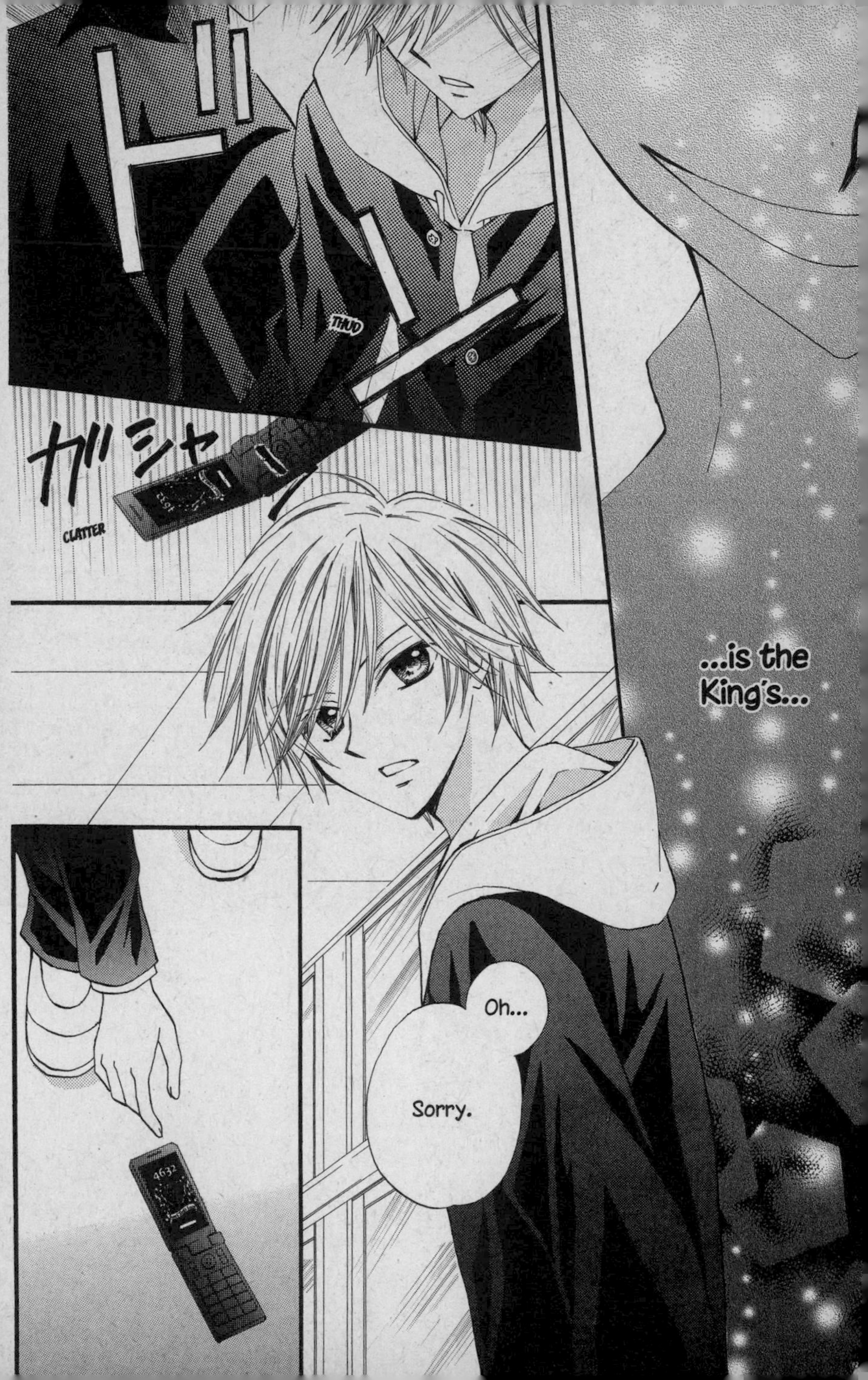
...is the King's...
THUD
ガシャ
CLATTER
Oh...
Sorry.

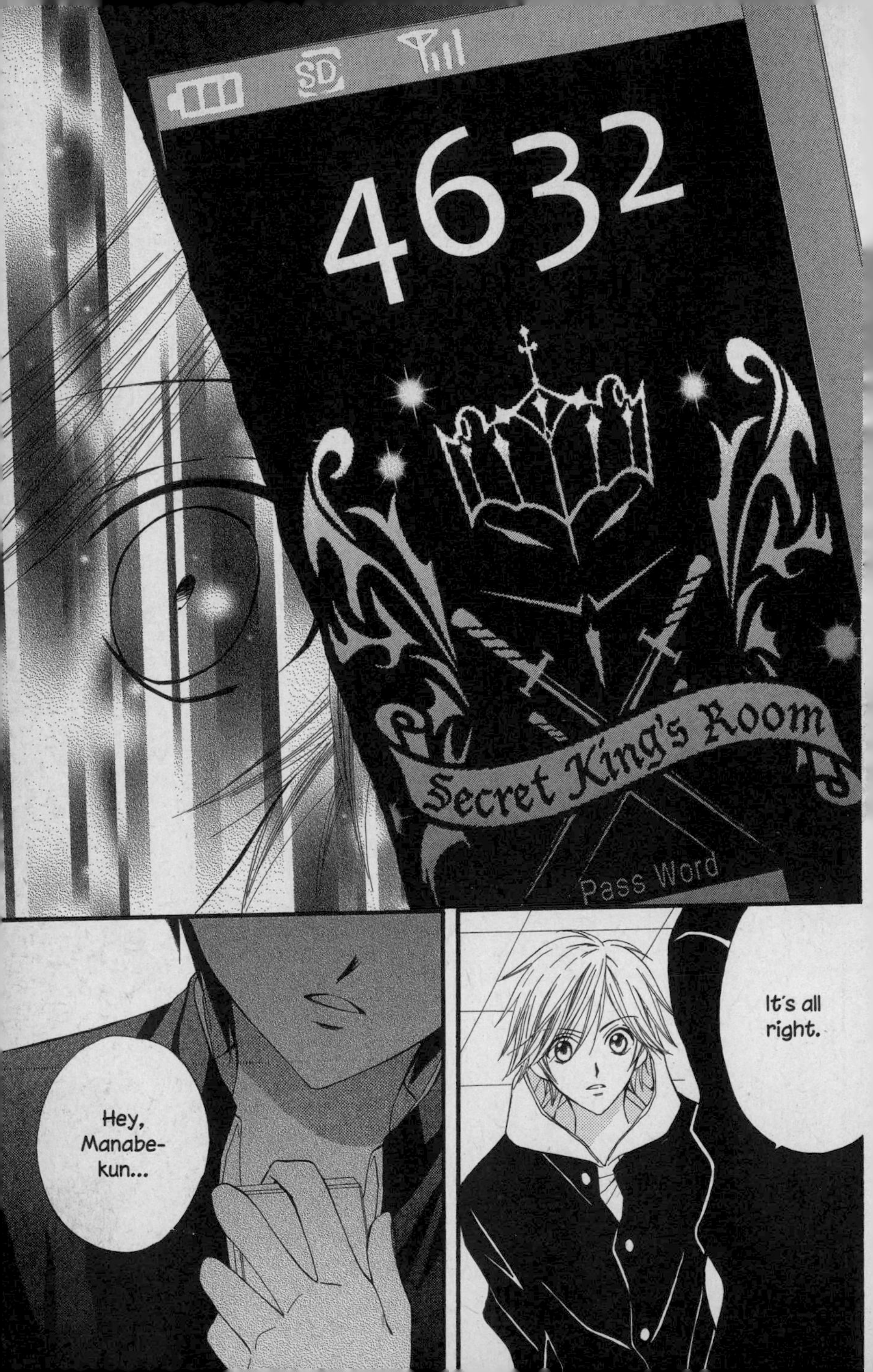
4632
Secret King's Room
Pass Word
It's all right.
Hey, Manabe-kun...

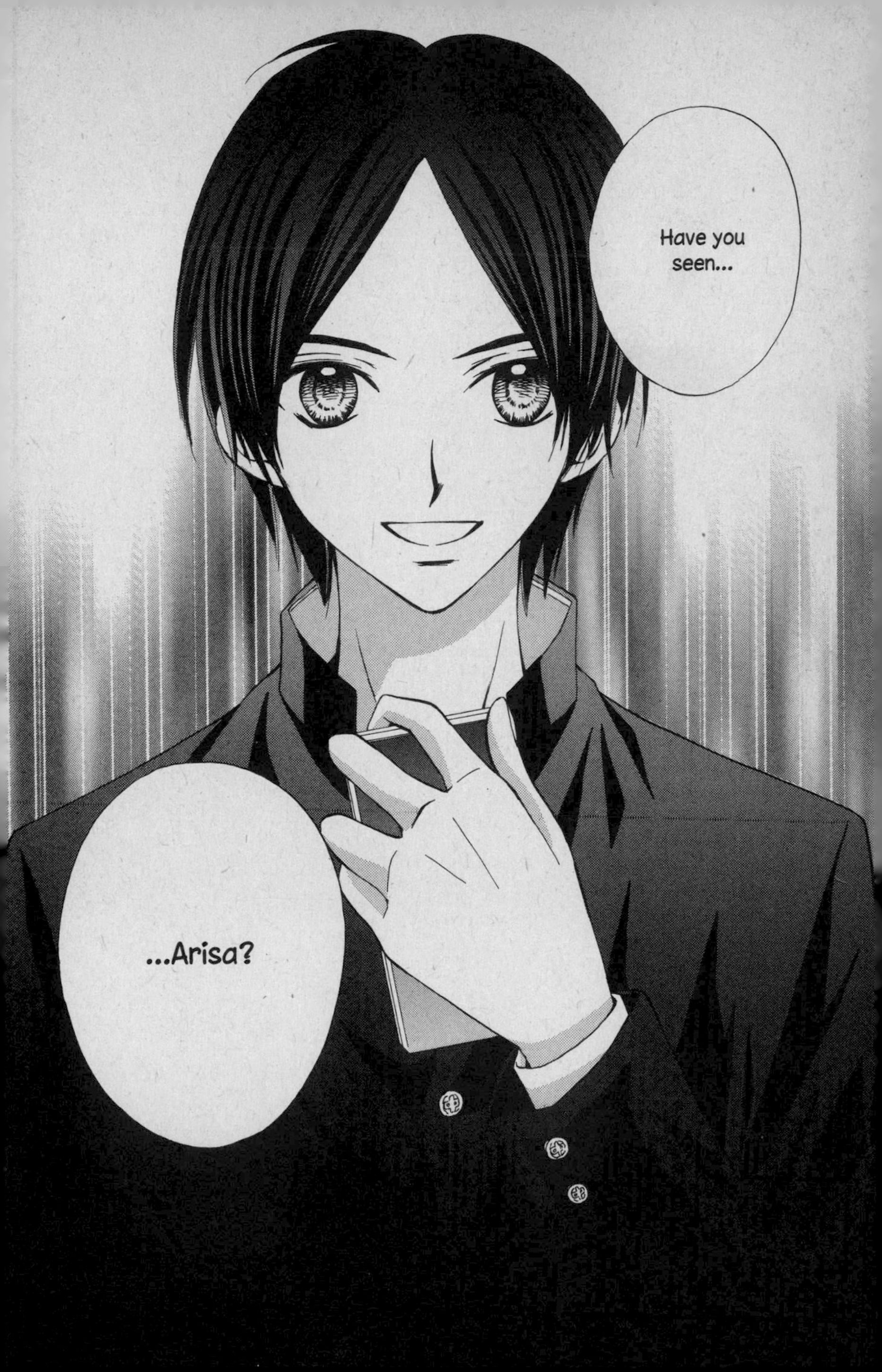
Have you seen...
...Arisa?

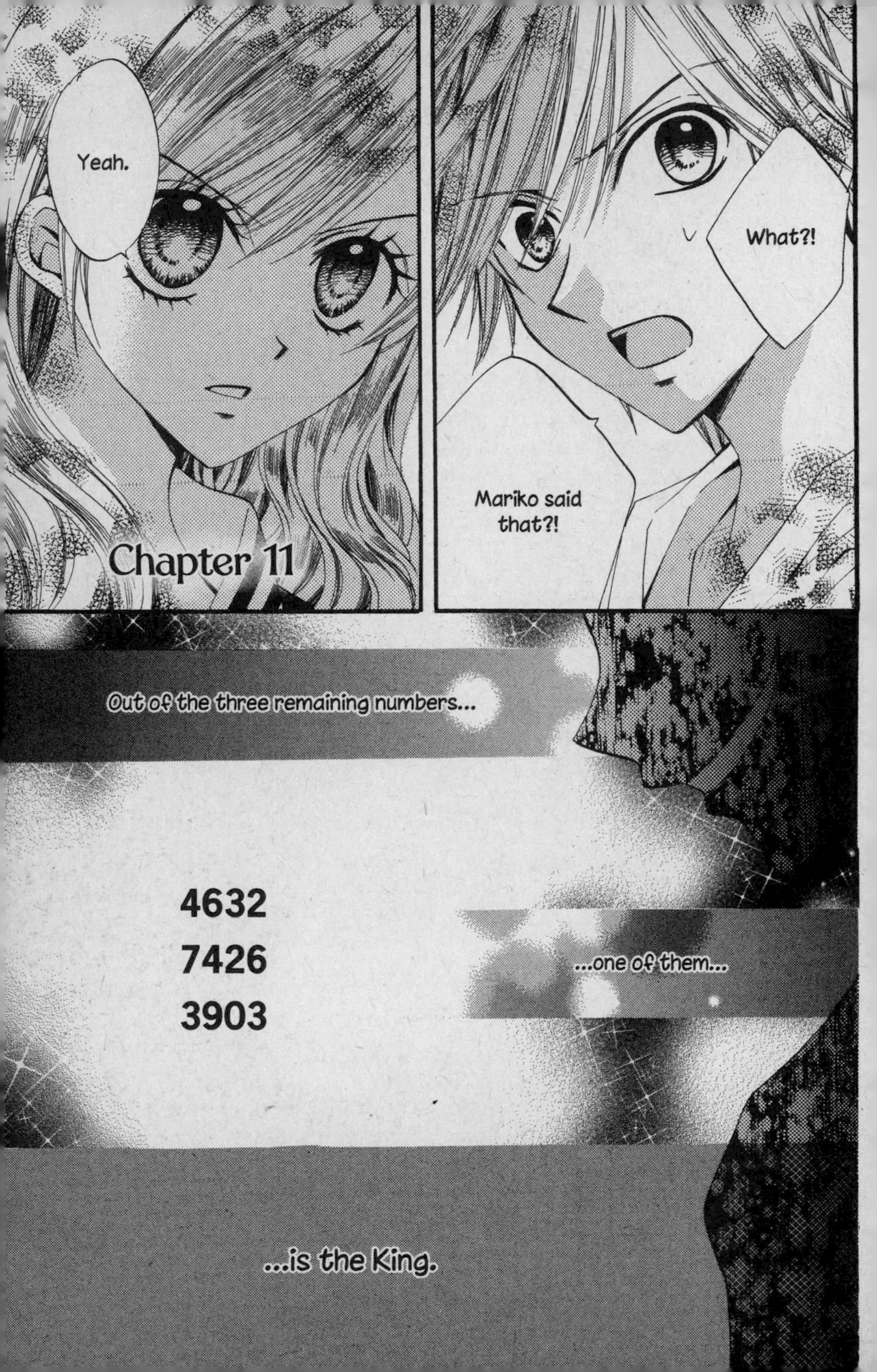
What?!
Mariko said that?!
Yeah.
Chapter 11
Out of the three remaining numbers...
...one of them...
4632
7426
3903
...is the King.

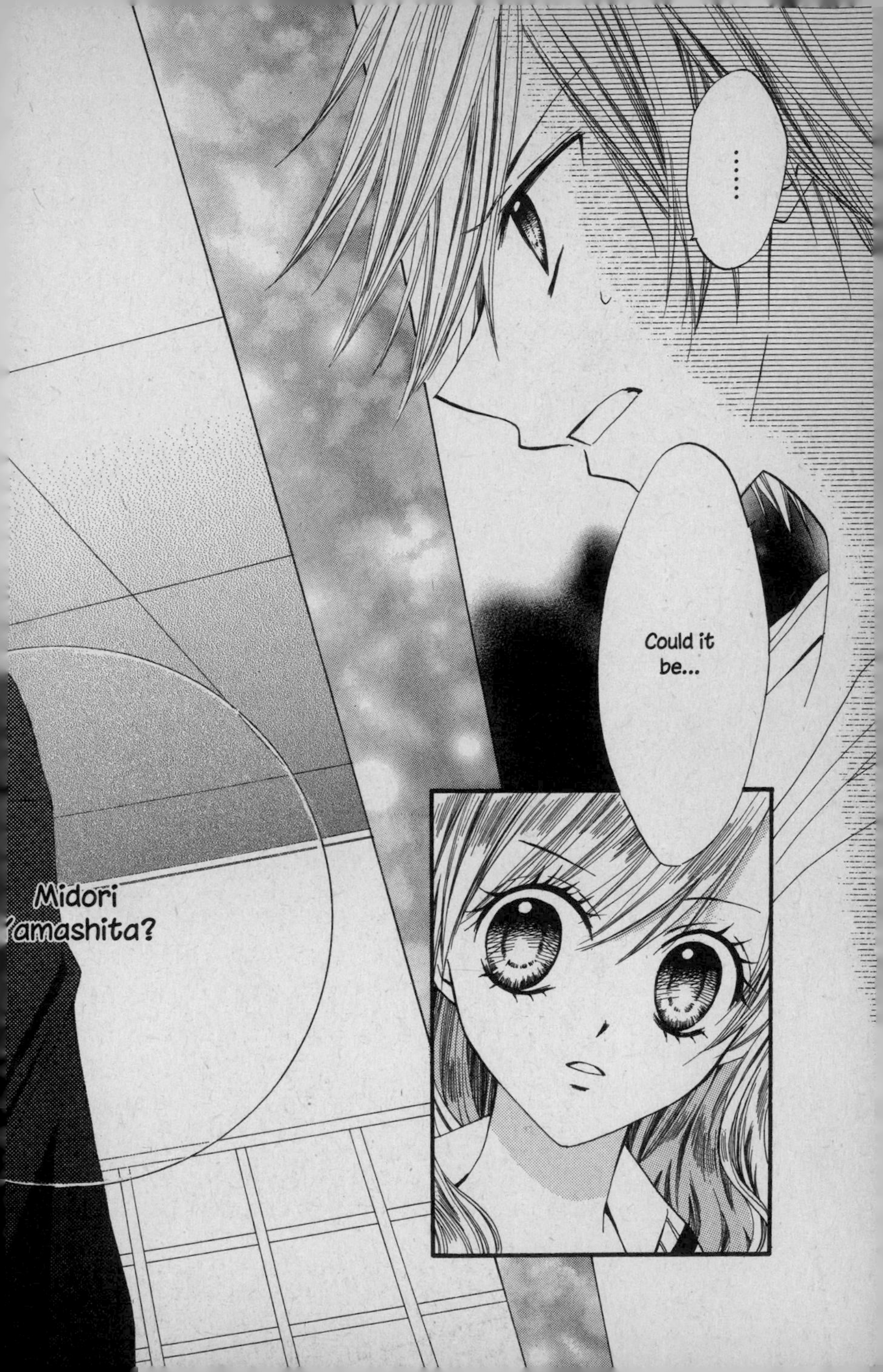
......
Could it be...
Midori
amashita?

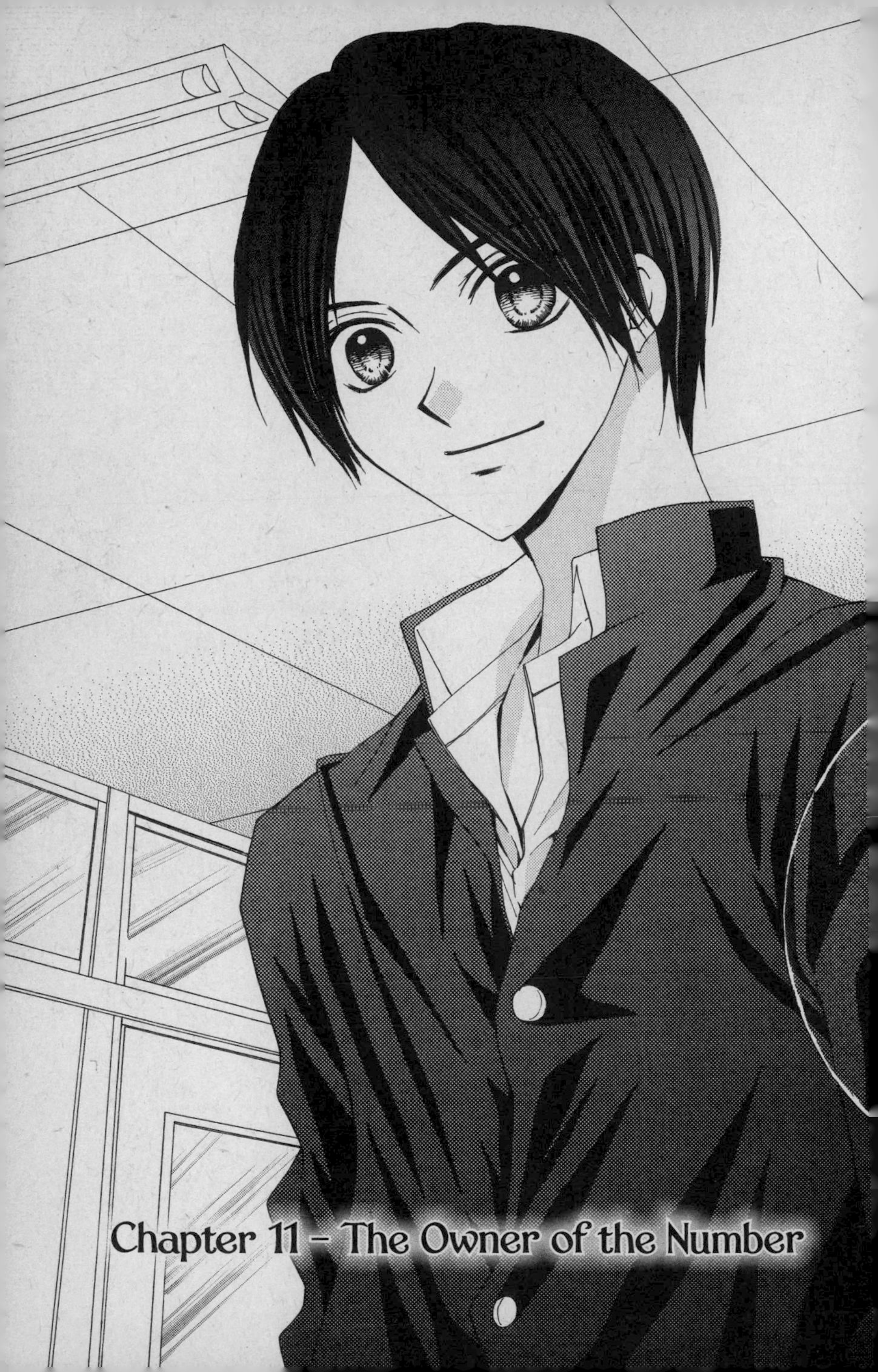
Chapter 11 - The Owner of the Number

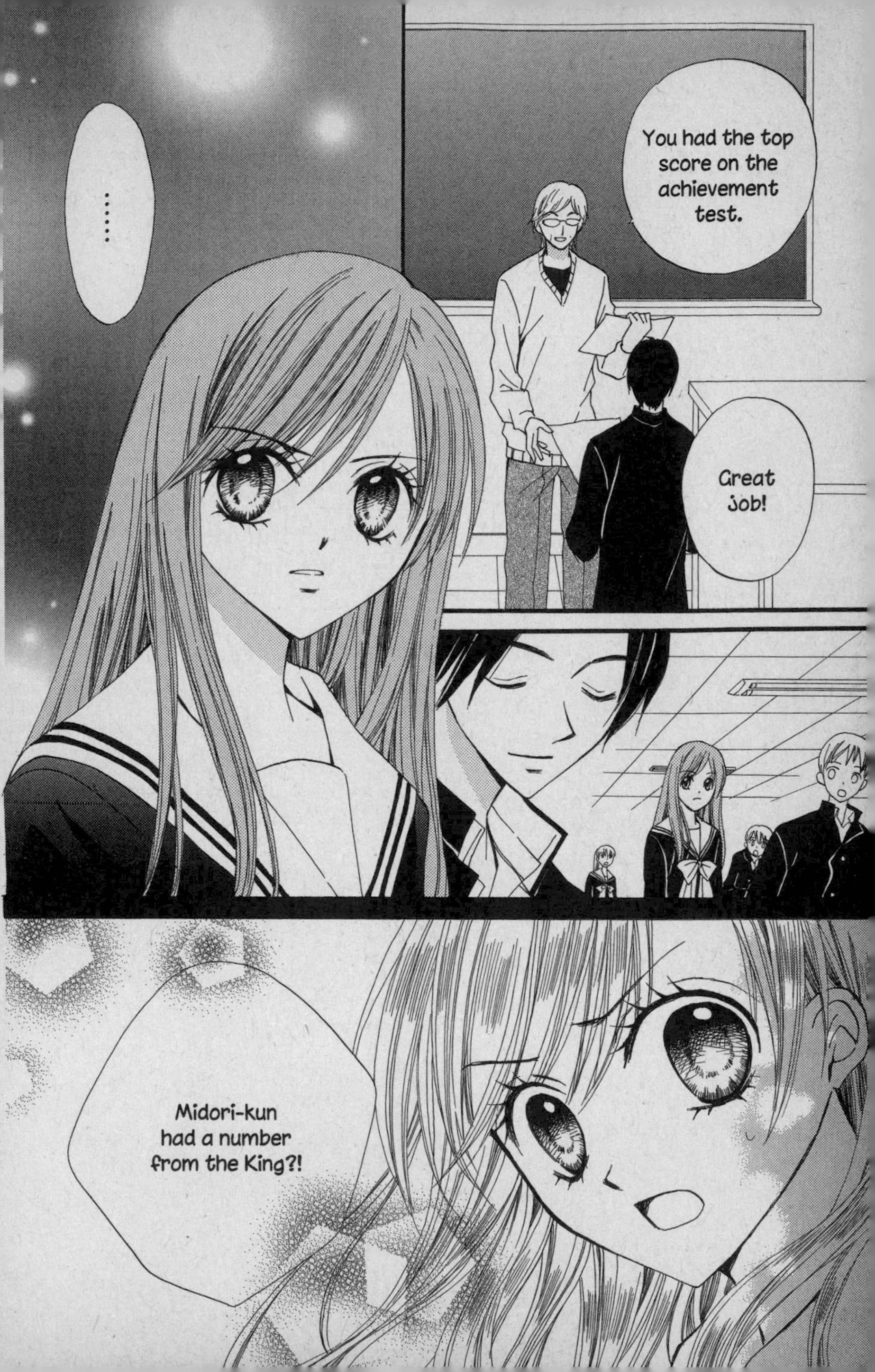
You had the top score on the achievement test.
Great job!
......
Midori-kun had a number from the King?!

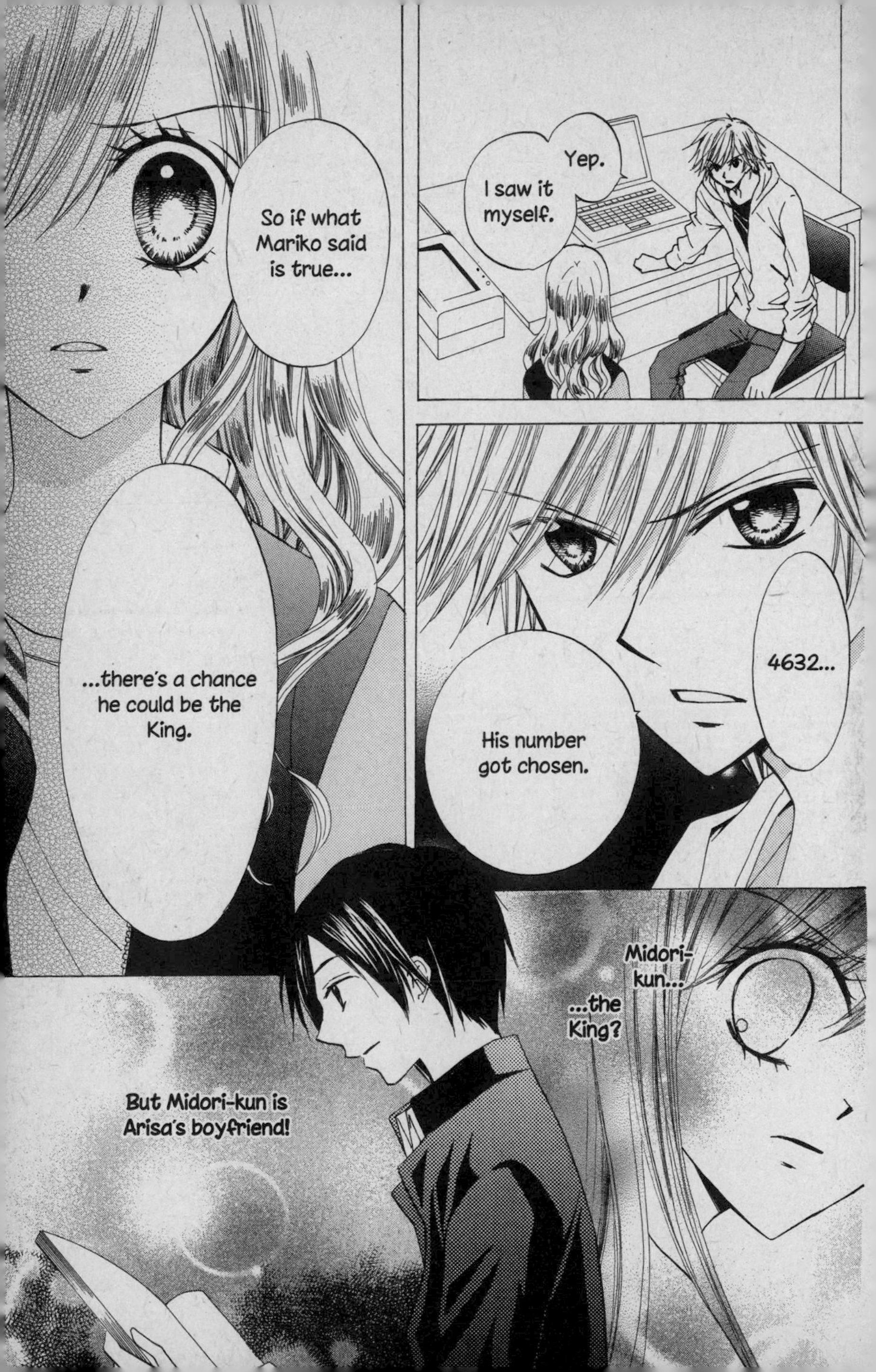
Yep.
I saw it myself.
4632...
His number got chosen.
So if what Mariko said is true...
...there's a chance he could be the King.
Midori-kun...
...the King?
But Midori-kun is Arisa's boyfriend!

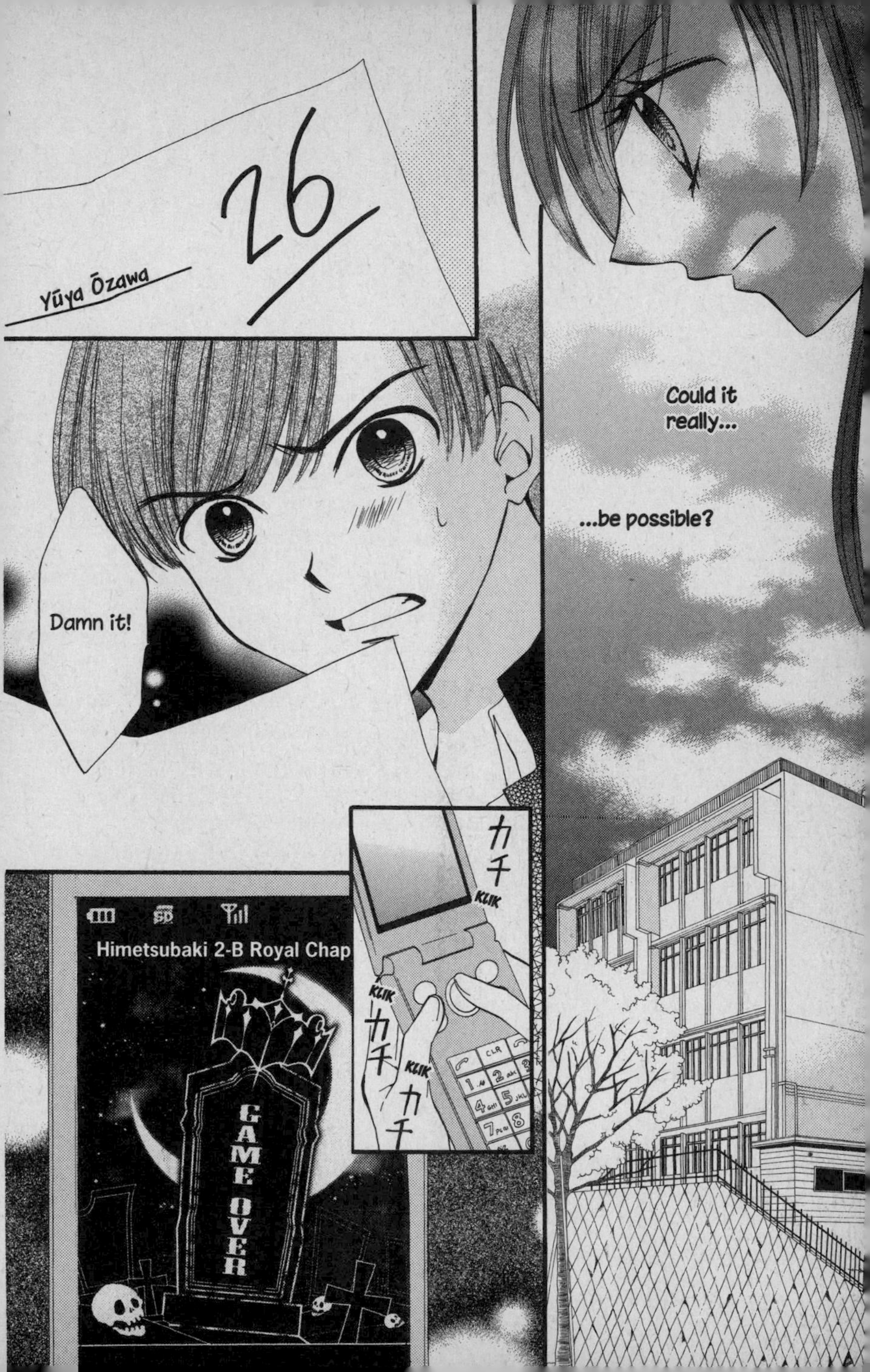
Could it really...
...be possible?
26
Yūya Ōzawa
Damn it!
カチ
KLIK
KLIK
カチ
KLIK
カチ
Himetsubaki 2-B Royal Chap
GAME OVER

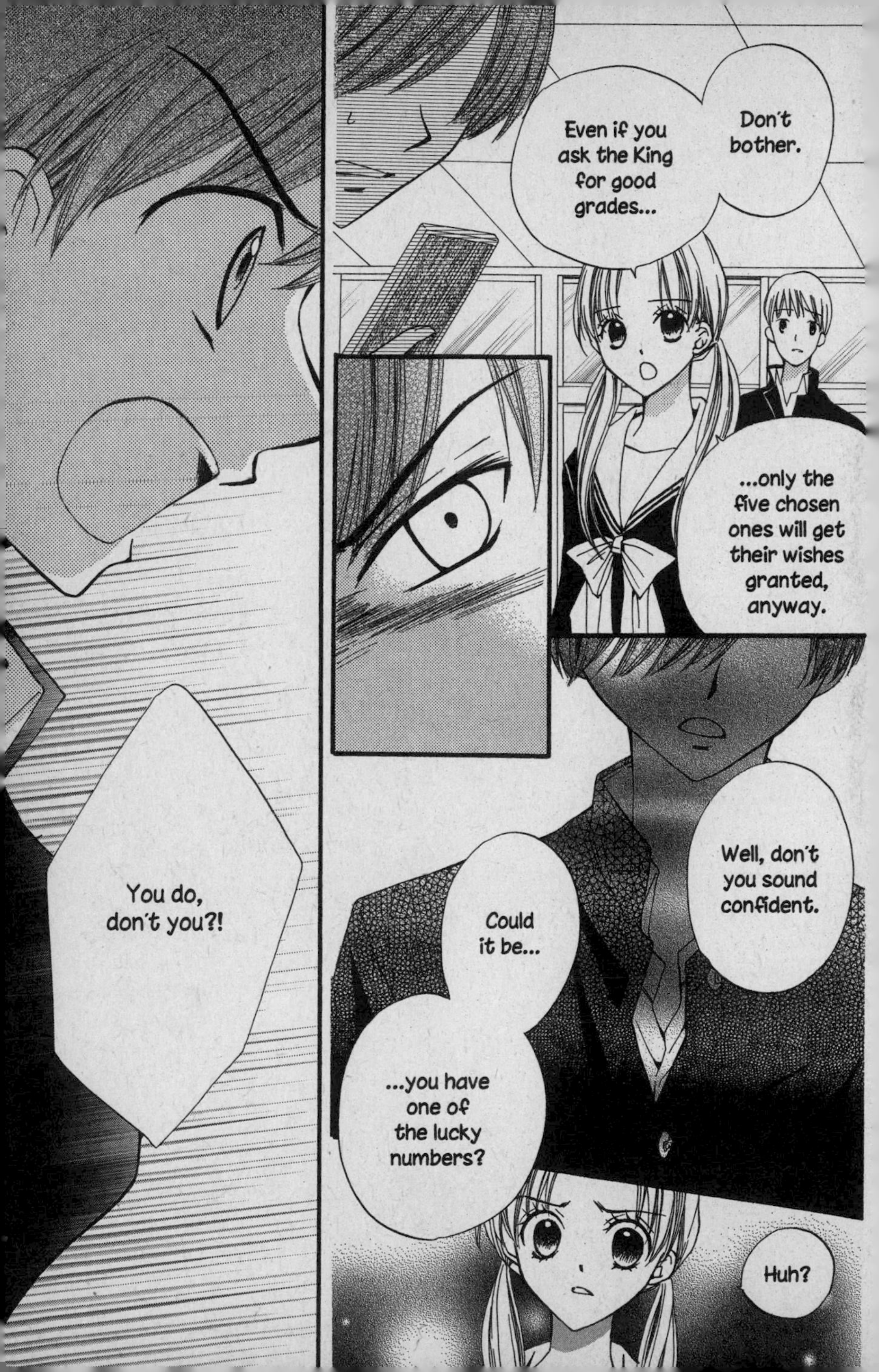
Don't bother.
Even if you ask the King for good grades...
...only the five chosen ones will get their wishes granted, anyway.
Well, don't you sound confident.
Could it be...
...you have one of the lucky numbers?
Huh?
You do, don't you?!

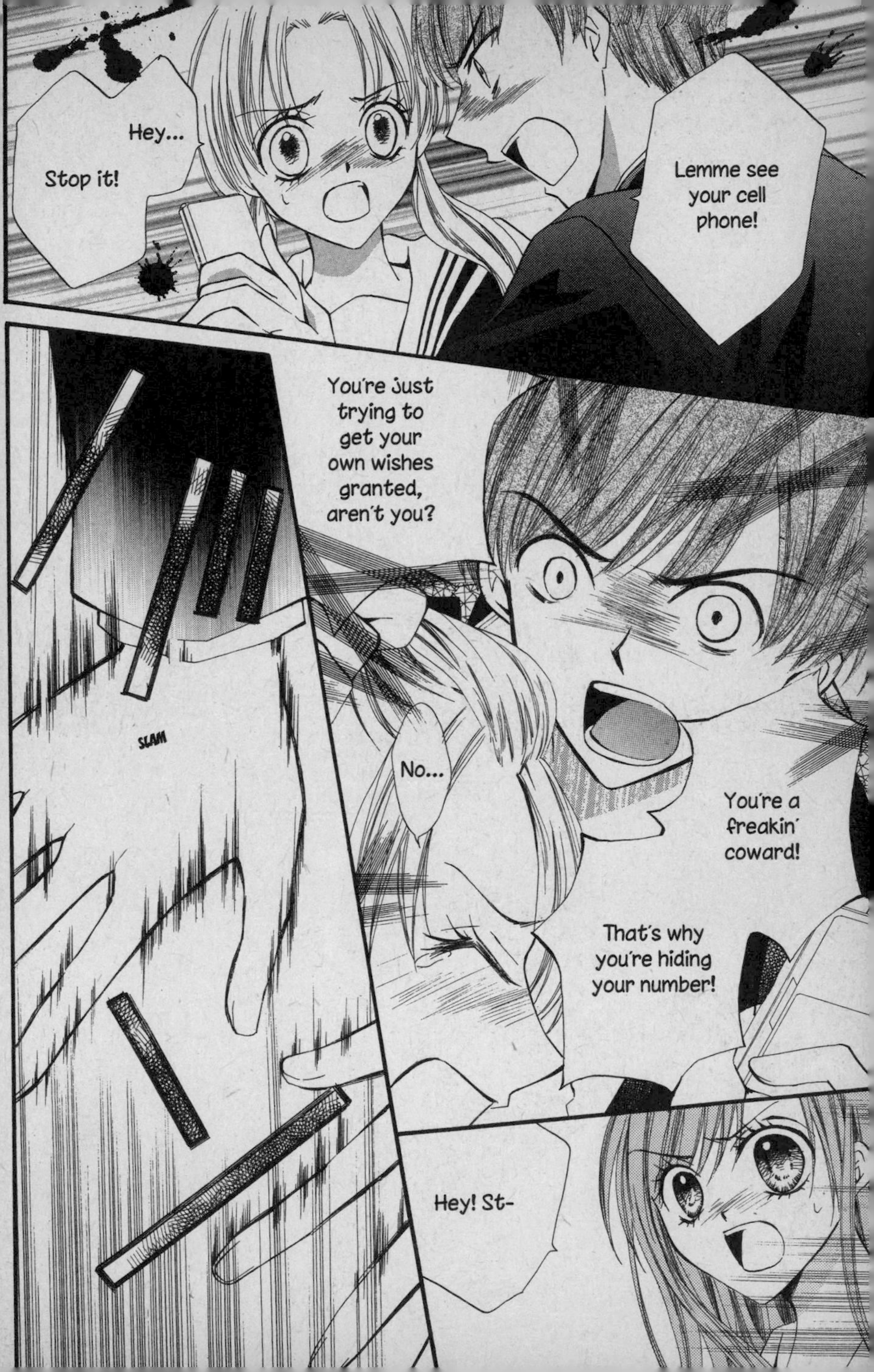
Lemme see your cell phone!
Hey...
Stop it!
You're just trying to get your own wishes granted, aren't you?
No...
You're a freakin' coward!
That's why you're hiding your number!
Hey! St-
SLAM

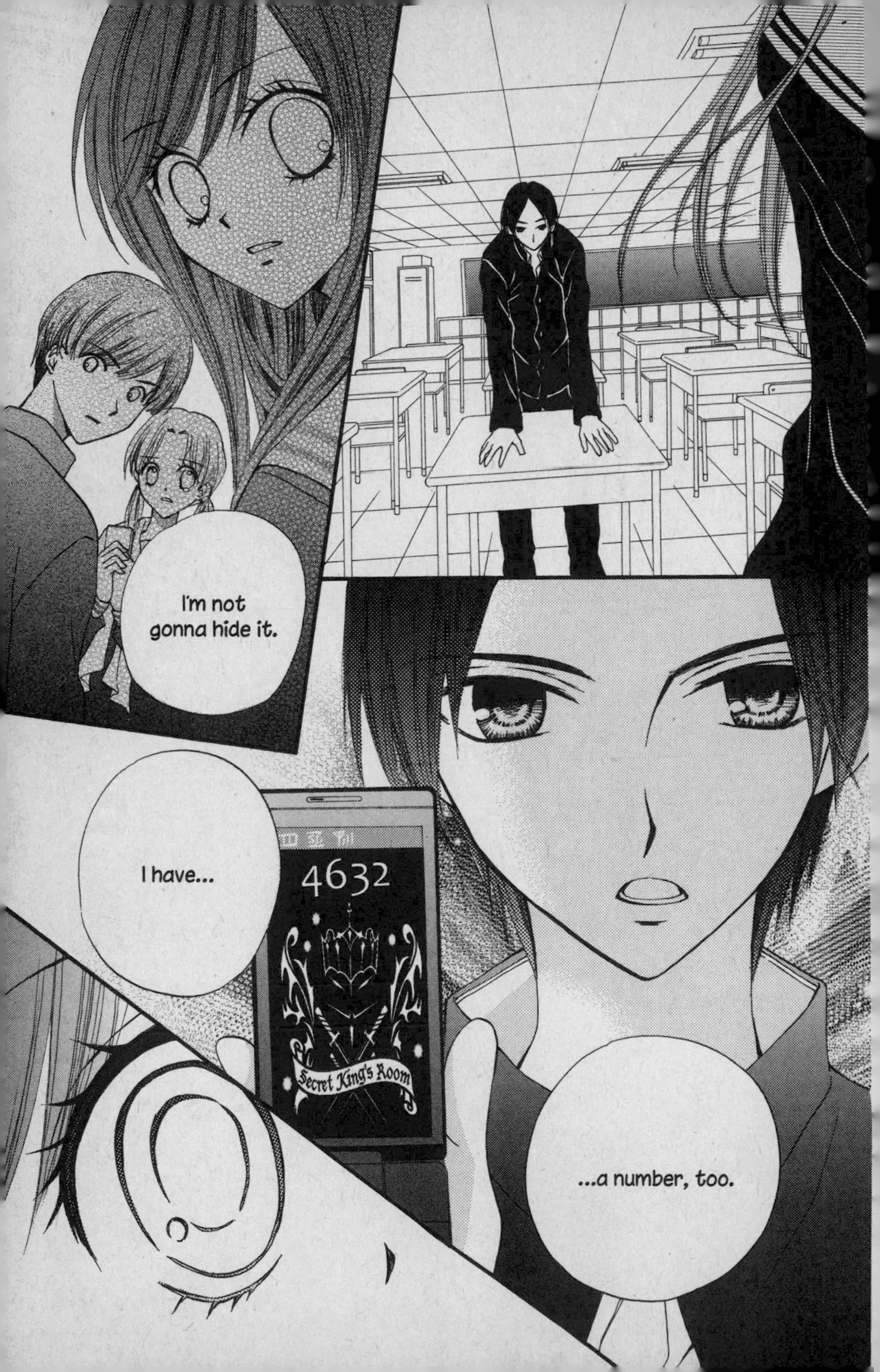
I'm not gonna hide it.
I have...
4632
Secret King's Room
...a number, too.

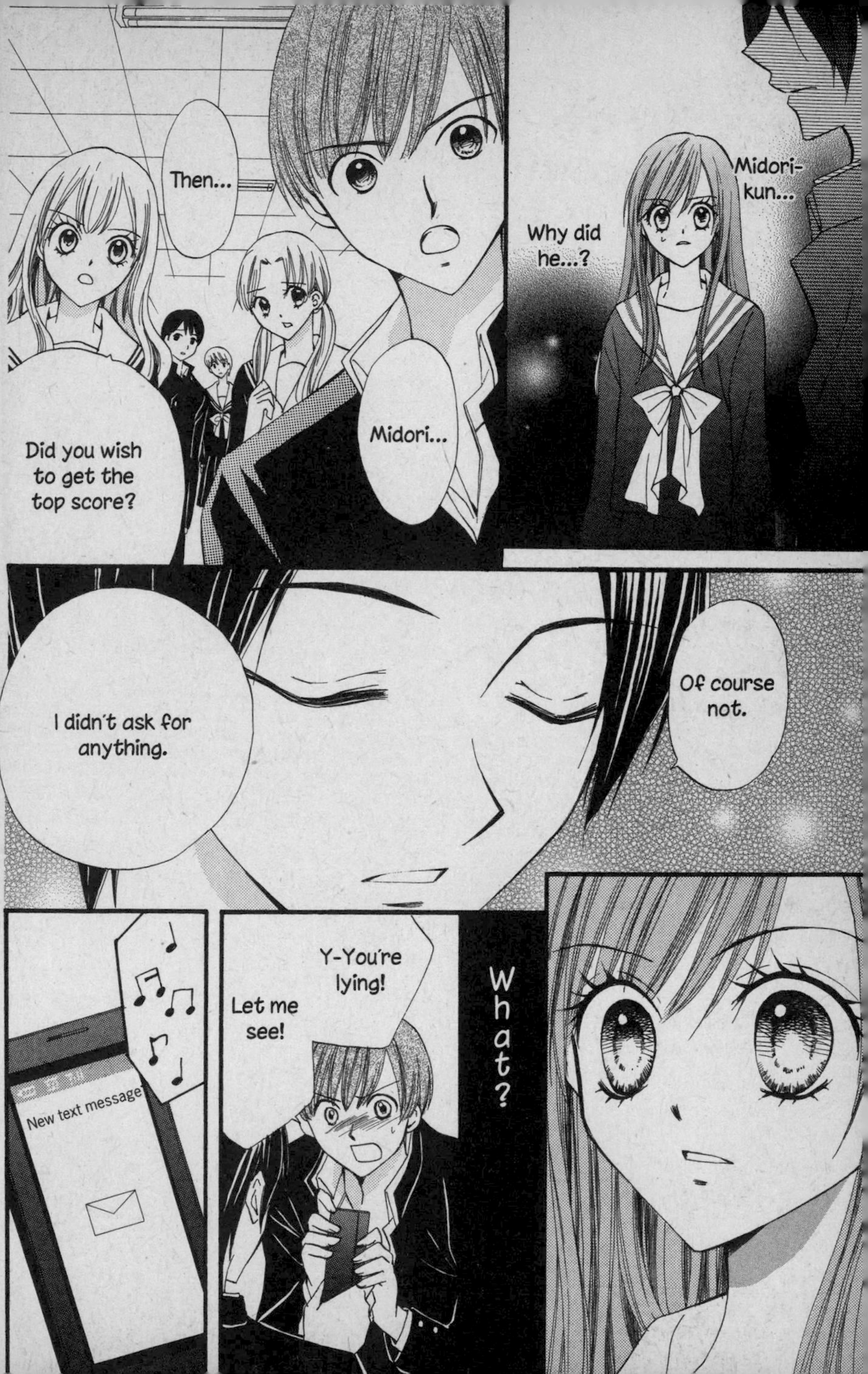
Midori-kun...
Why did he...?
Then...
Midori...
Did you wish to get the top score?
Of course not.
I didn't ask for anything.
What?
Y-You're lying!
Let me see!
New text message

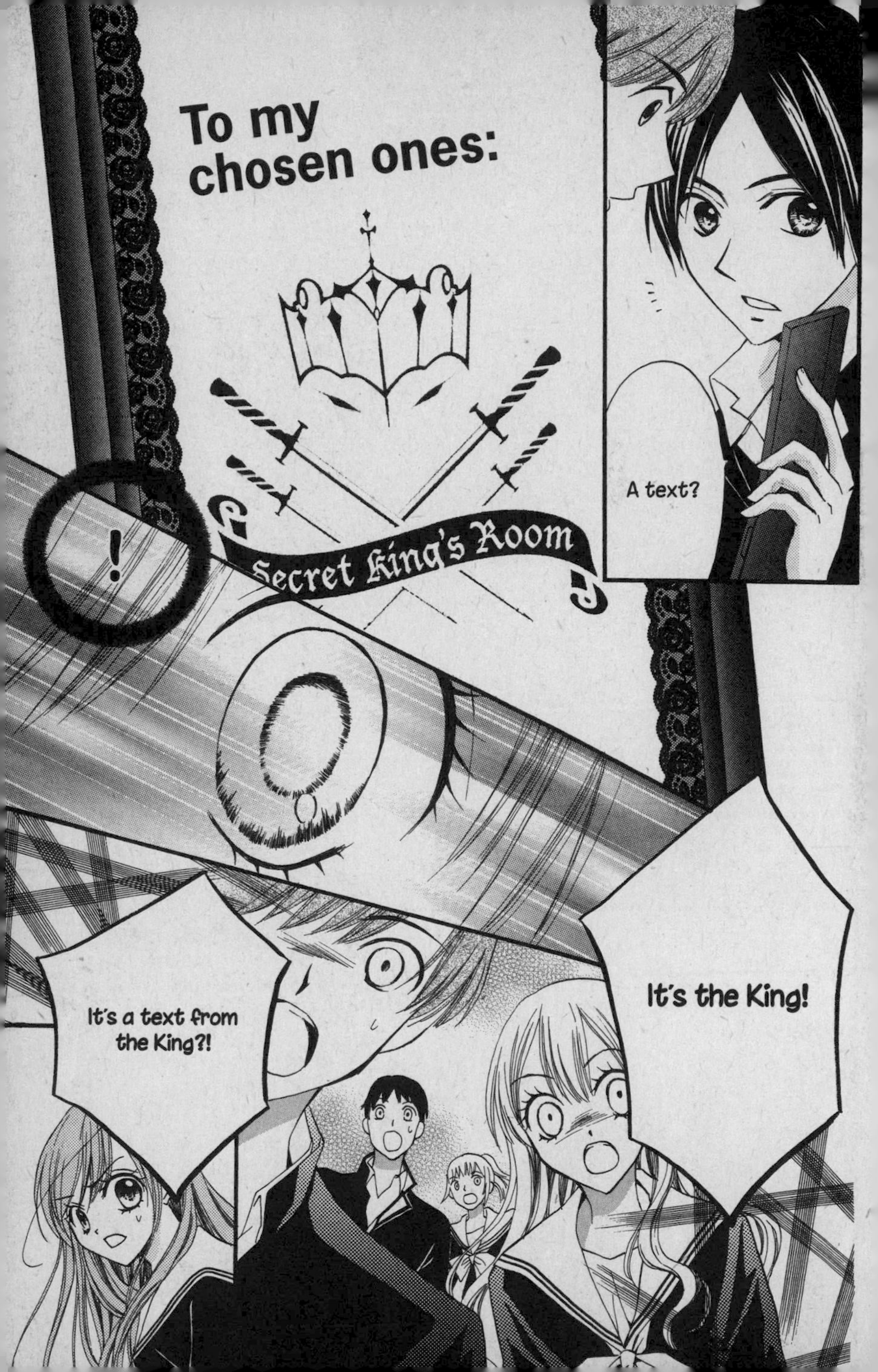
A text?
To my chosen ones:
Secret King's Room
!
It's the King!
It's a text from the King?!

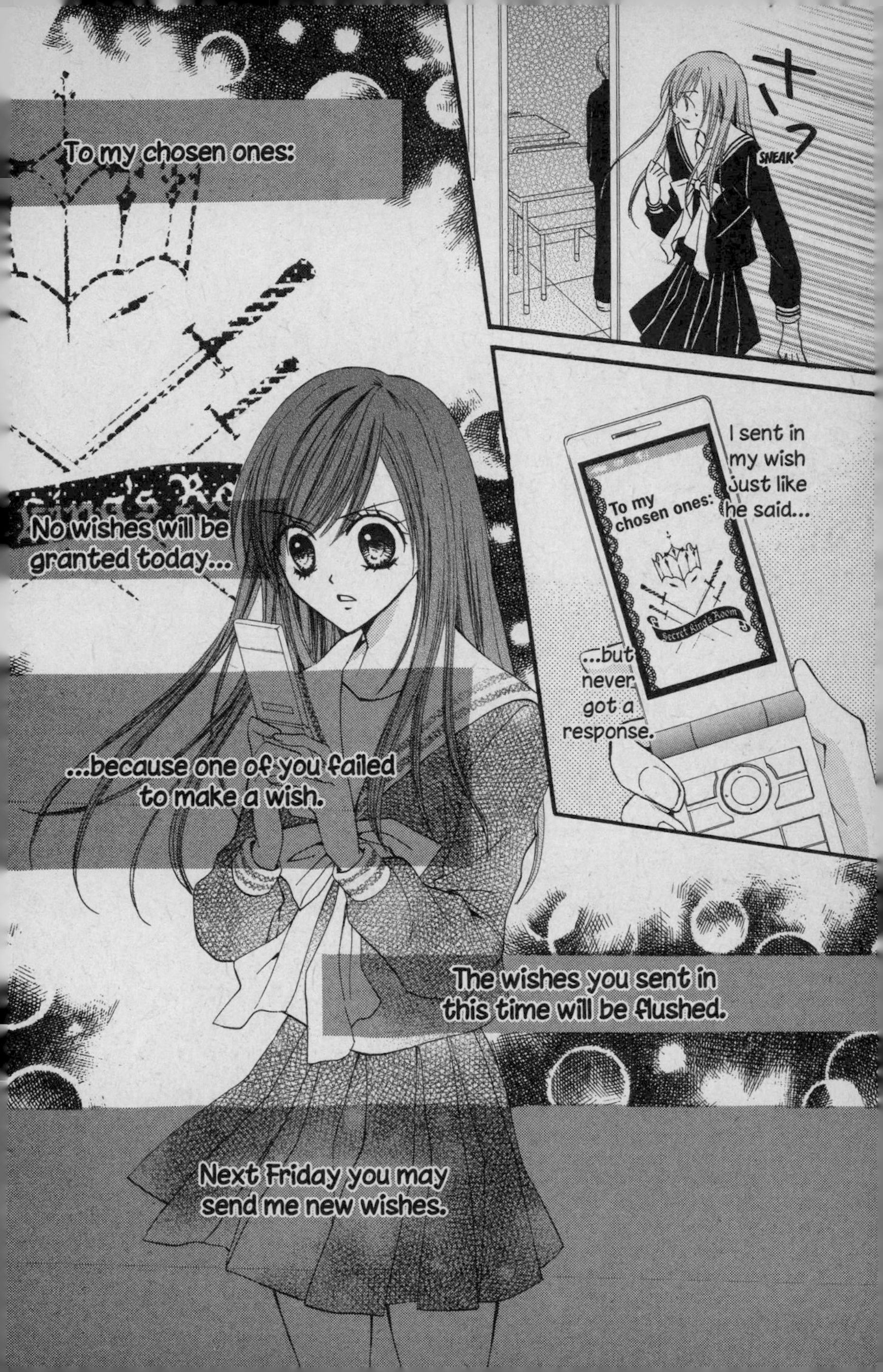
さッ
SNEAK
I sent in my wish just like he said...
To my chosen ones:
Secret King's Room
...but never got a response.
To my chosen ones:
No wishes will be granted today...
...because one of you failed to make a wish.
The wishes you sent in this time will be flushed.
Next Friday you may send me new wishes.

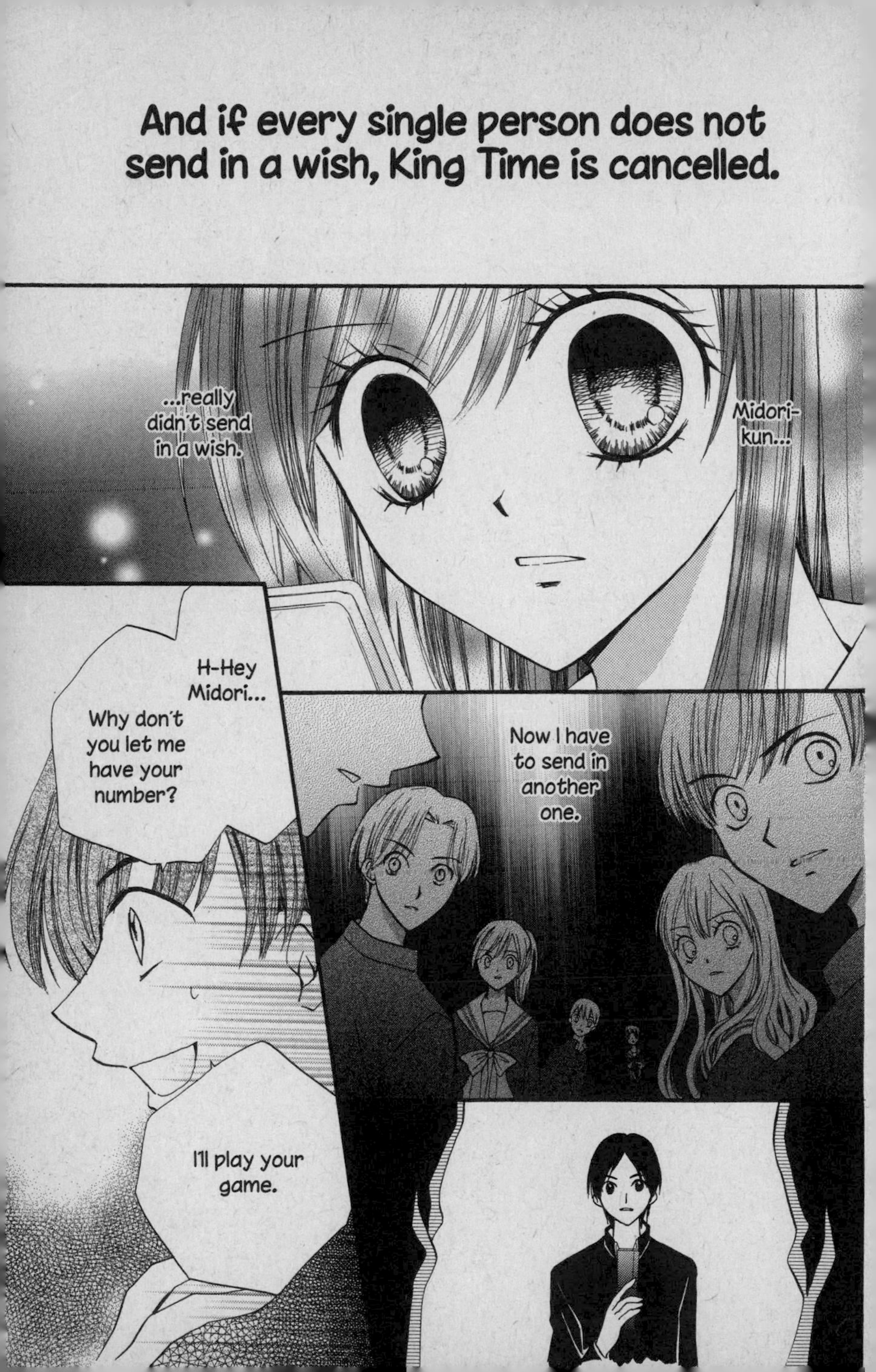
And if every single person does not send in a wish, King Time is cancelled.
Midori-kun...
...really didn't send in a wish.
Now I have to send in another one.
H-Hey Midori... Why don't you let me have your number?
I'll play your game.

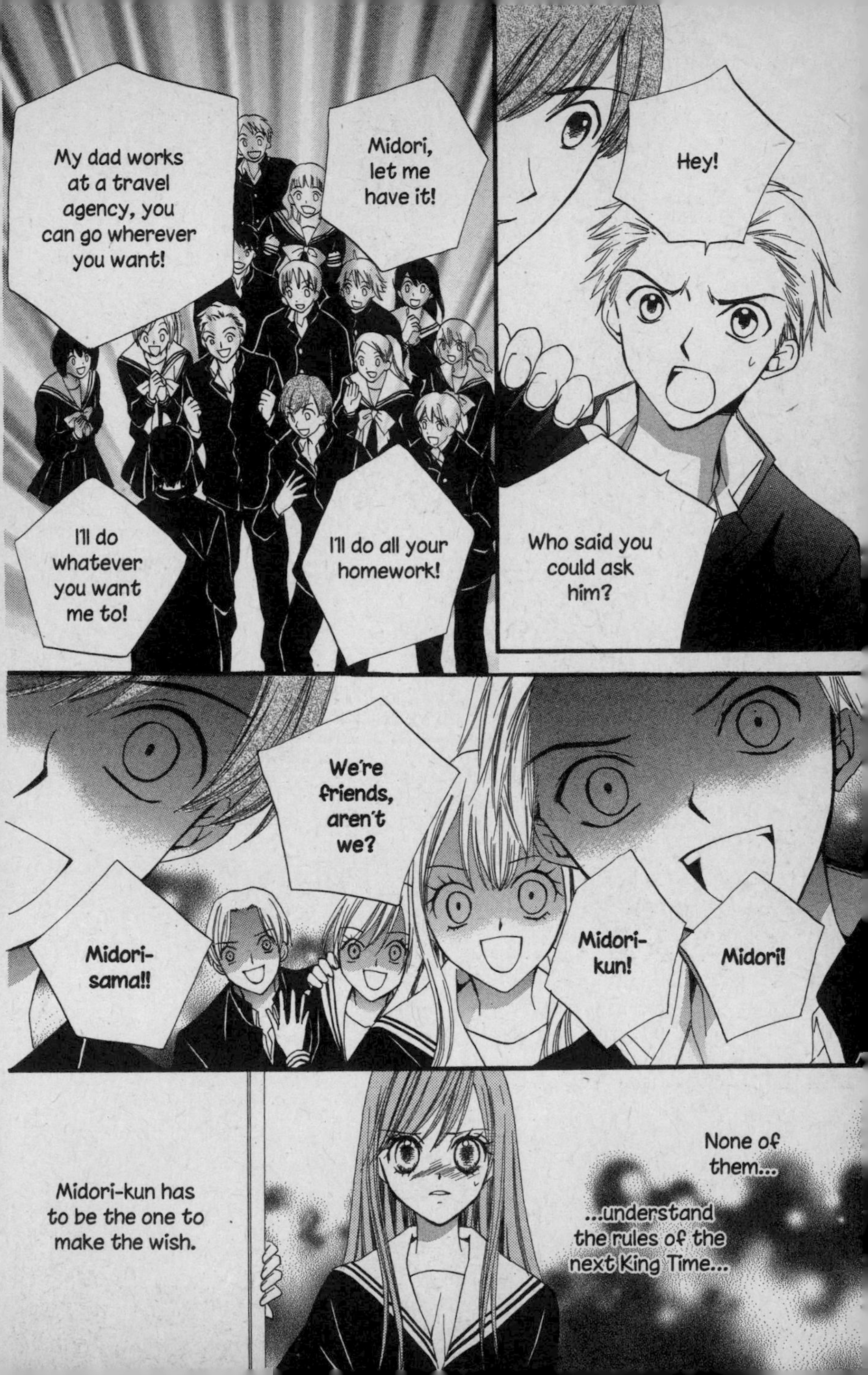
Hey!
Who said you could ask him?
Midori, let me have it!
My dad works at a travel agency, you can go wherever you want!
I'll do all your homework!
I'll do whatever you want me to!
Midori!
Midori-kun!
We're friends, aren't we?
Midori-sama!!
None of them...
...understand the rules of the next King Time...
Midori-kun has to be the one to make the wish.

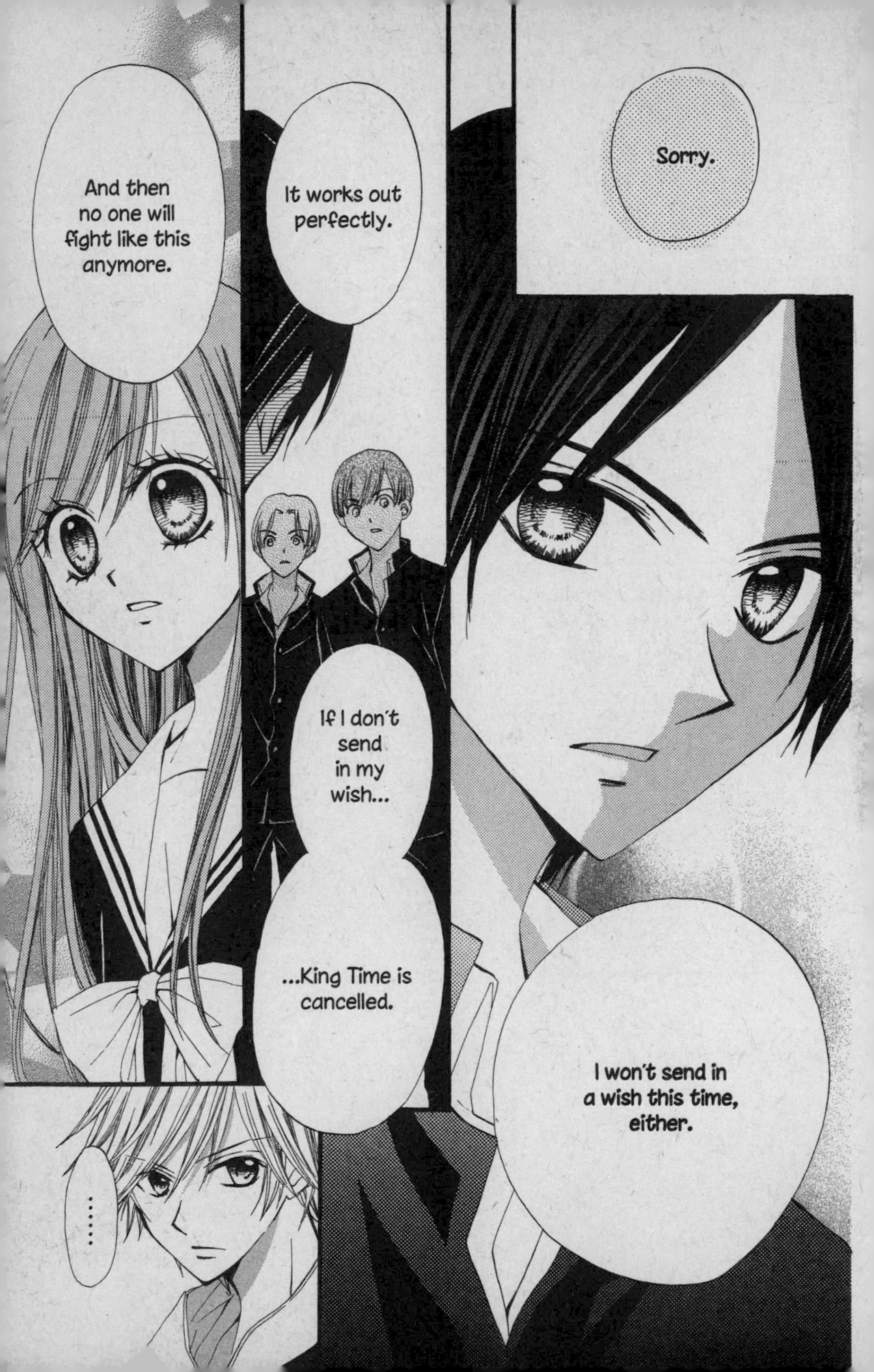
Sorry.
I won't send in a wish this time, either.
If I don't send in my wish...
...King Time is cancelled.
It works out perfectly.
And then no one will fight like this anymore.
......

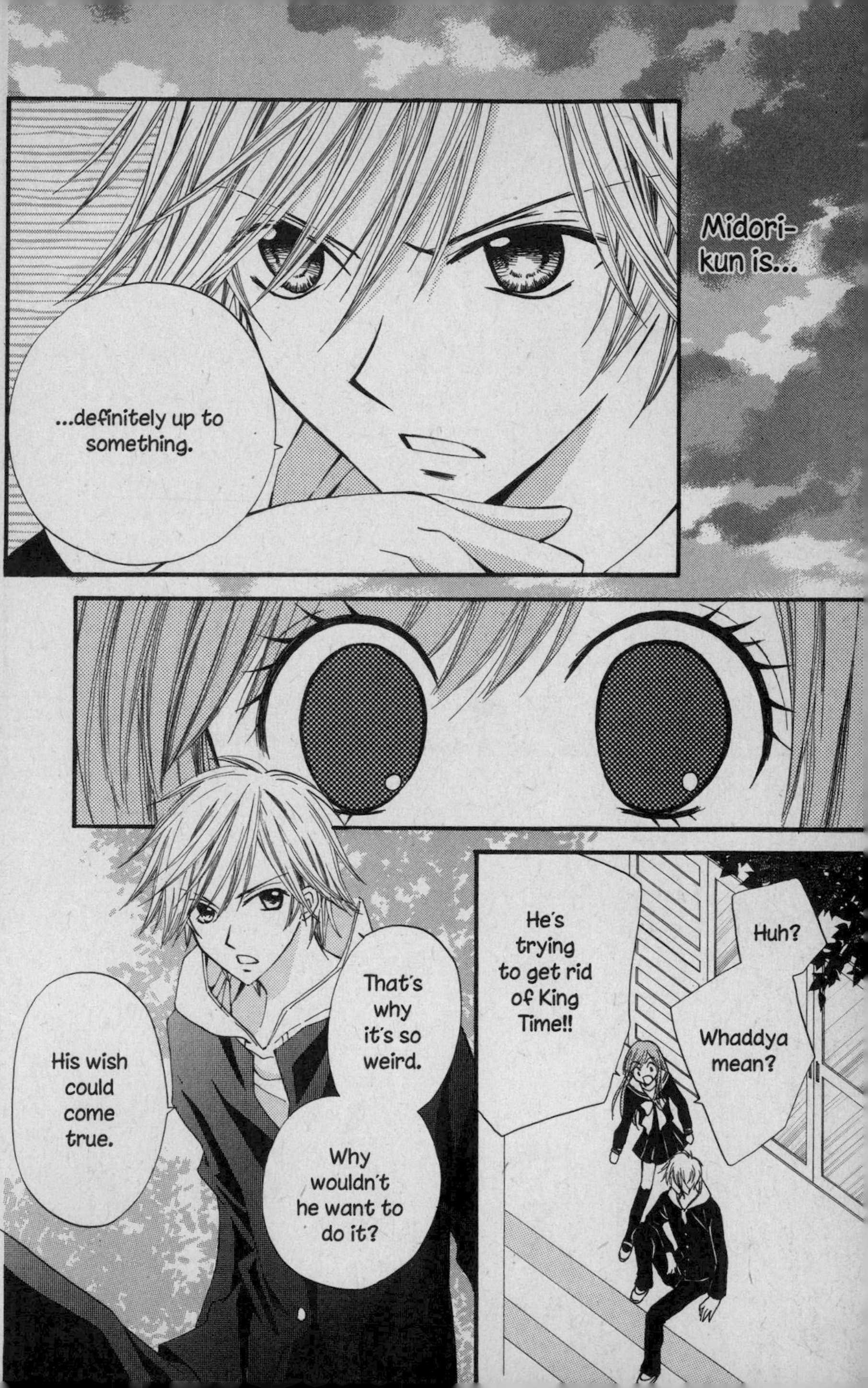

Midori-kun is...
...definitely up to something.
Huh?
Whaddya mean?
He's trying to get rid of King Time!!
That's why it's so weird.
His wish could come true.
Why wouldn't he want to do it?

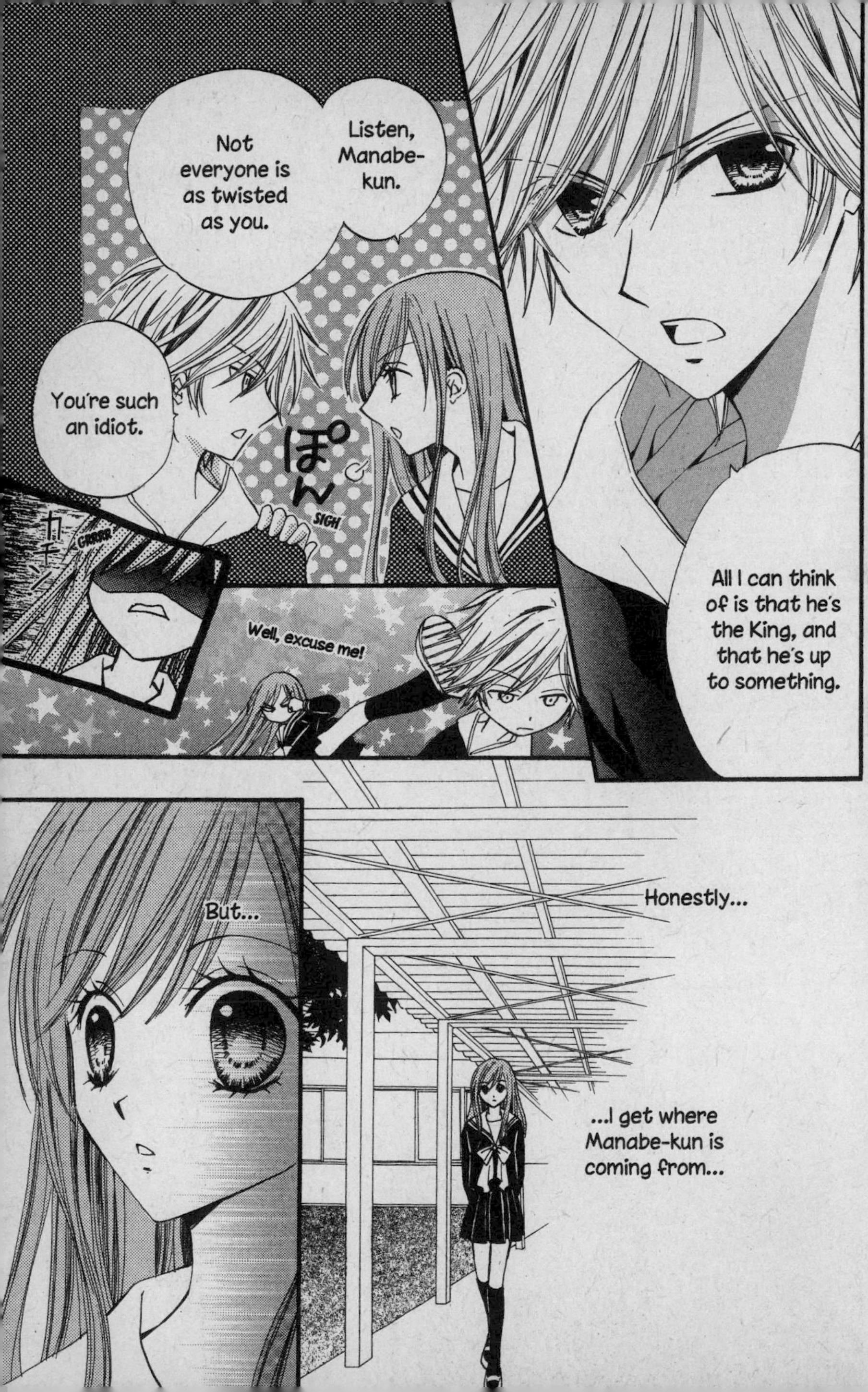
All I can think of is that he's the King, and that he's up to something.
Listen, Manabe-kun.
Not everyone is as twisted as you.
You're such an idiot.
ぽん
SIGH
GRRRR
Well, excuse me!
Honestly...
...I get where Manabe-kun is coming from...
But...

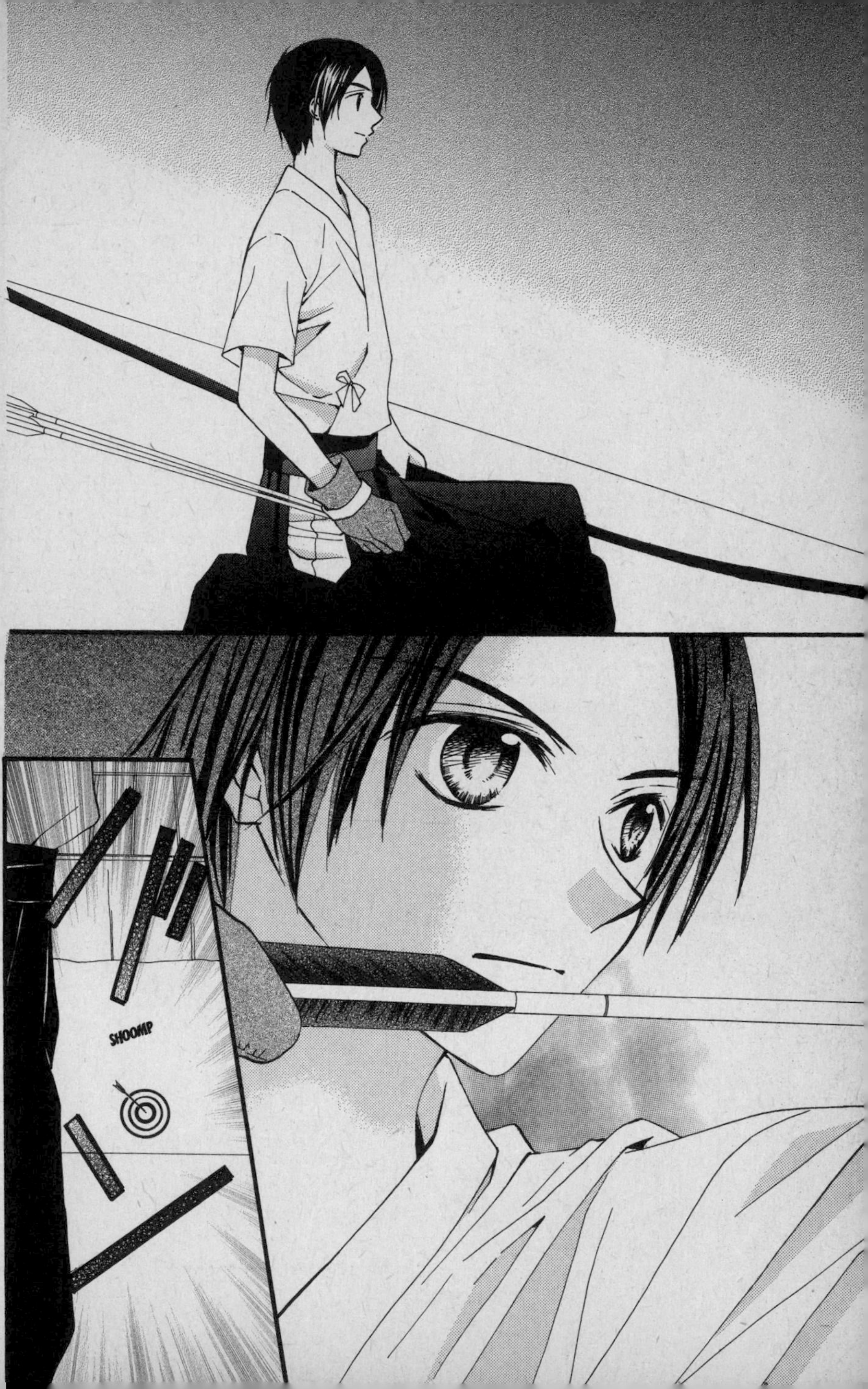
SHOOMP

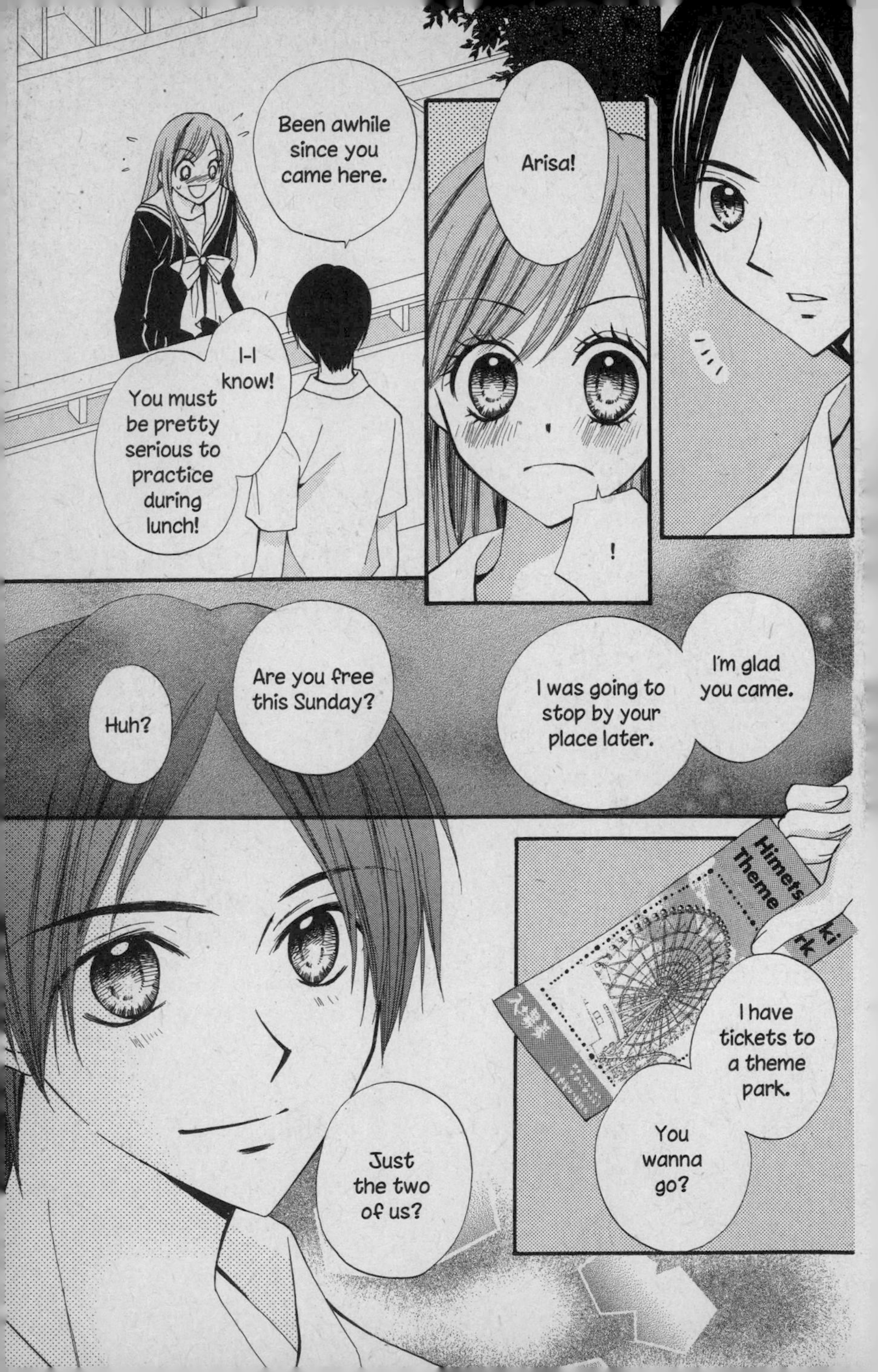
Arisa!
!
Been awhile since you came here.
I-I know! You must be pretty serious to practice during lunch!
I'm glad you came.
I was going to stop by your place later.
Are you free this Sunday?
Huh?
I have tickets to a theme park.
You wanna go?
Just the two of us?

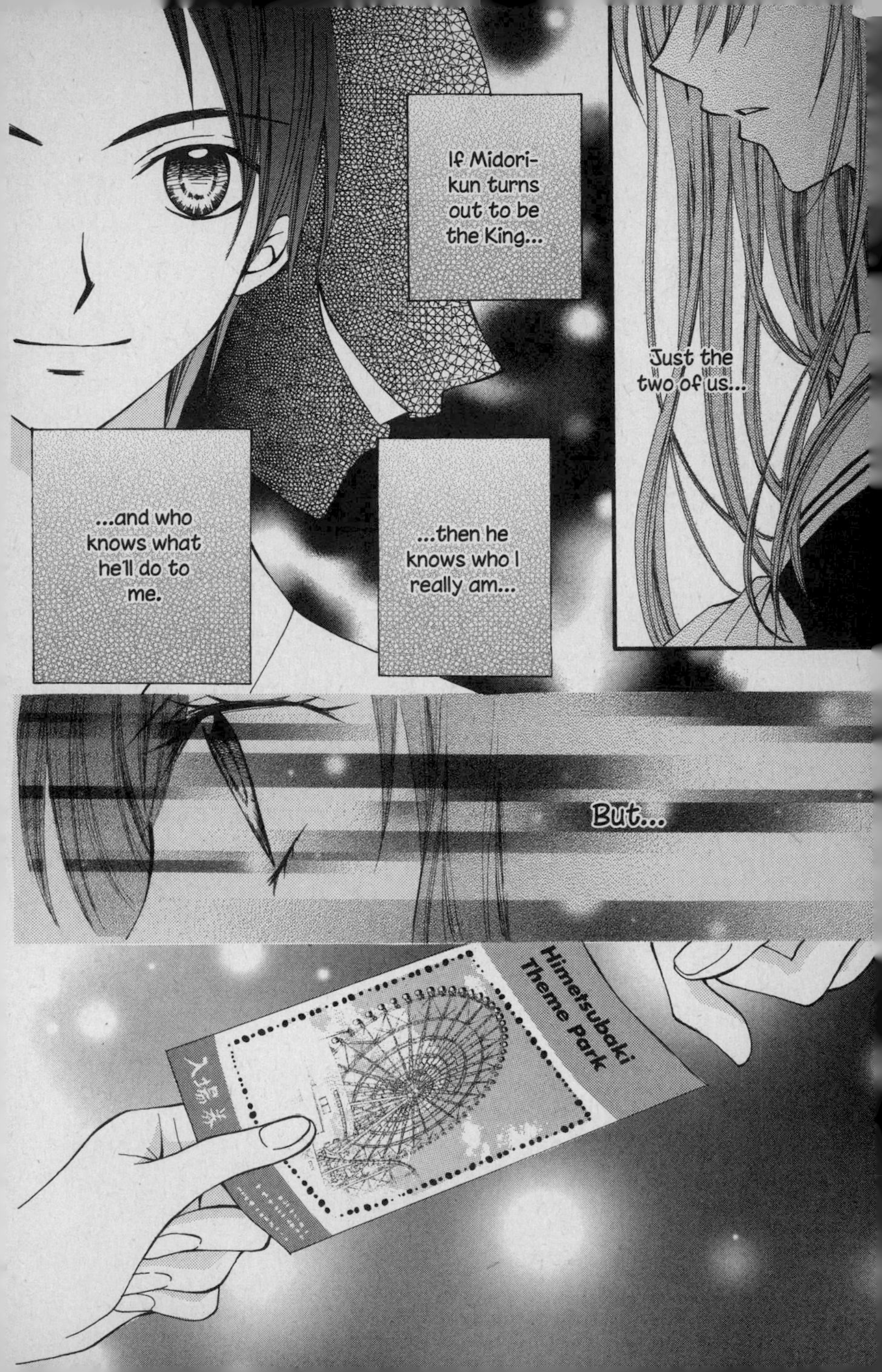
Just the two of us...
If Midori-kun turns out to be the King...
...then he knows who I really am...
...and who knows what he'll do to me.
But...
Himetsubaki Theme Park
入場券

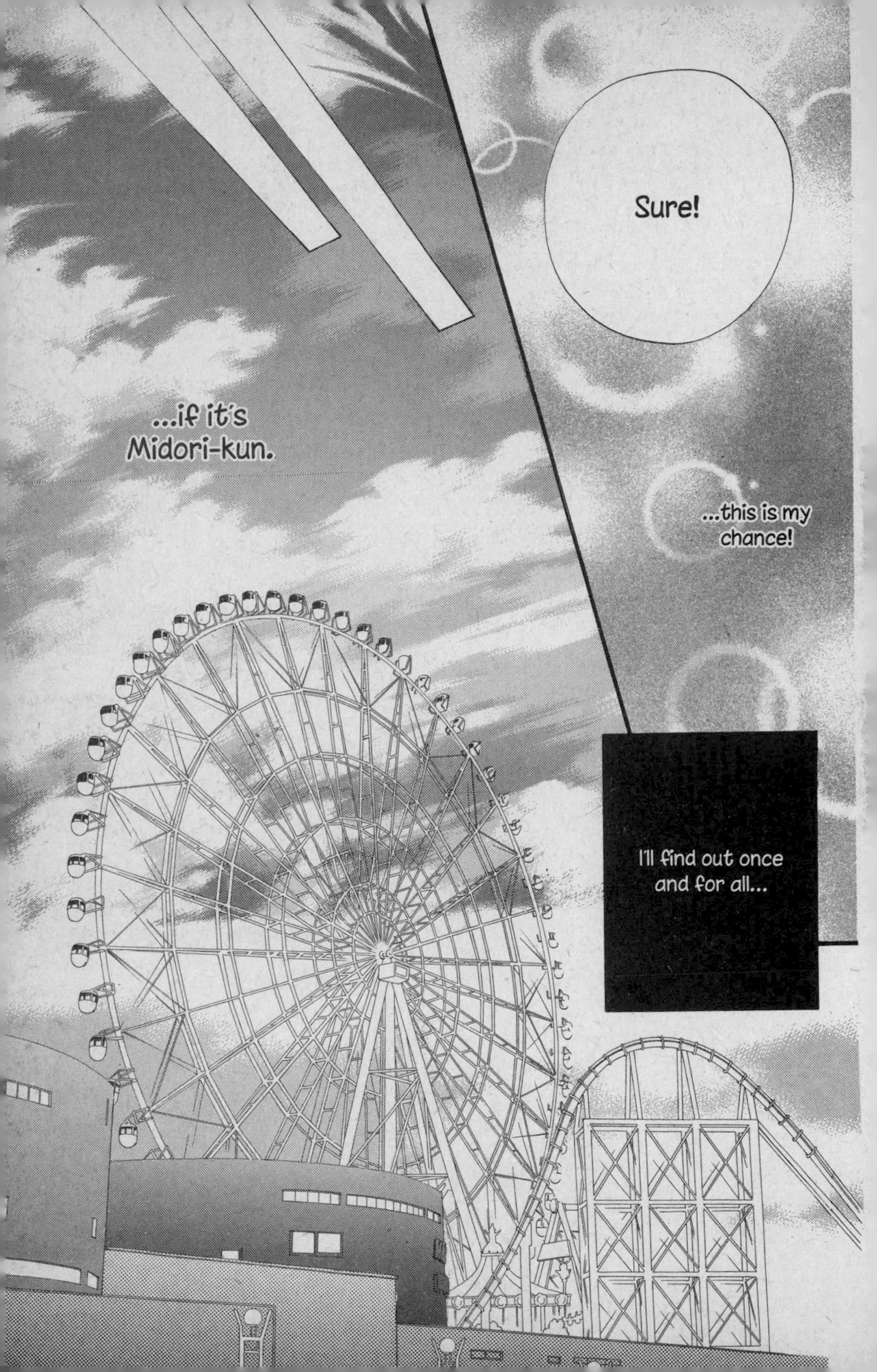
Sure!
...this is my chance!
I'll find out once and for all...
...if it's Midori-kun.

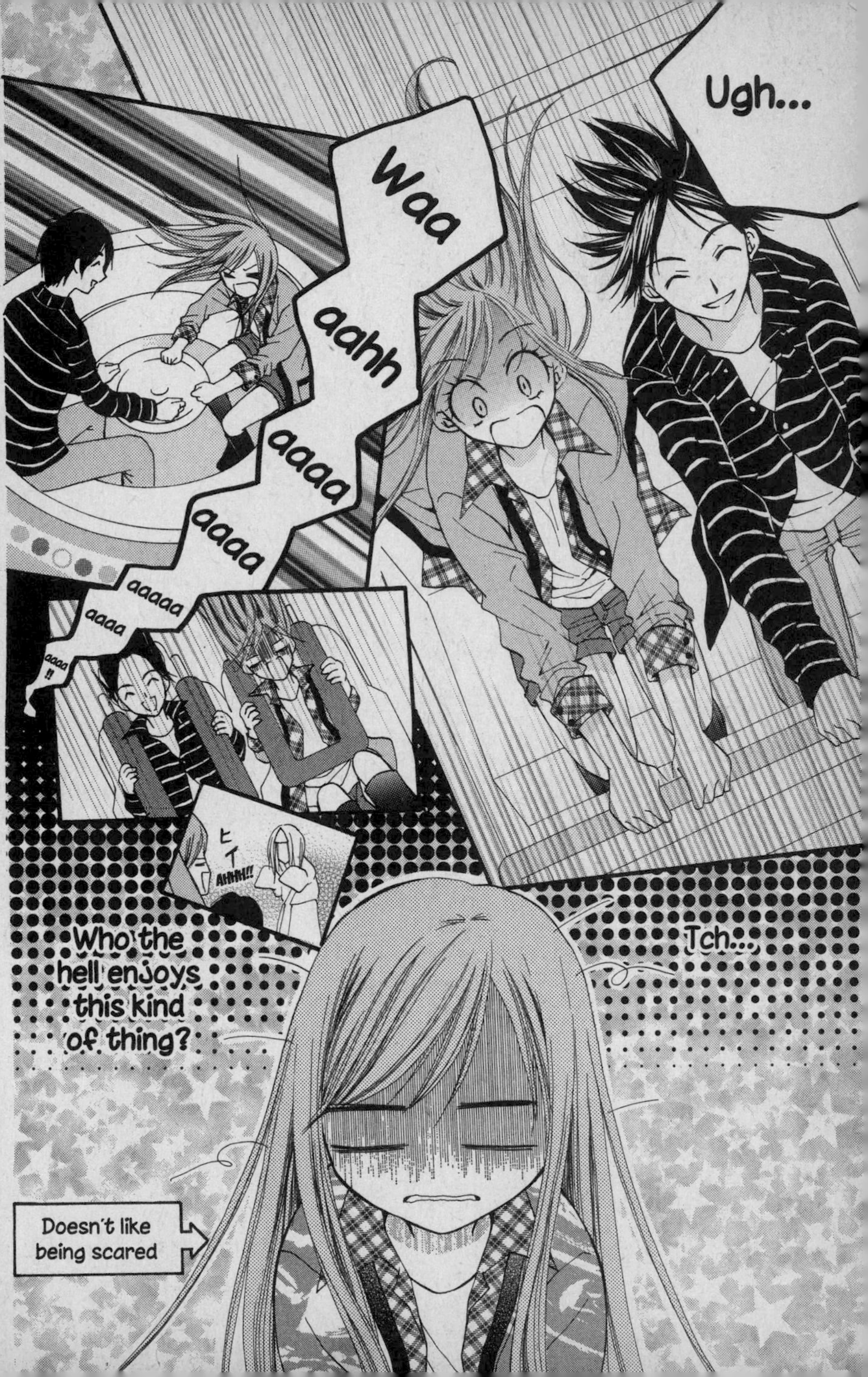
Ugh...
Waa aahh aaaa aaaa aaaaa aaaa aaaa!!
ヒイ
AHHH!!
Tch...
Who the hell enjoys this kind of thing?
Doesn't like being scared

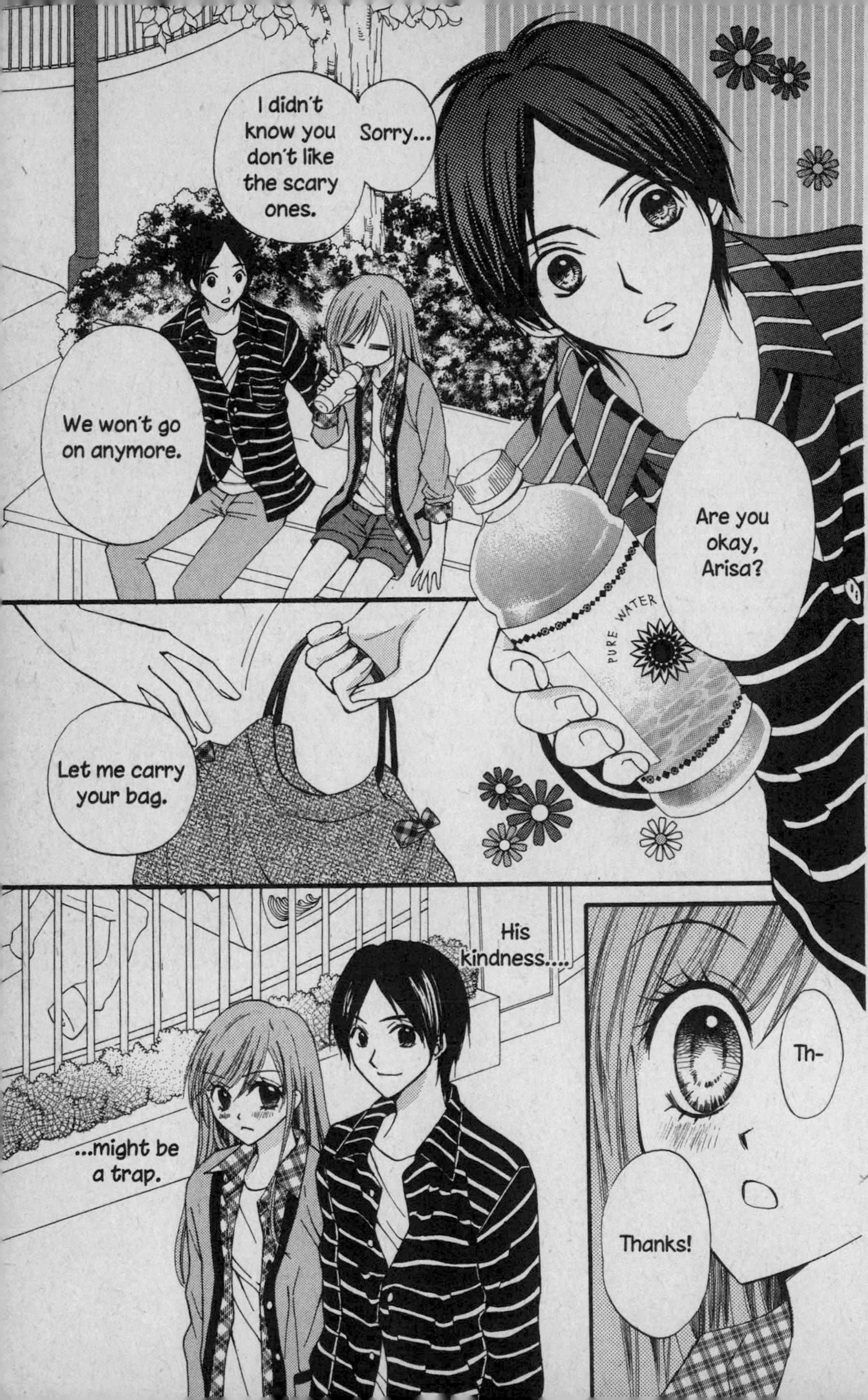
Are you okay, Arisa?
Sorry...
I didn't know you don't like the scary ones.
We won't go on anymore.
Let me carry your bag.
Th-
Thanks!
His kindness....
...might be a trap.

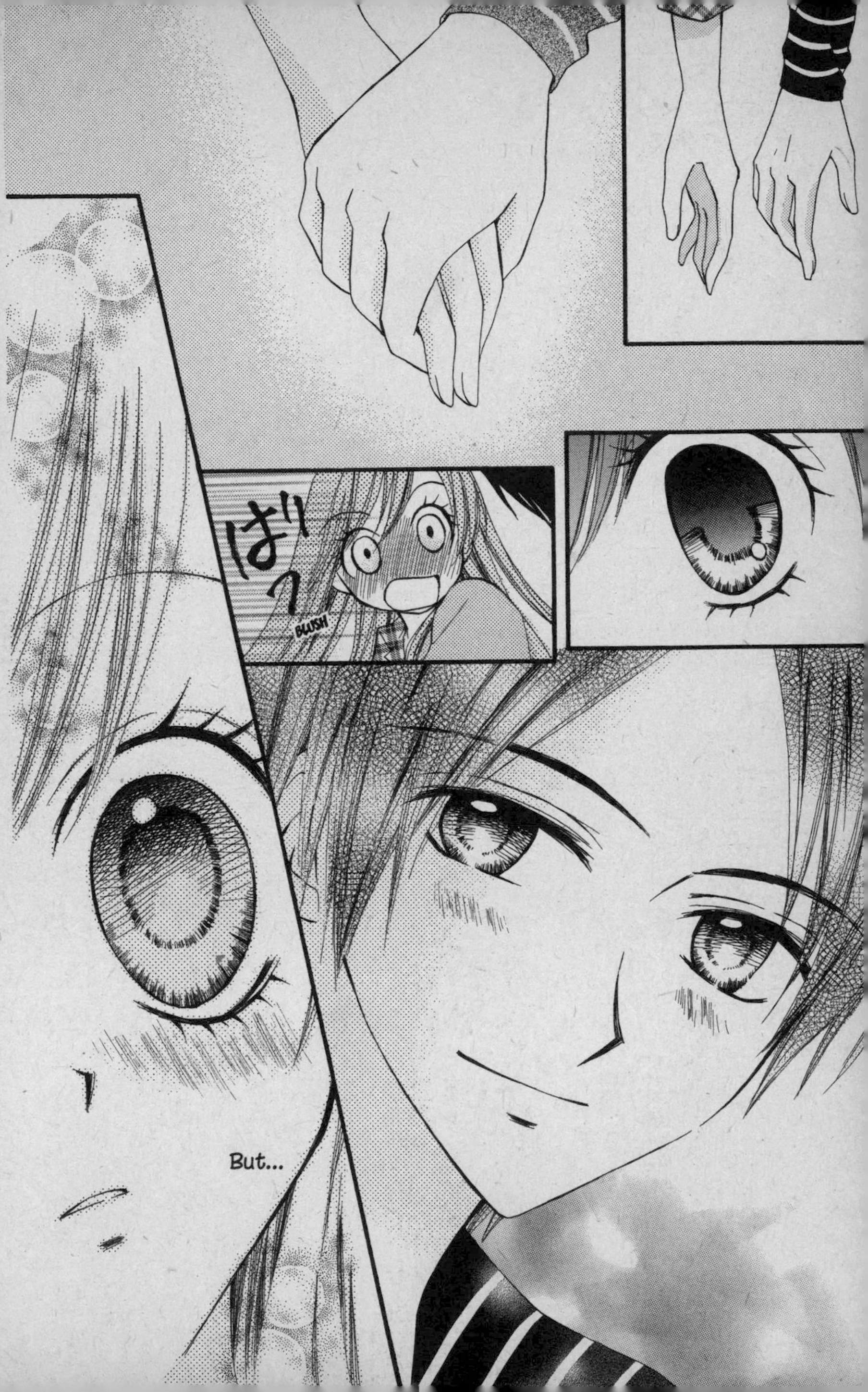
ぱっ
BLUSH
But...

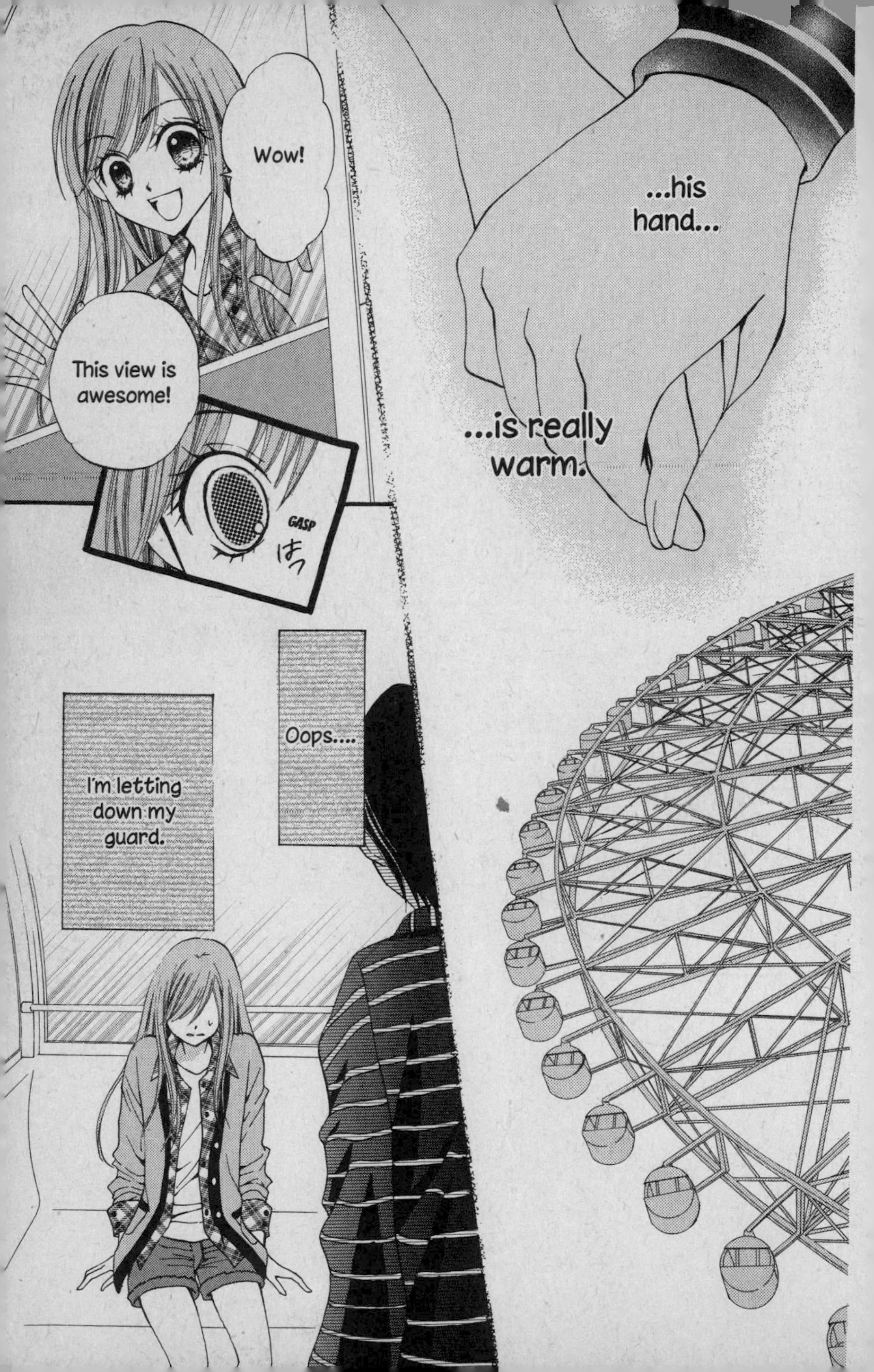
...his hand...
...is really warm.
Wow!
This view is awesome!
GASP
はっ
Oops....
I'm letting down my guard.

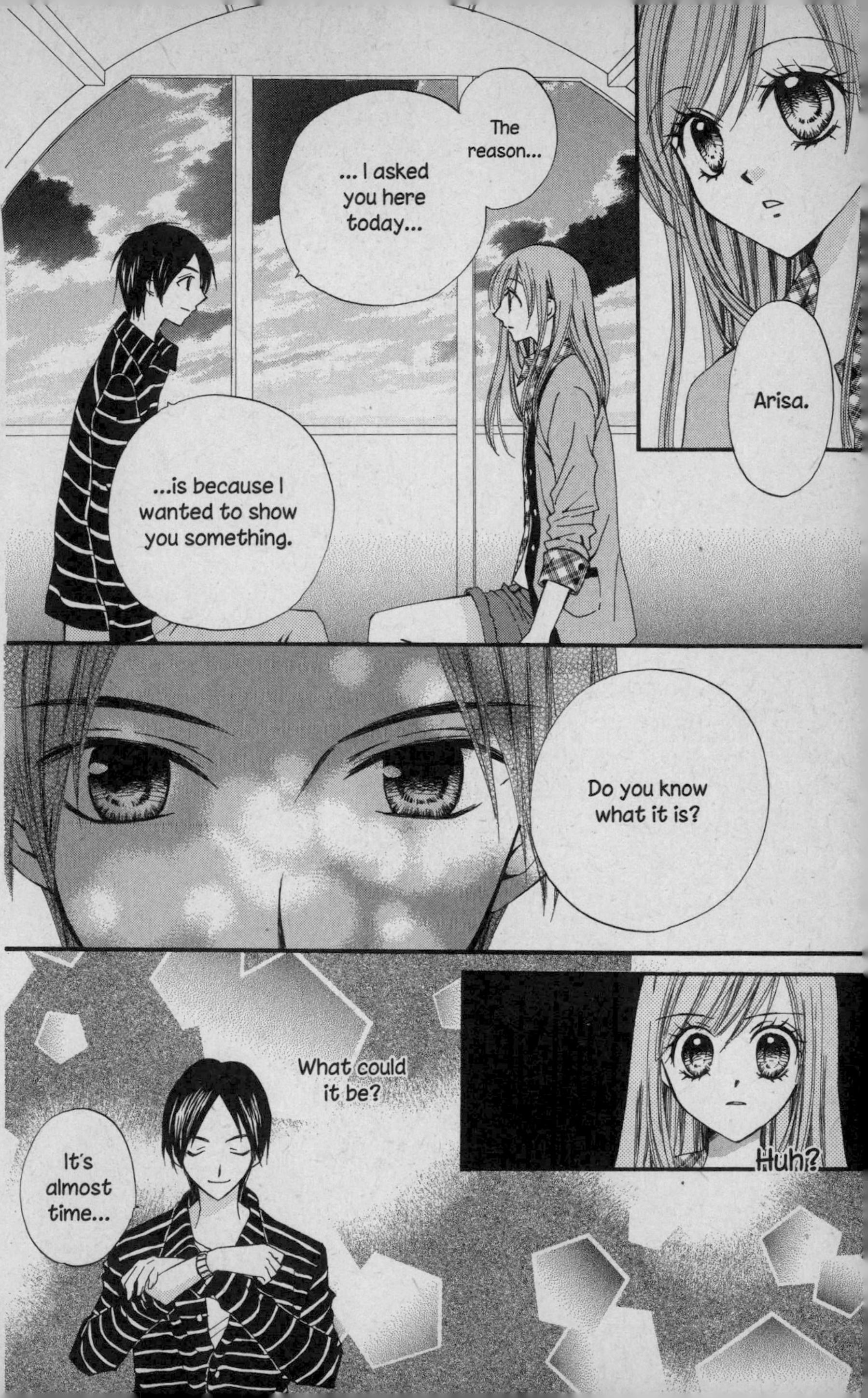
Arisa.
The reason...
... I asked you here today...
...is because I wanted to show you something.
Do you know what it is?
Huh?
What could it be?
It's almost time...

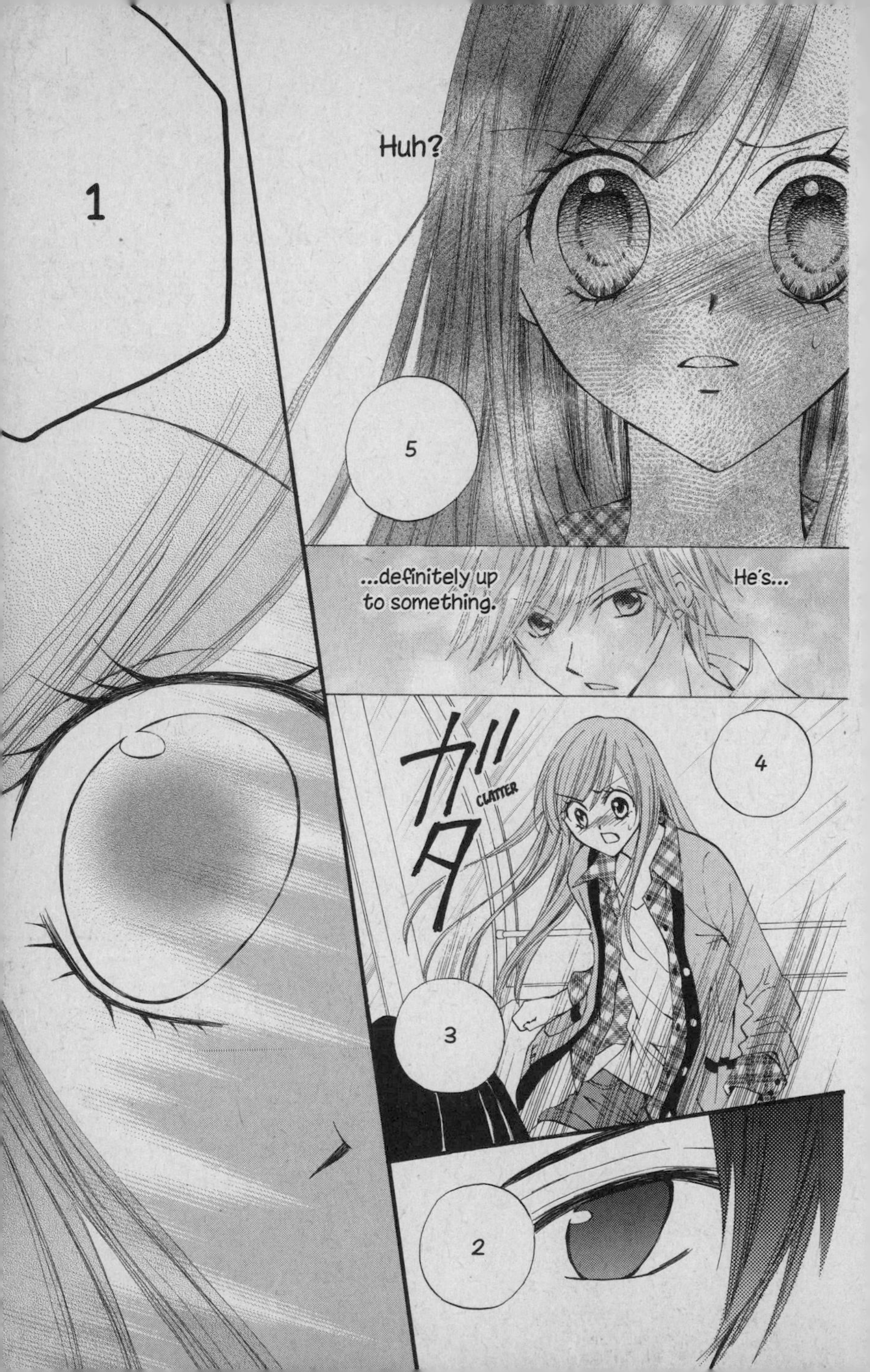
Huh?
5
He's...
...definitely up to something.
4
ガタ
CLATTER
3
2
1

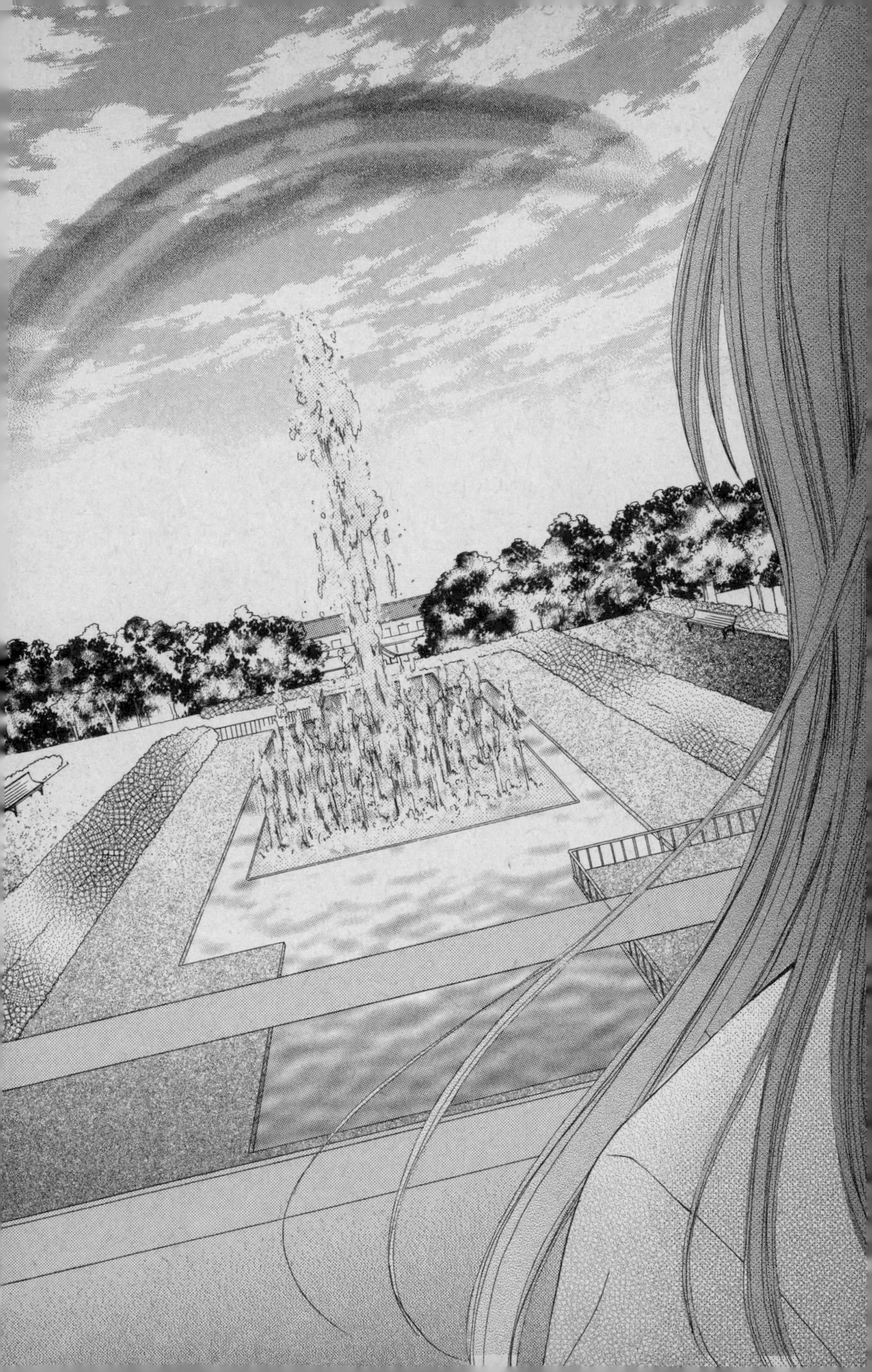

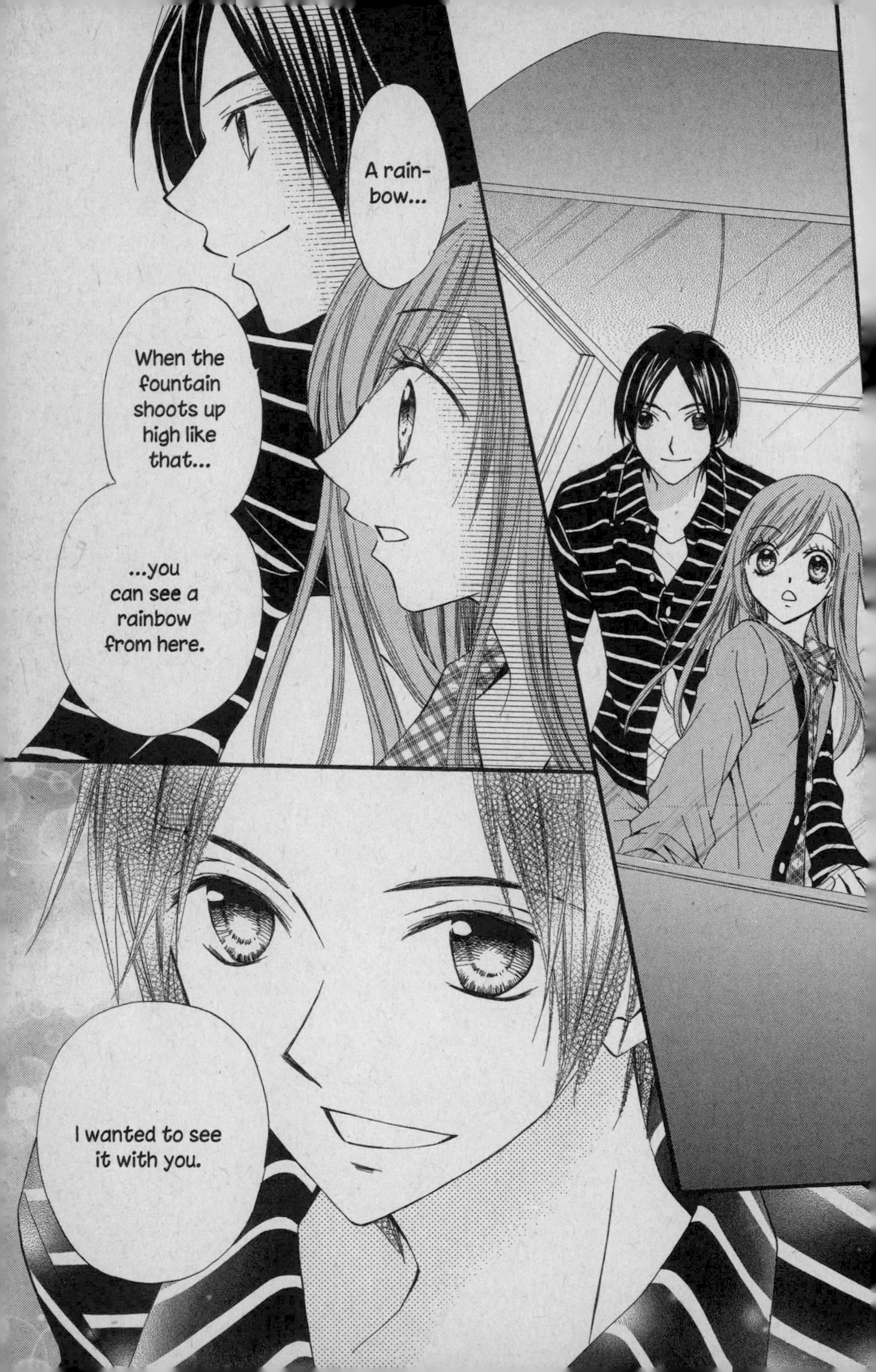
A rain-bow...
When the fountain shoots up high like that...
...you can see a rainbow from here.
I wanted to see it with you.

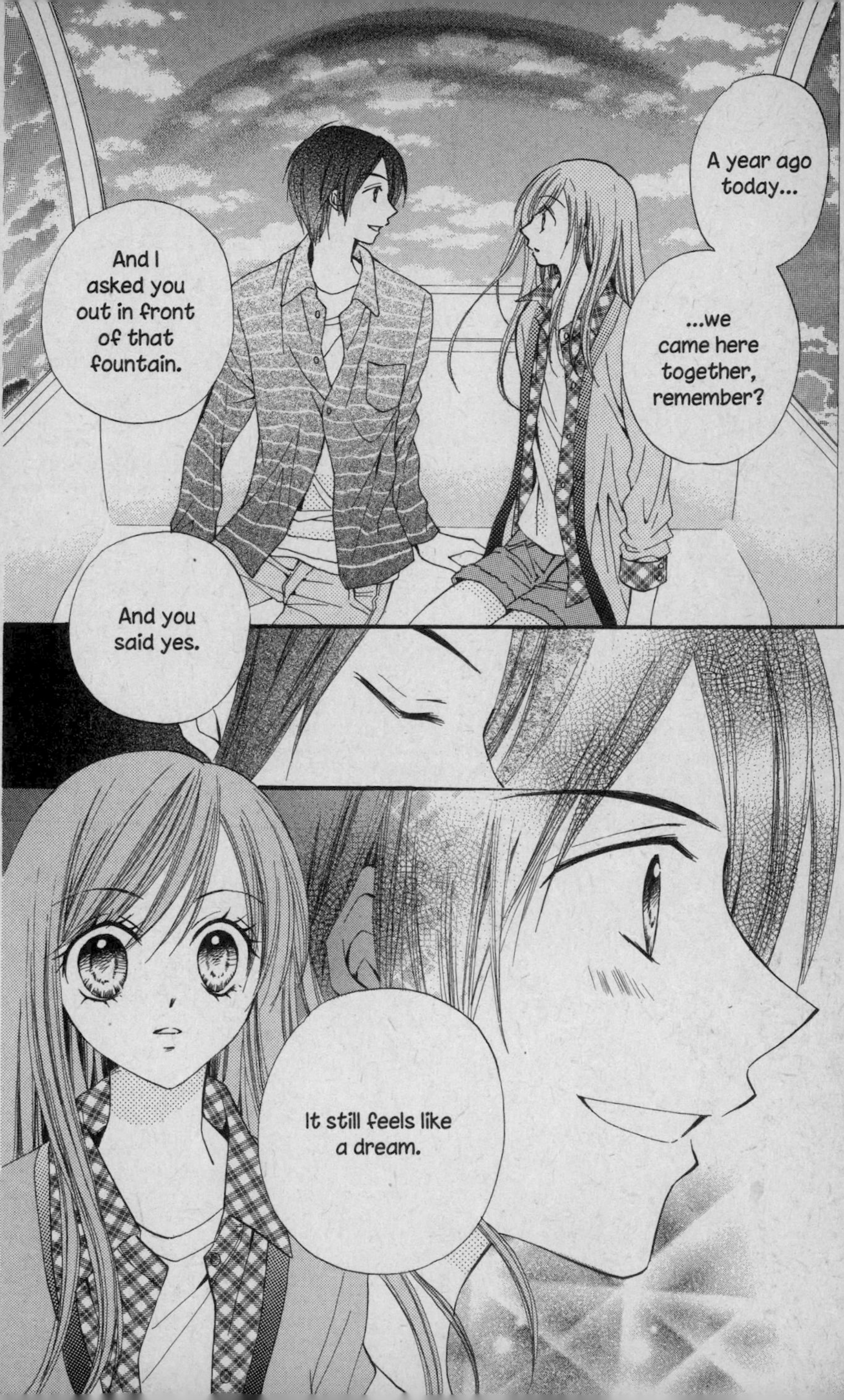
A year ago today...
...we came here together, remember?
And I asked you out in front of that fountain.
And you said yes.
It still feels like a dream.

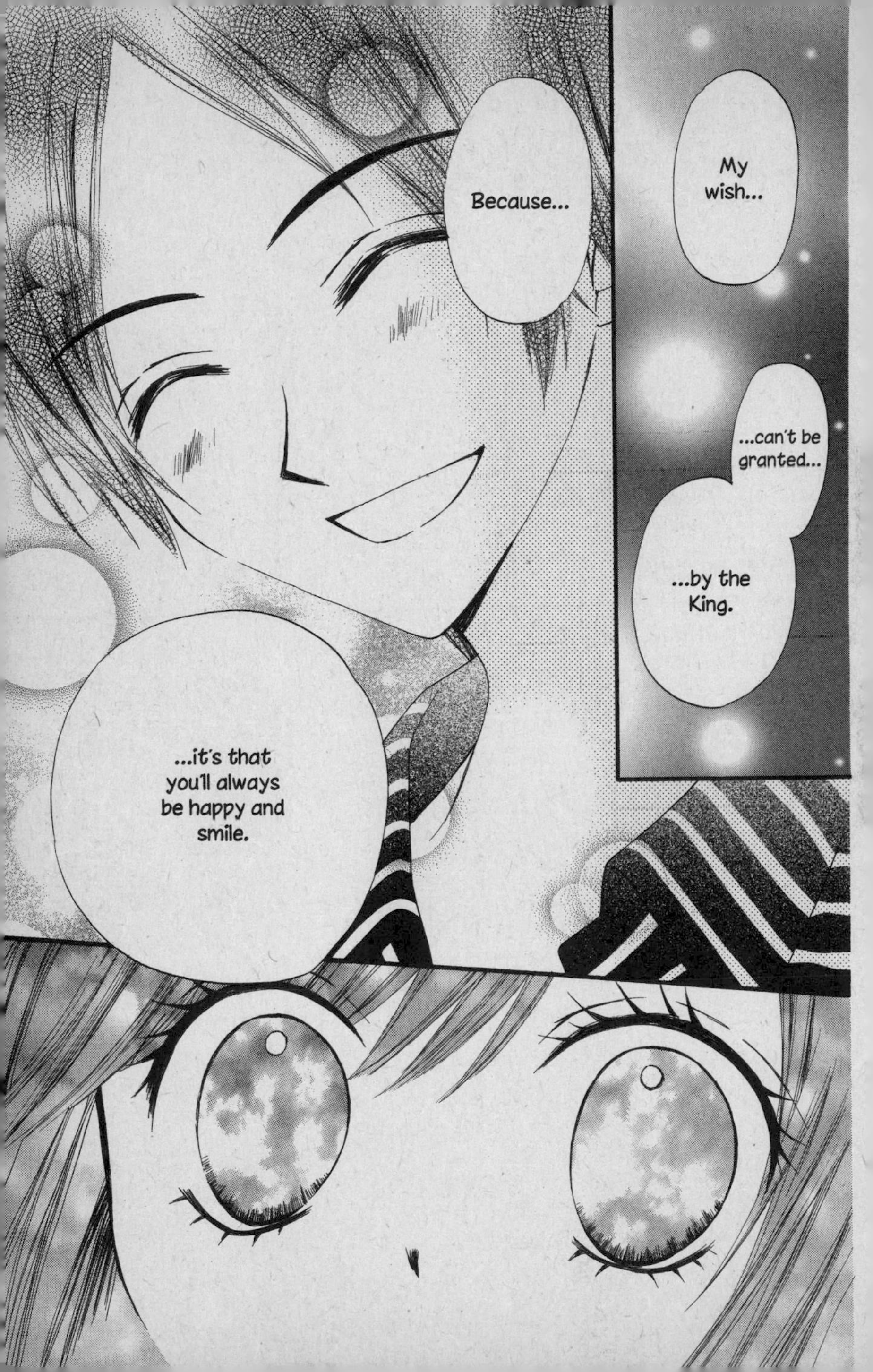
My wish...
...can't be granted...
...by the King.
Because...
...it's that you'll always be happy and smile.

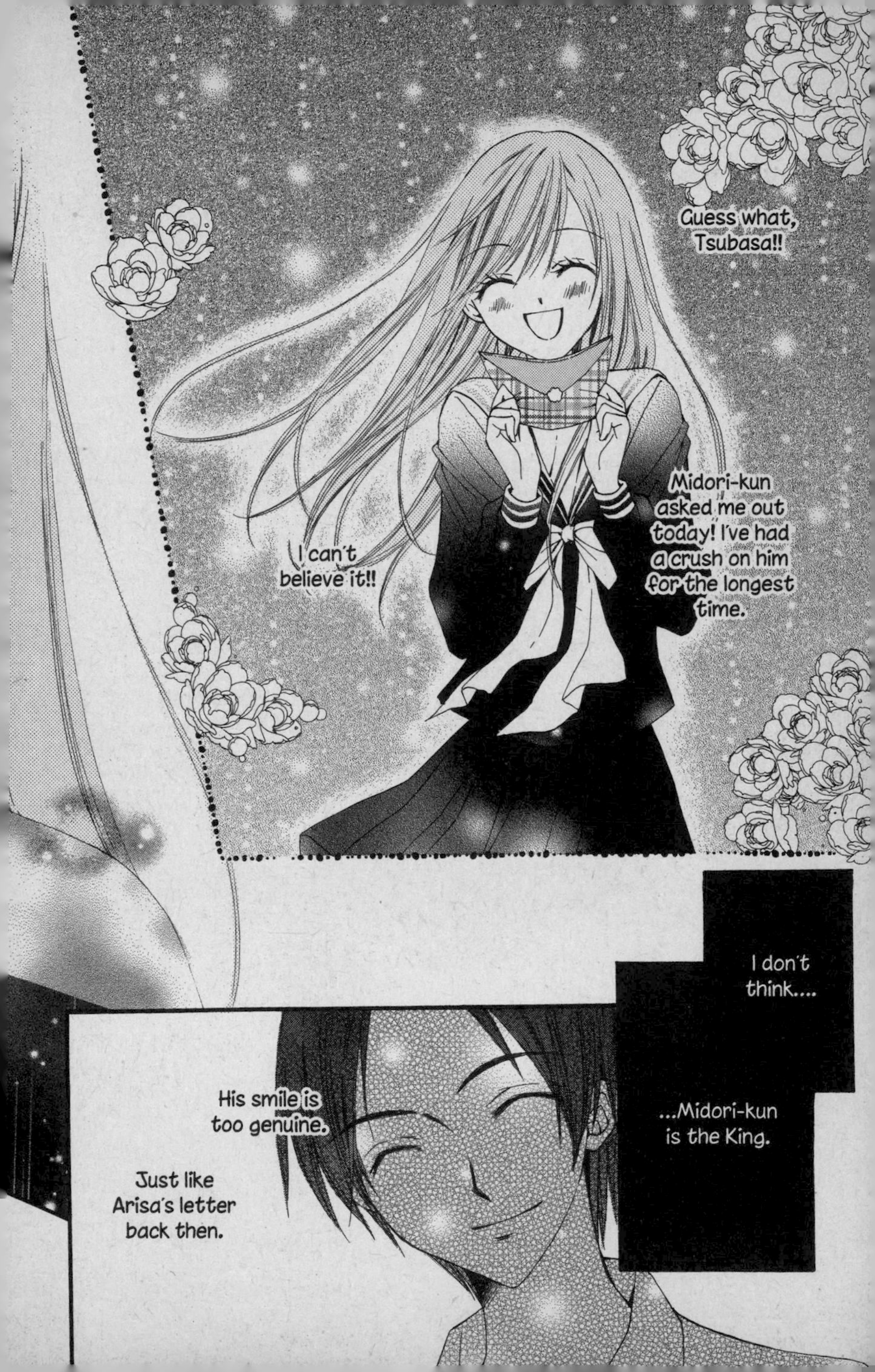
Guess what, Tsubasa!!
Midori-kun asked me out today! I've had a crush on him for the longest time.
I can't believe it!!
I don't think....
...Midori-kun is the King.
His smile is too genuine.
Just like Arisa's letter back then.

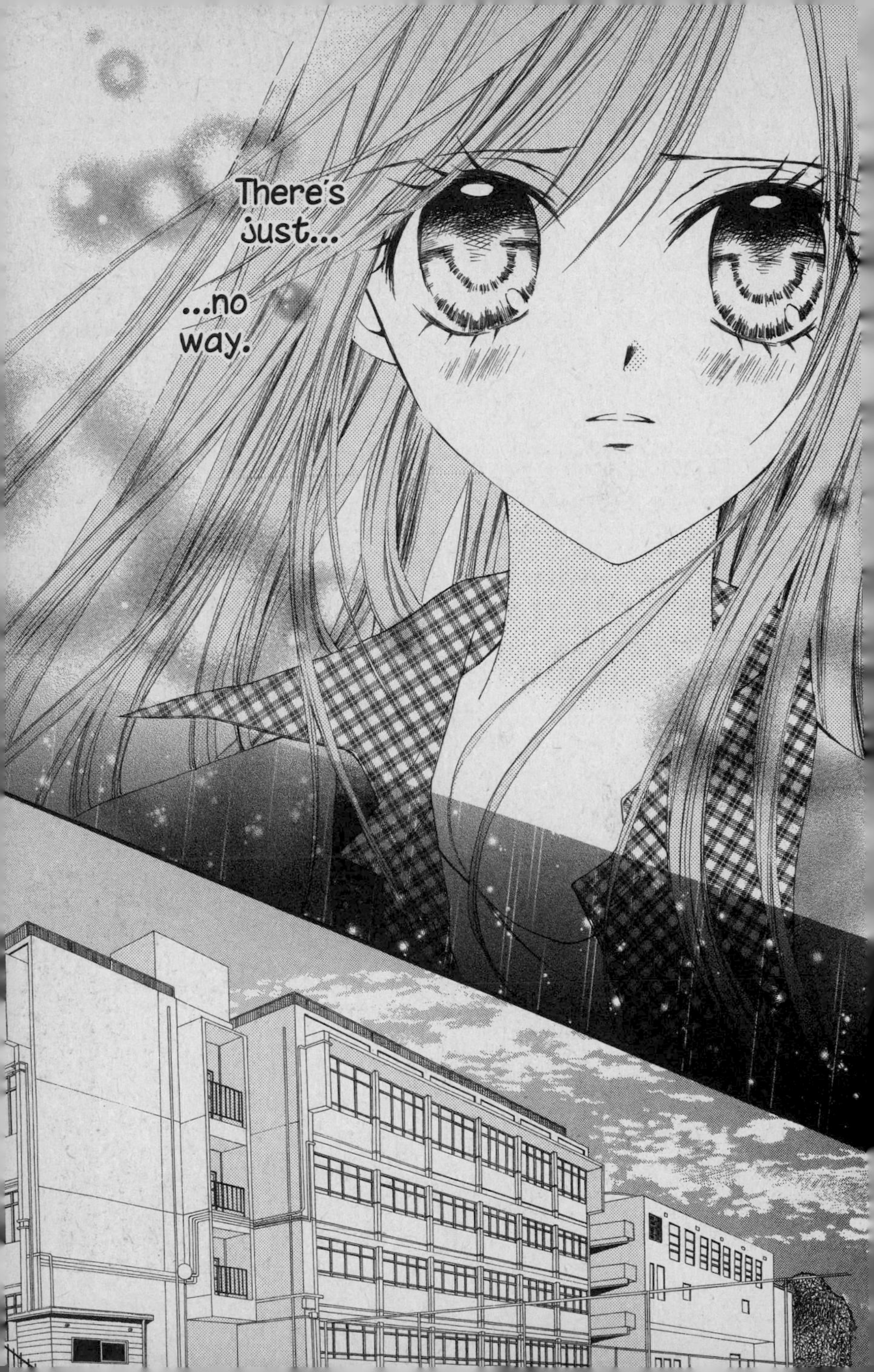
There's just...
...no way.

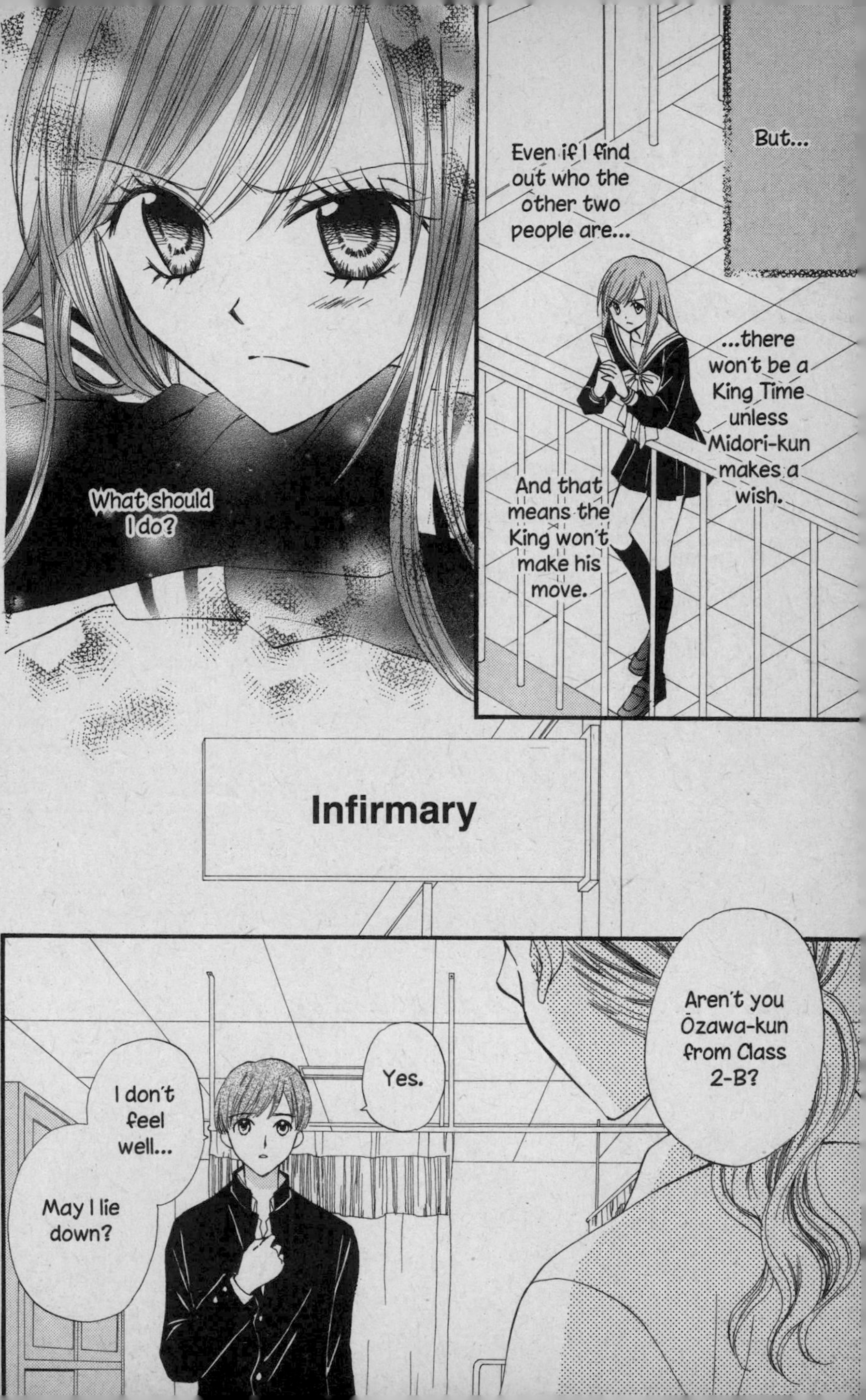
But...
Even if I find out who the other two people are...
...there won't be a King Time unless Midori-kun makes a wish.
And that means the King won't make his move.
What should I do?
Infirmary
Aren't you Ōzawa-kun from Class 2-B?
Yes.
I don't feel well...
May I lie down?

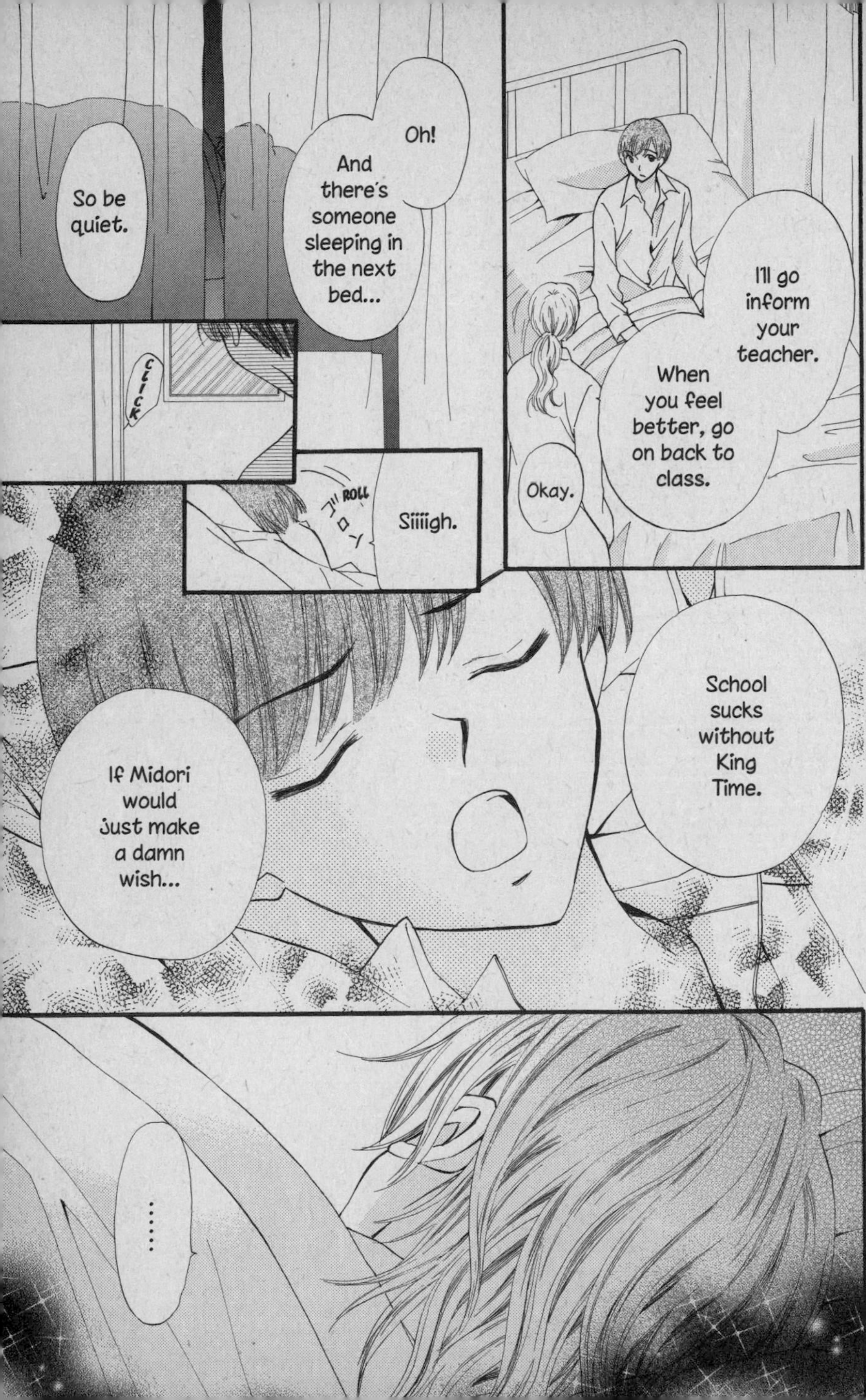
I'll go inform your teacher.
When you feel better, go on back to class.
Okay.
Oh! And there's someone sleeping in the next bed...
So be quiet.
CLICK
ROLL
Siiiigh.
School sucks without King Time.
If Midori would just make a damn wish...
......

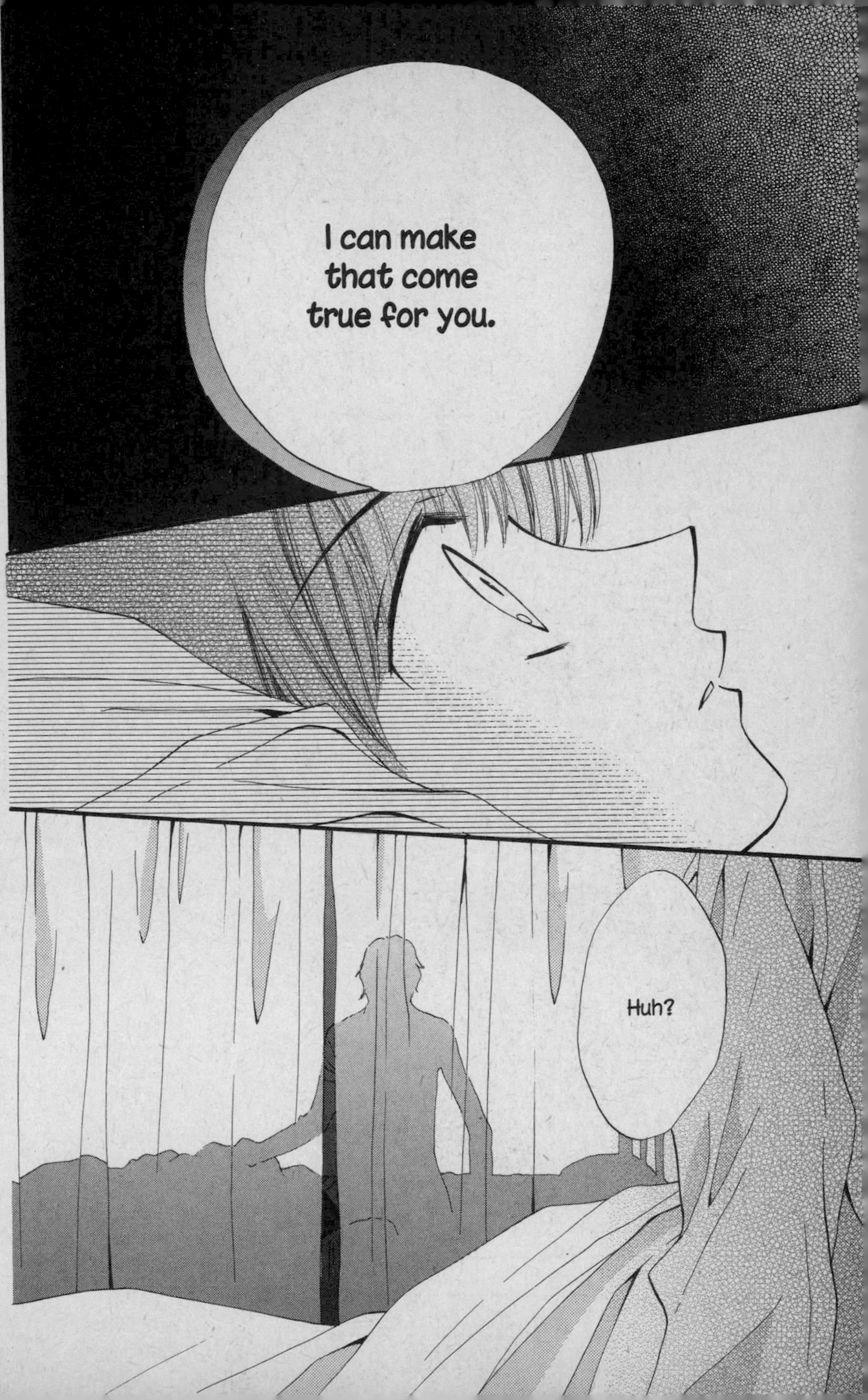
I can make that come true for you.
Huh?

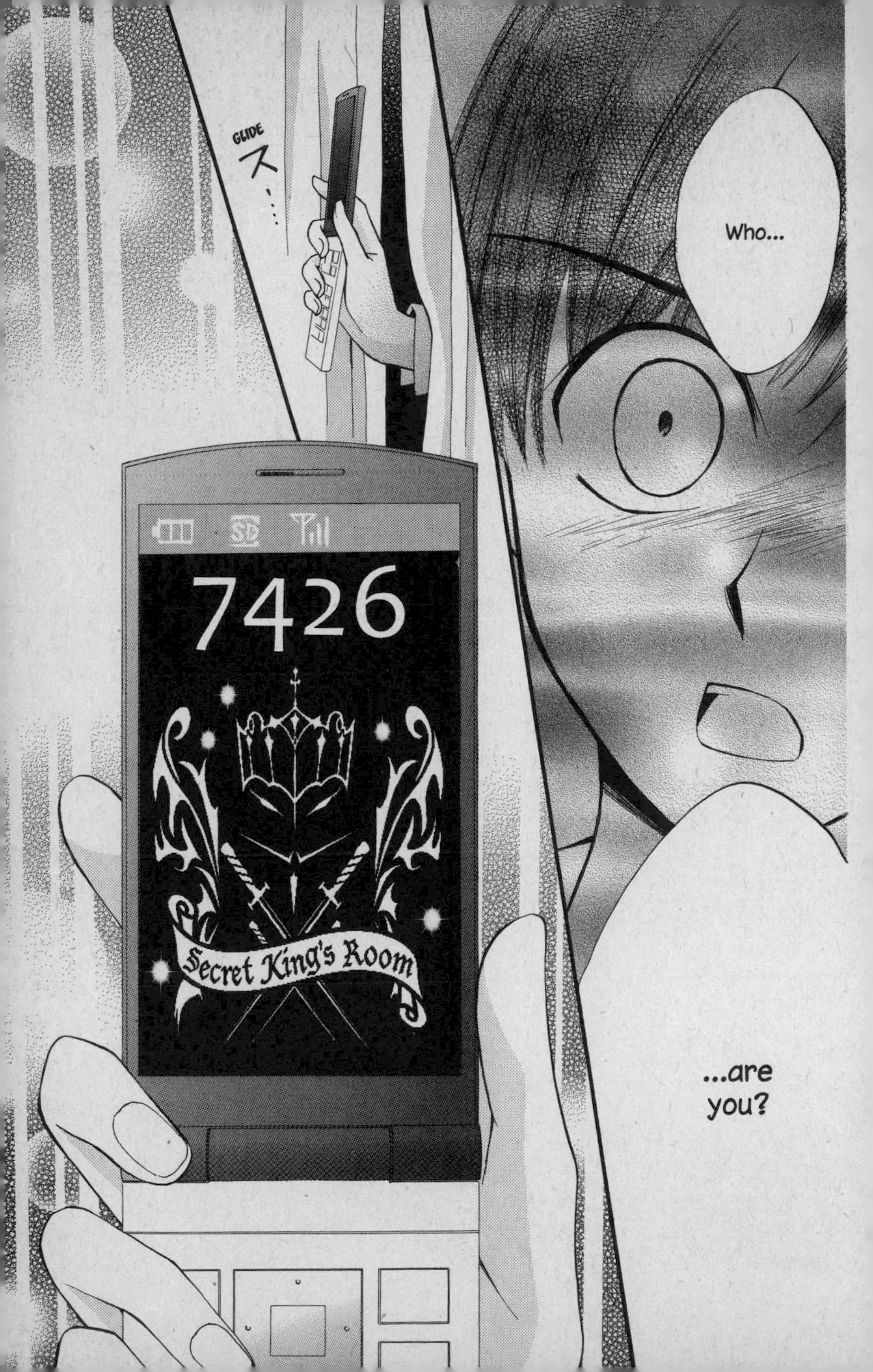
Who...
GLIDE
ス...
7426
Secret King's Room
...are you?

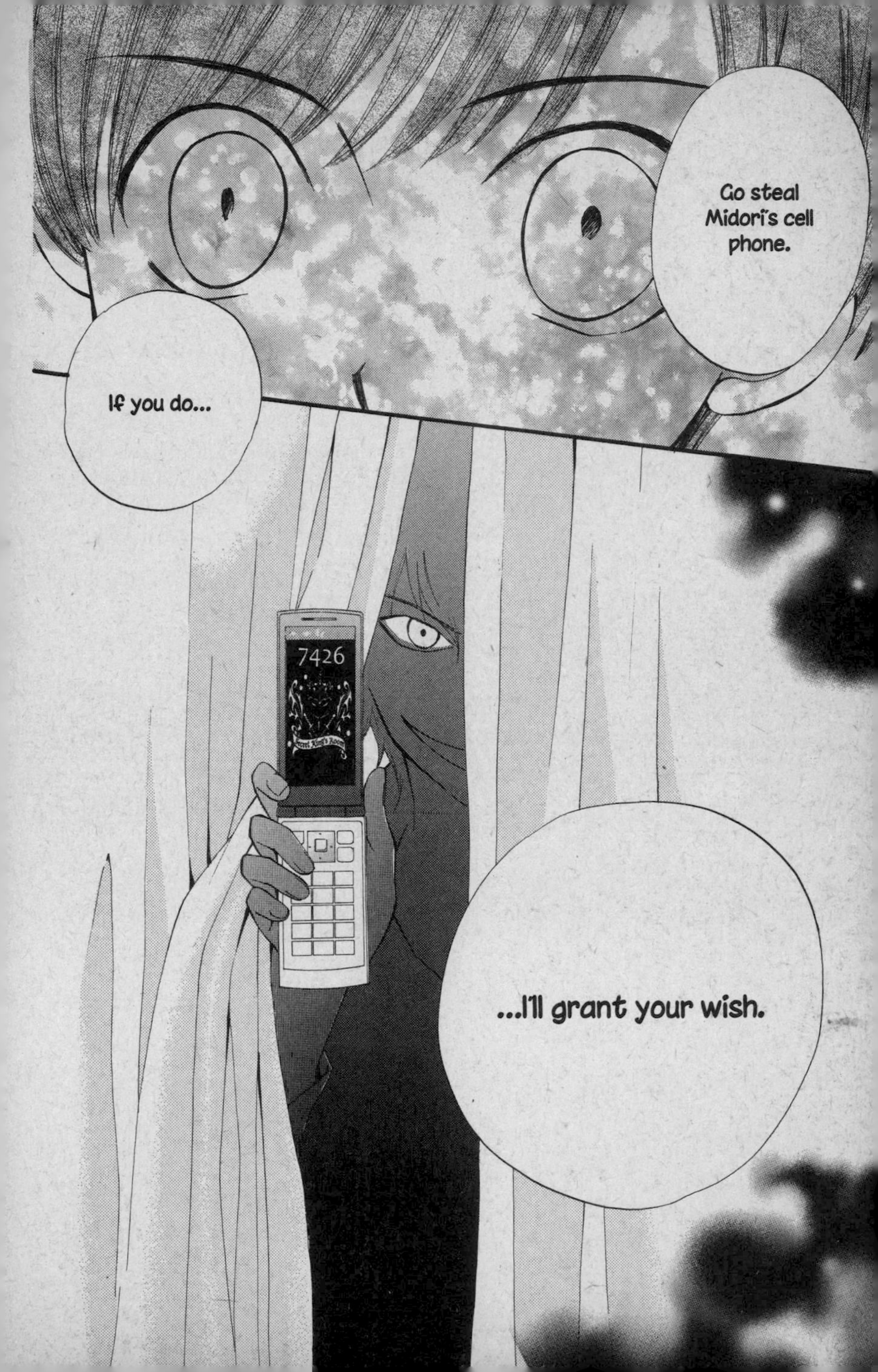
Go steal Midori's cell phone.
If you do...
7426
...I'll grant your wish.

ARISA

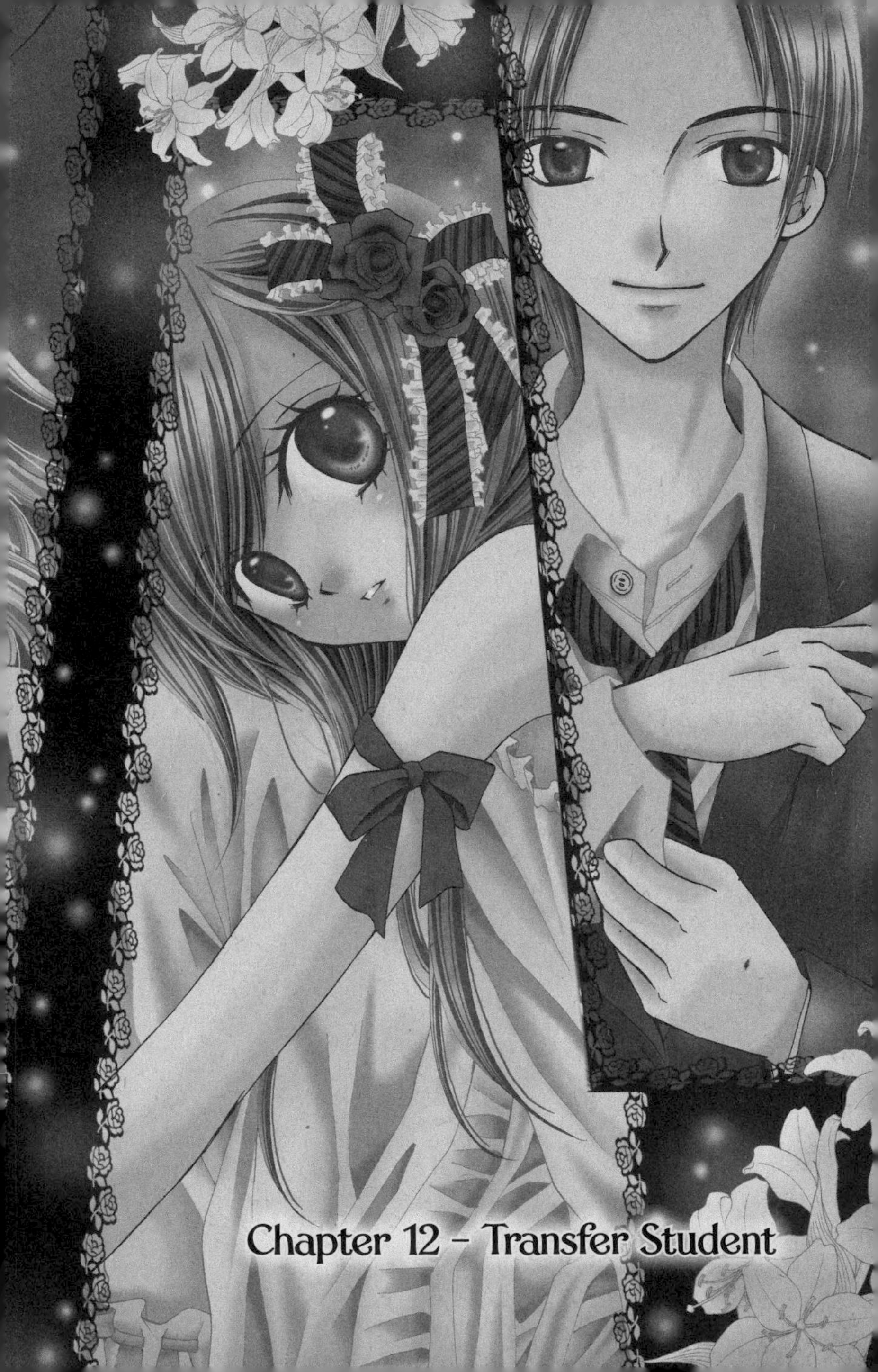
Chapter 12 - Transfer Student

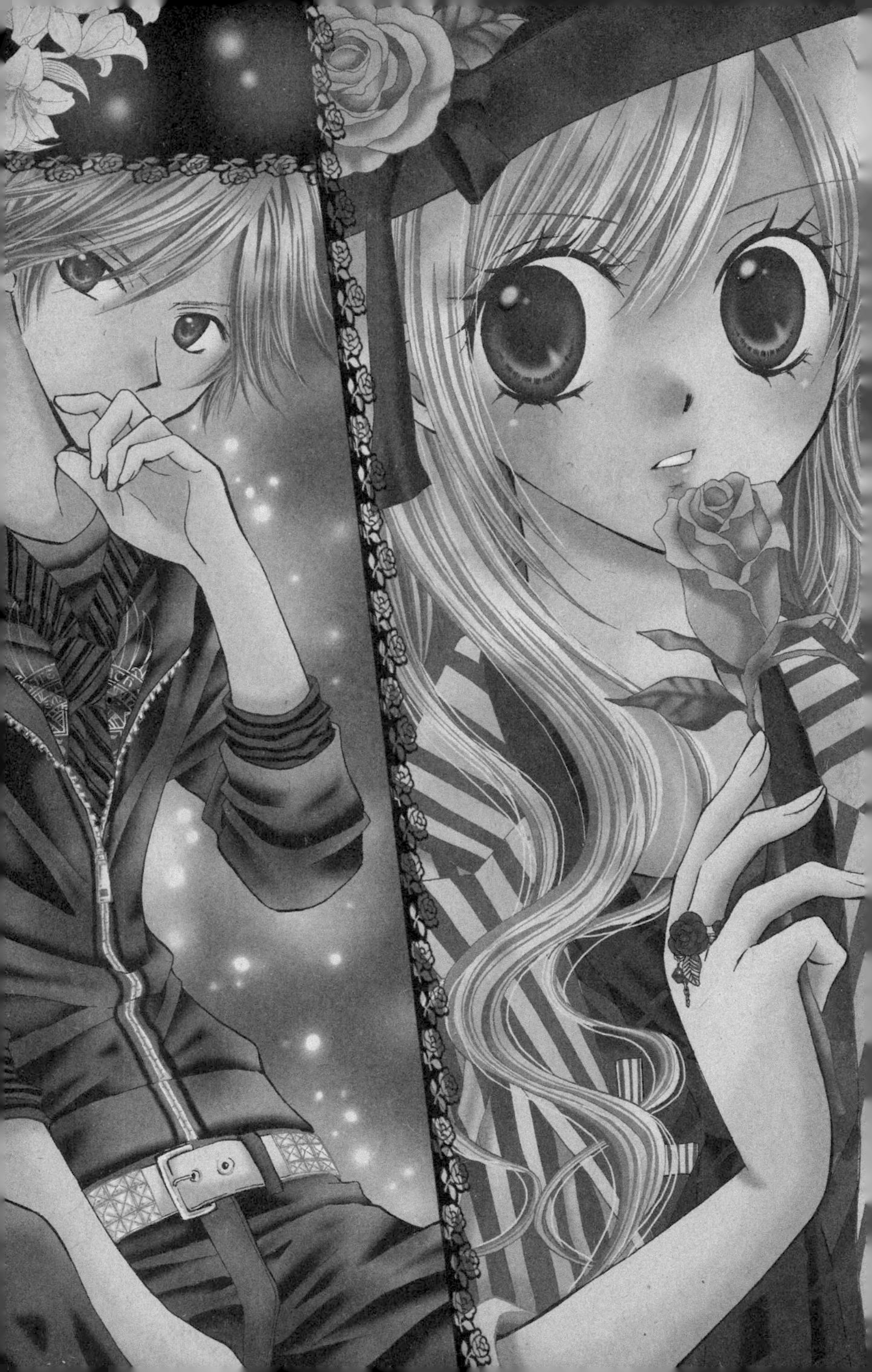

SPECIAL THANKS:

T. Nakamura

S. Okada

H. Kishimoto

M. Nakata

M. Shirasawa

A. Nakamura

My assistants and
editors at Nakayoshi

Red rooster

Takashi Shimoyama

GINNANSHA

Toriumi-sama

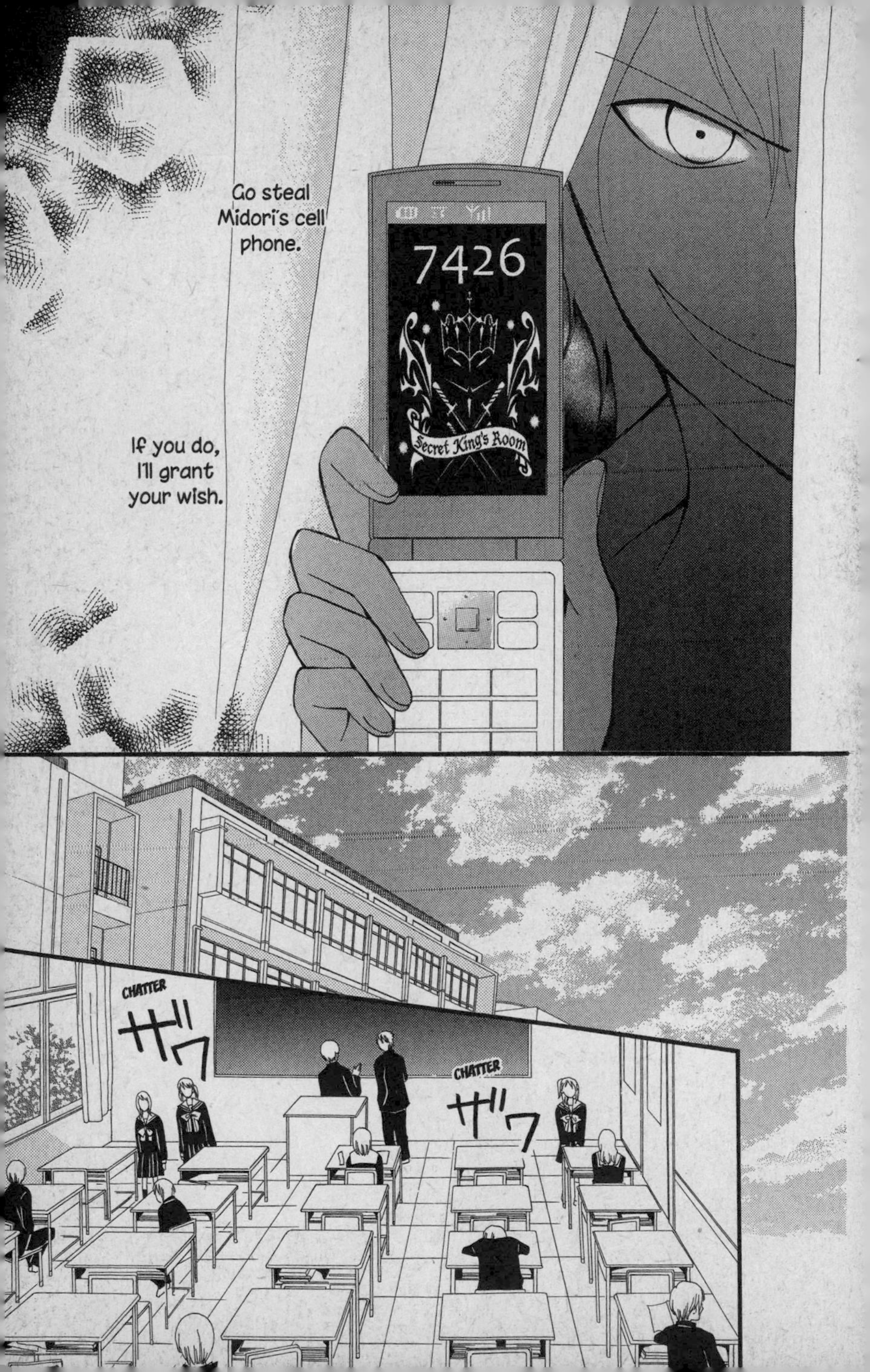
Go steal Midori's cell phone.
7426
Secret King's Room
If you do, I'll grant your wish.
CHATTER
ザワ
CHATTER
ザワ

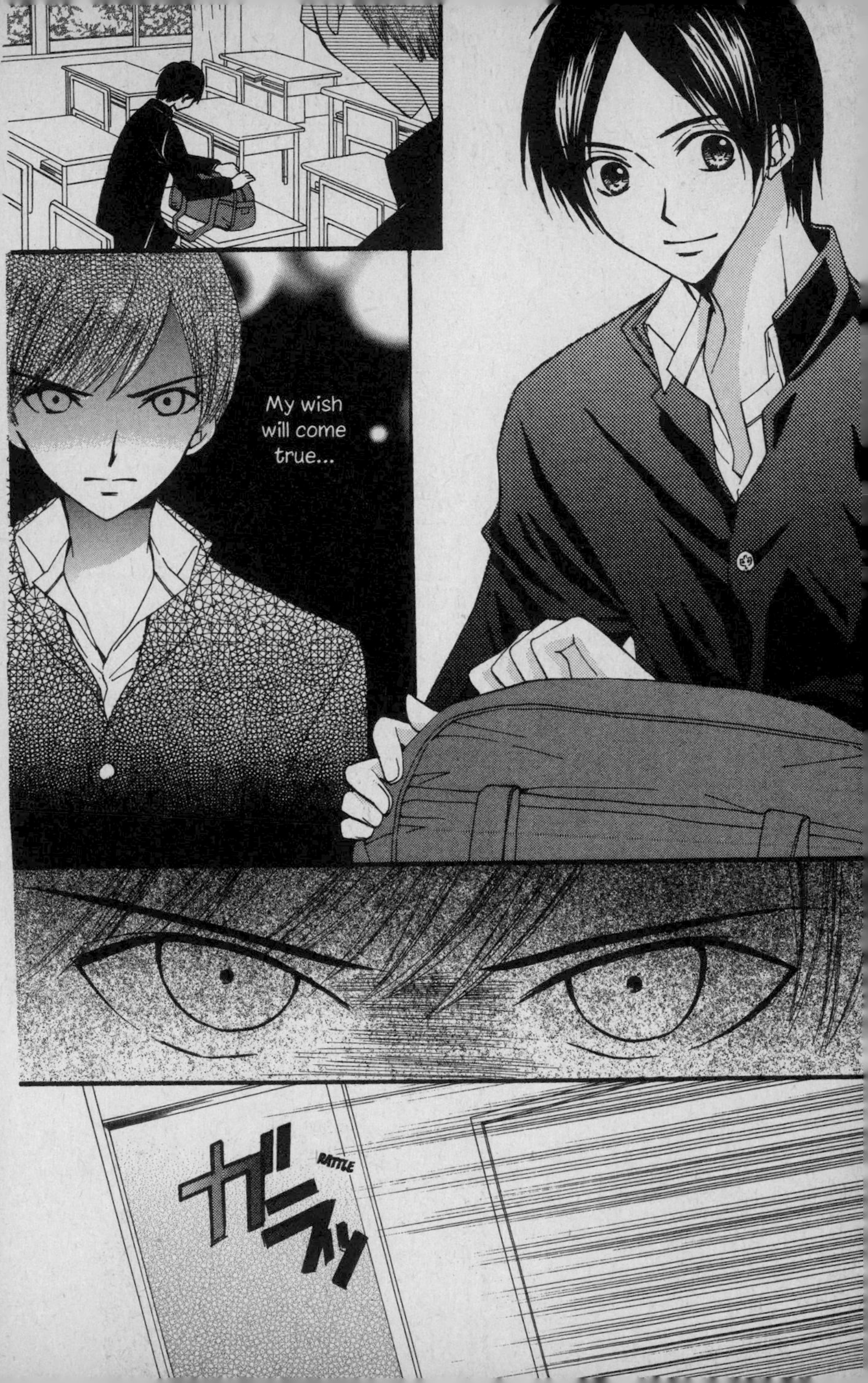
My wish will come true...
RATTLE

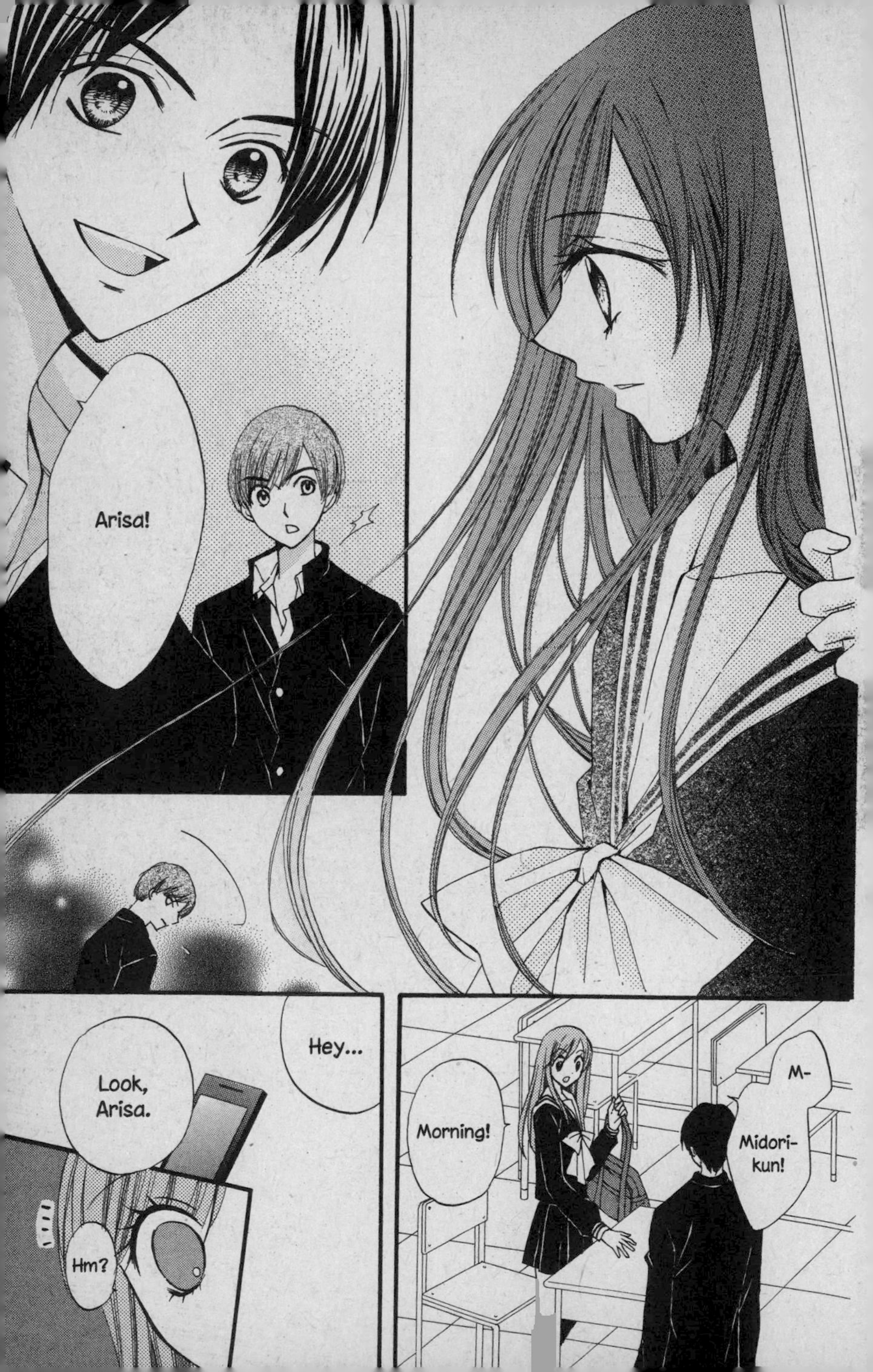
Arisa!
M- Midori-kun!
Morning!
Hey...
Look, Arisa.
Hm?

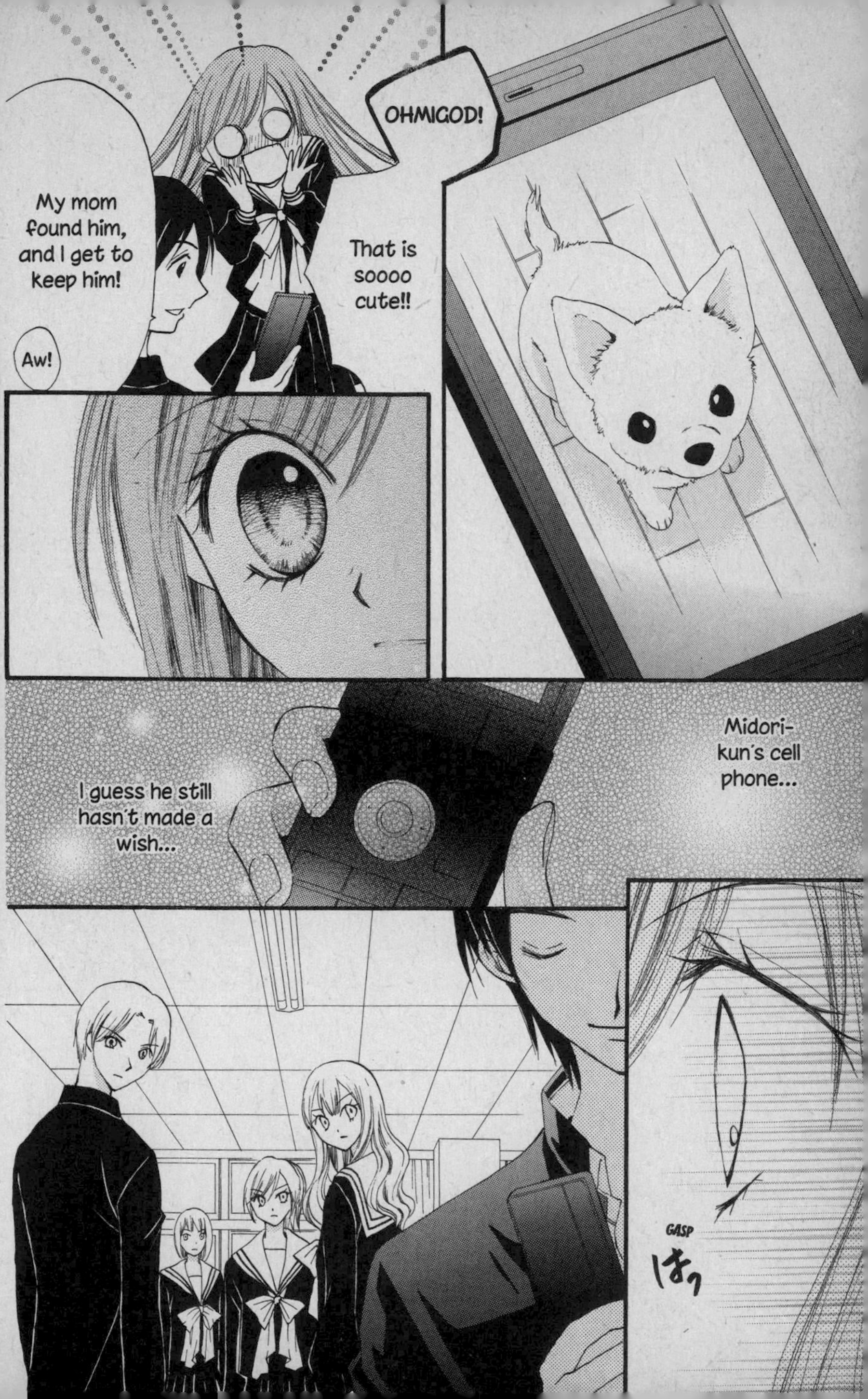
OHMIGOD!
That is soooo cute!!
My mom found him, and I get to keep him!
Aw!
Midori-kun's cell phone...
I guess he still hasn't made a wish...
GASP
はっ

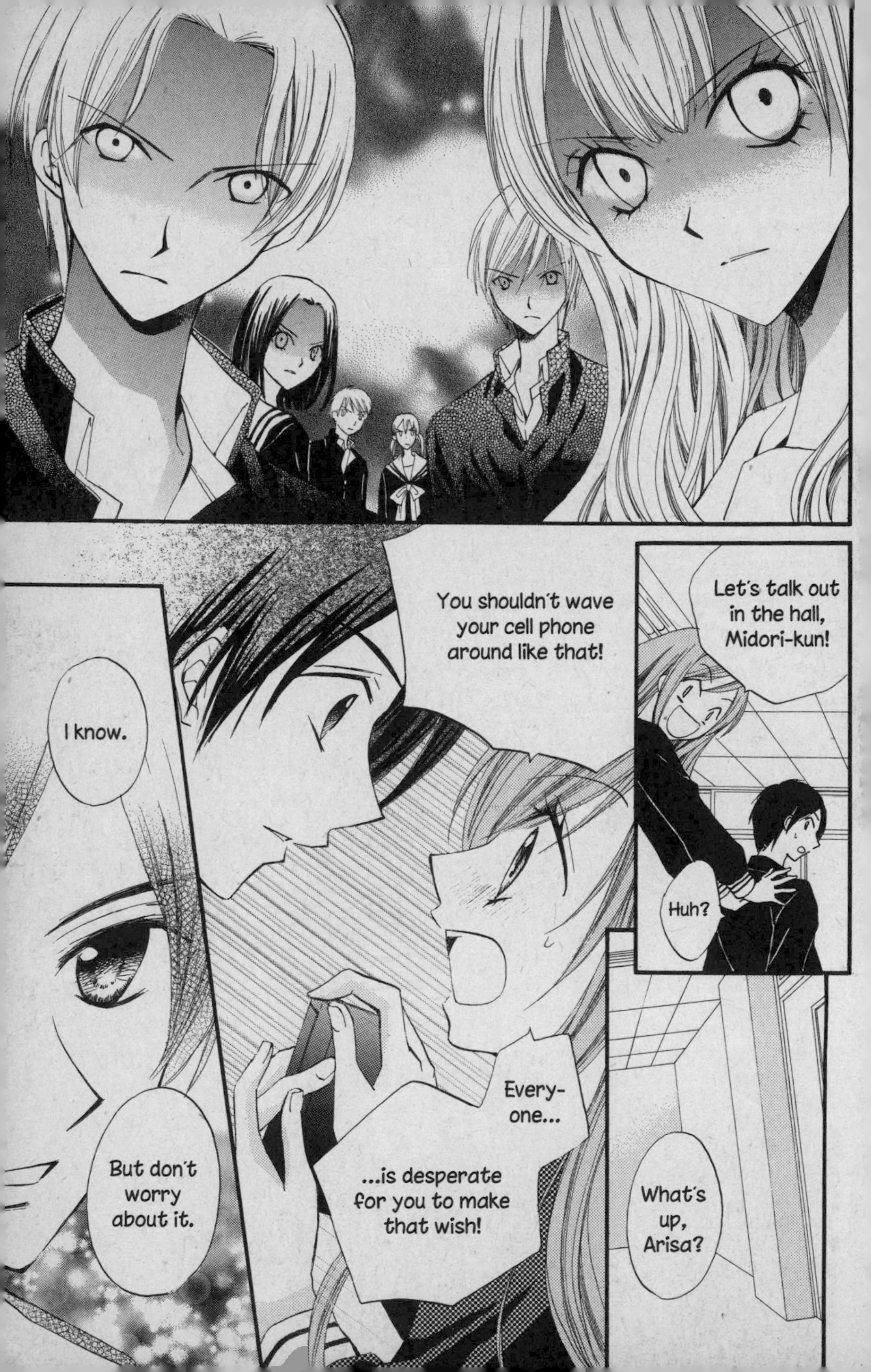
Let's talk out in the hall, Midori-kun!
Huh?
What's up, Arisa?
You shouldn't wave your cell phone around like that!
I know.
Every-one...
...is desperate for you to make that wish!
But don't worry about it.

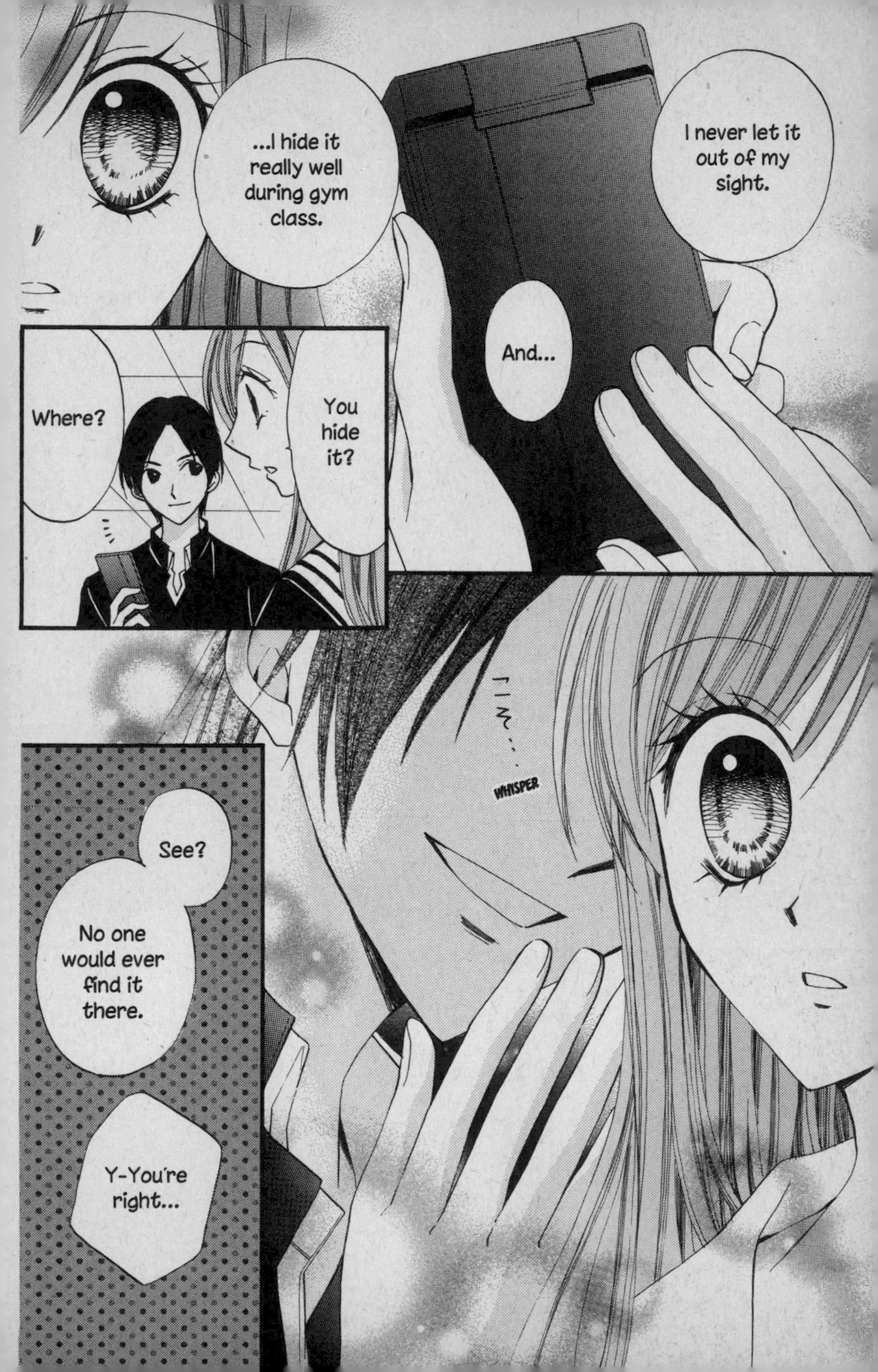
I never let it out of my sight.
And...
...I hide it really well during gym class.
You hide it?
Where?
WHISPER
See?
No one would ever find it there.
Y-You're right...

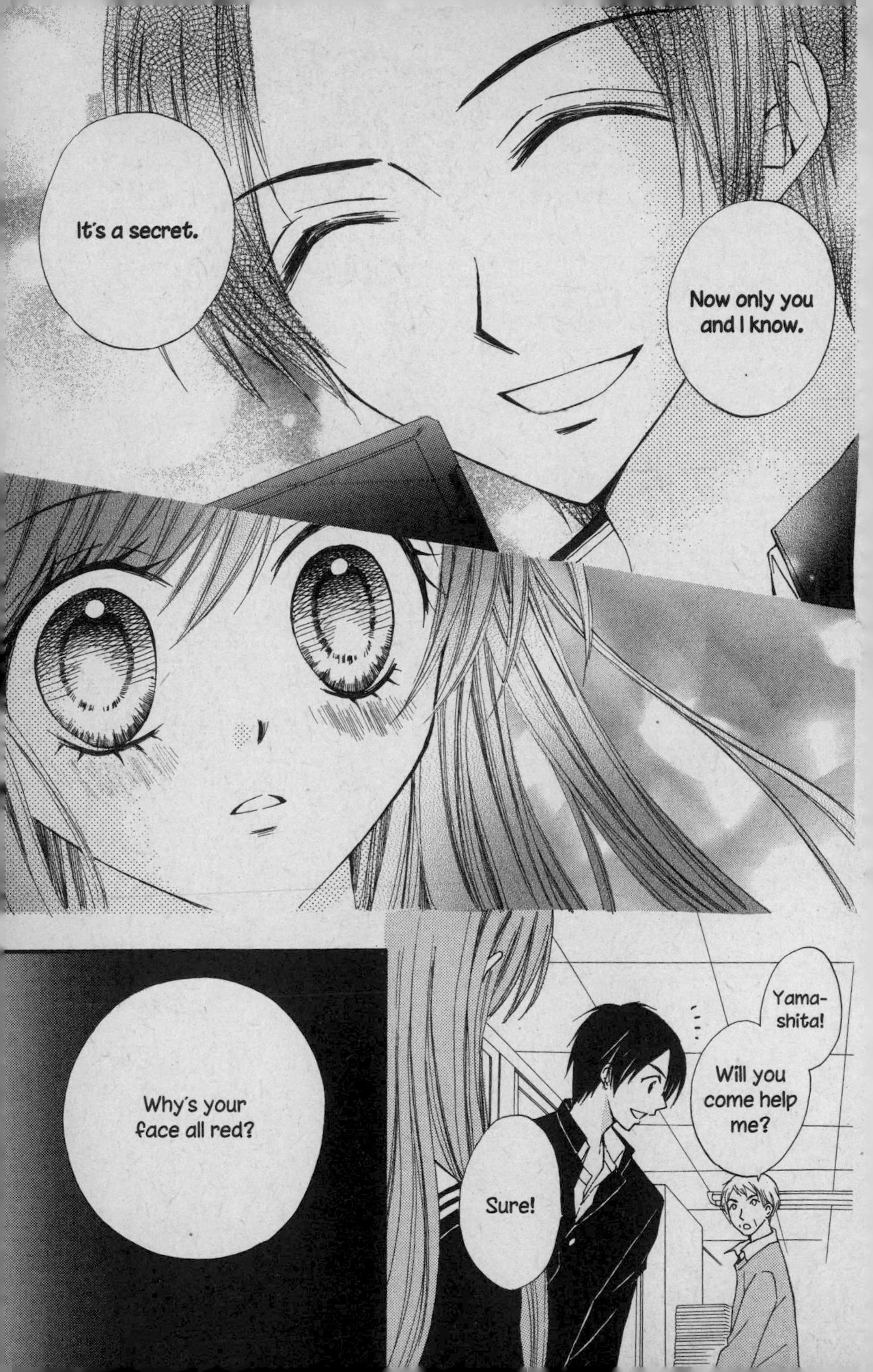
It's a secret.
Now only you and I know.
Yama-shita!
Will you come help me?
Sure!
Why's your face all red?

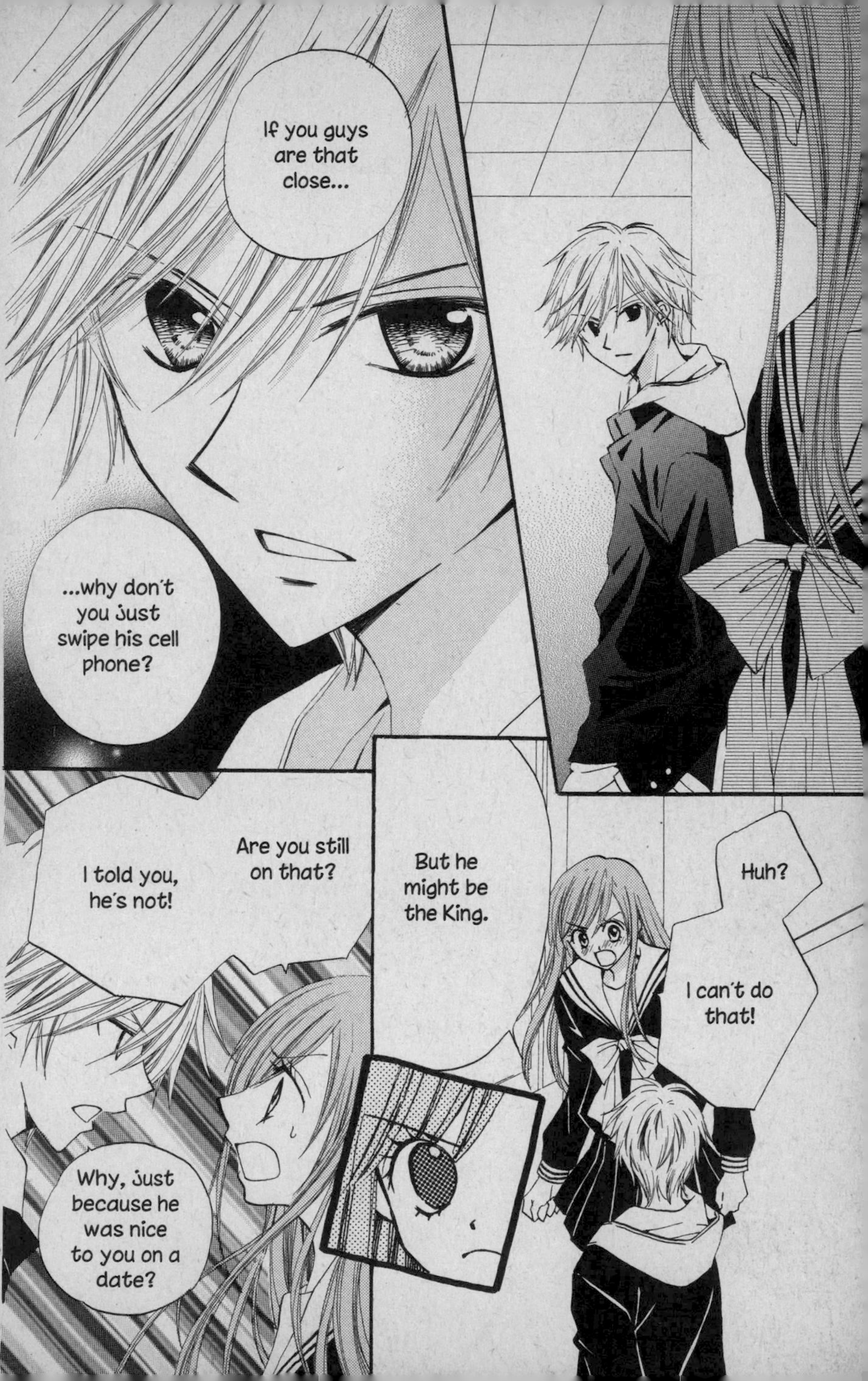
If you guys are that close...
...why don't you just swipe his cell phone?
Huh?
I can't do that!
But he might be the King.
Are you still on that?
I told you, he's not!
Why, just because he was nice to you on a date?

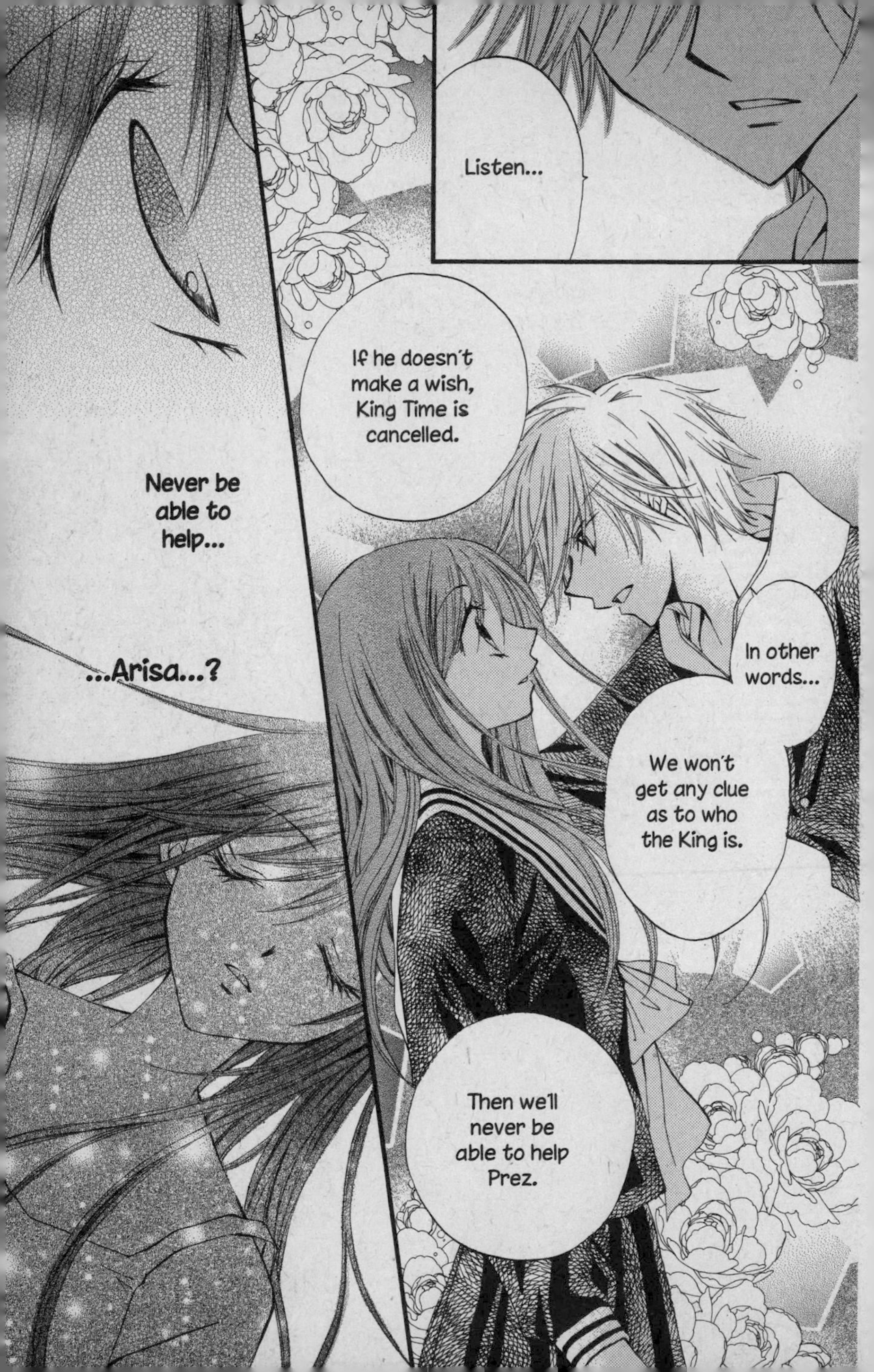
Listen...
If he doesn't make a wish, King Time is cancelled.
In other words...
We won't get any clue as to who the King is.
Then we'll never be able to help Prez.
Never be able to help...
...Arisa...?

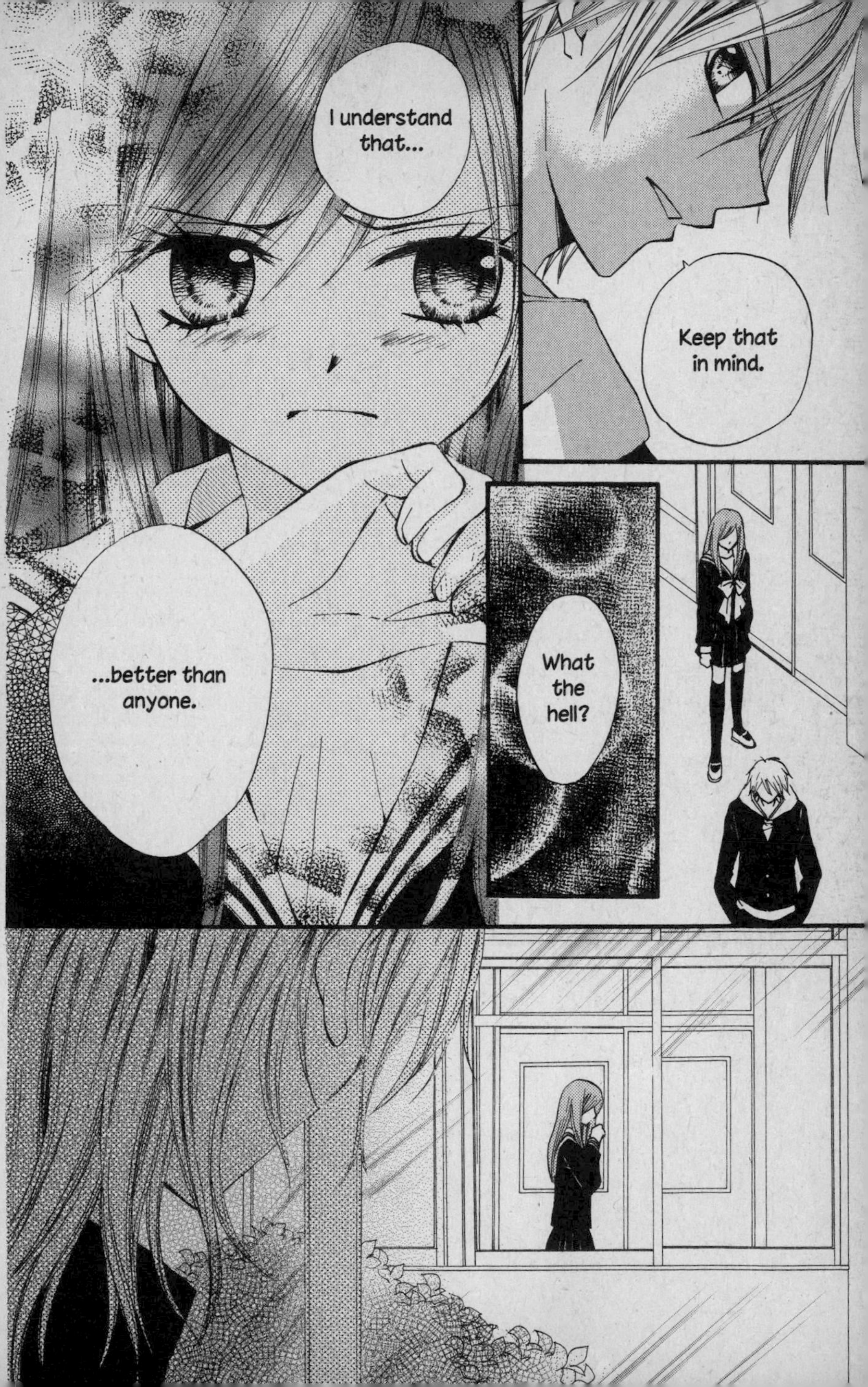
Keep that in mind.
What the hell?
I understand that...
...better than anyone.

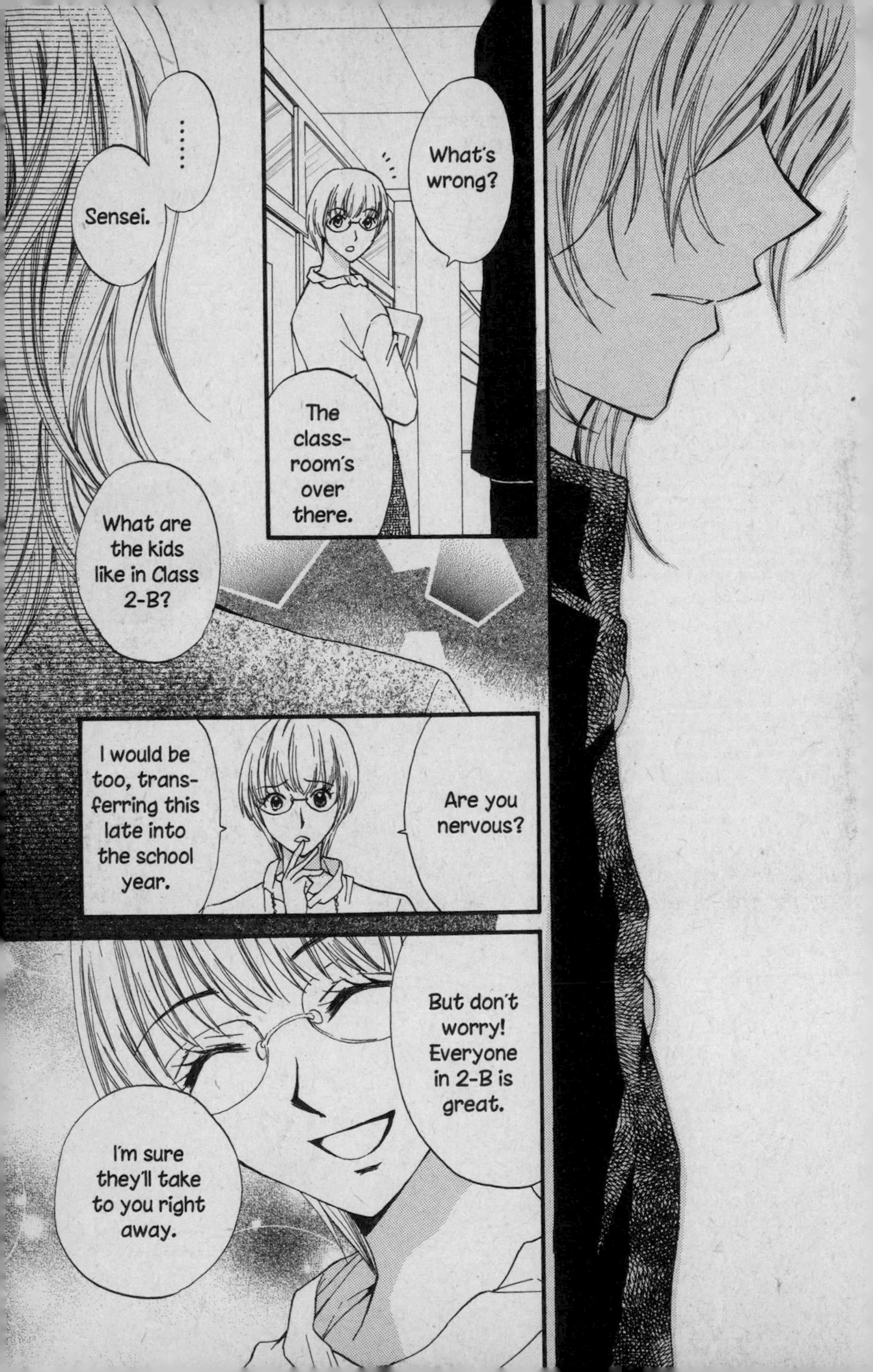
What's wrong?
The class-room's over there.
......
Sensei.
What are the kids like in Class 2-B?
Are you nervous?
I would be too, trans-ferring this late into the school year.
But don't worry! Everyone in 2-B is great.
I'm sure they'll take to you right away.

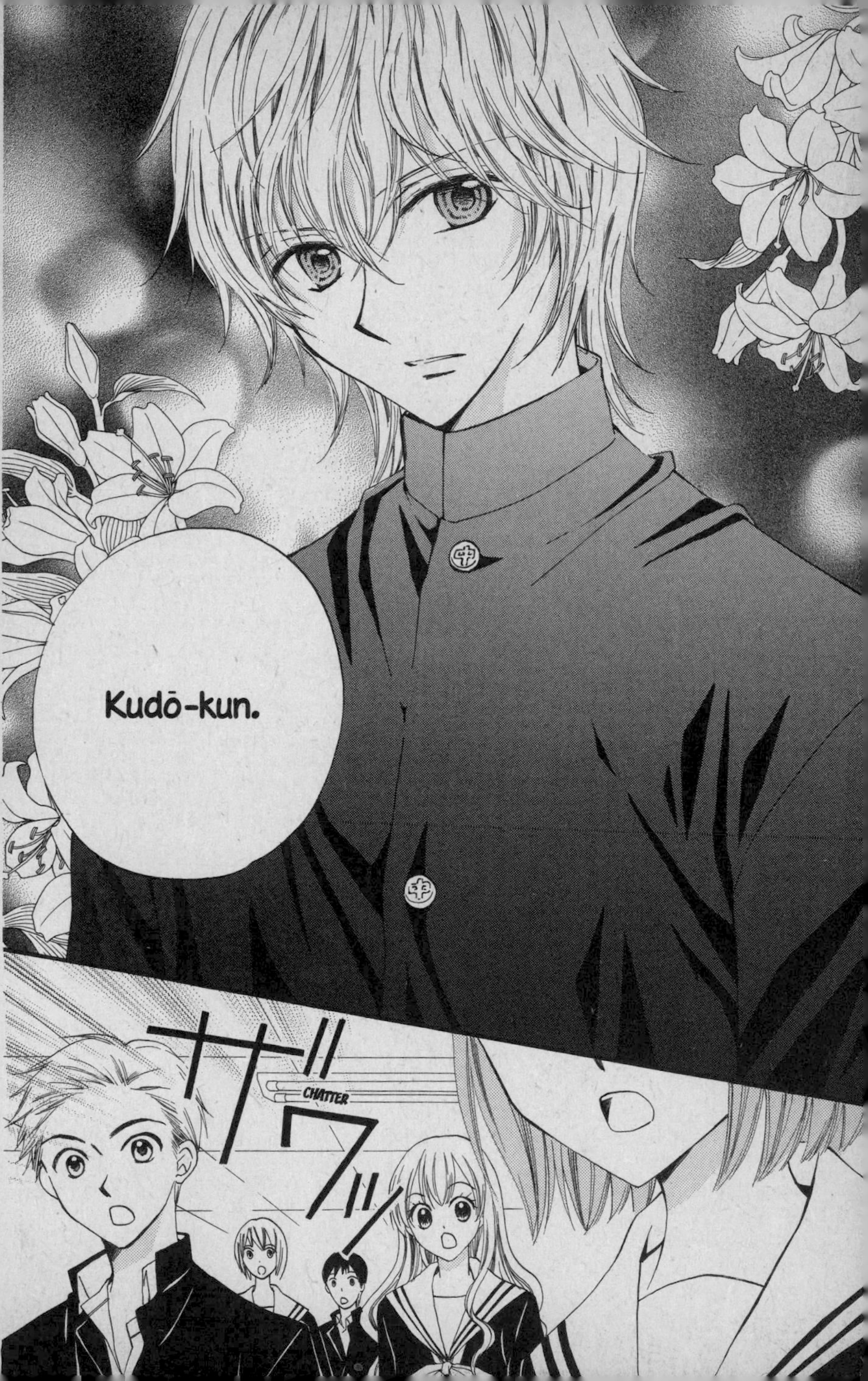
Kudō-kun.
CHATTER

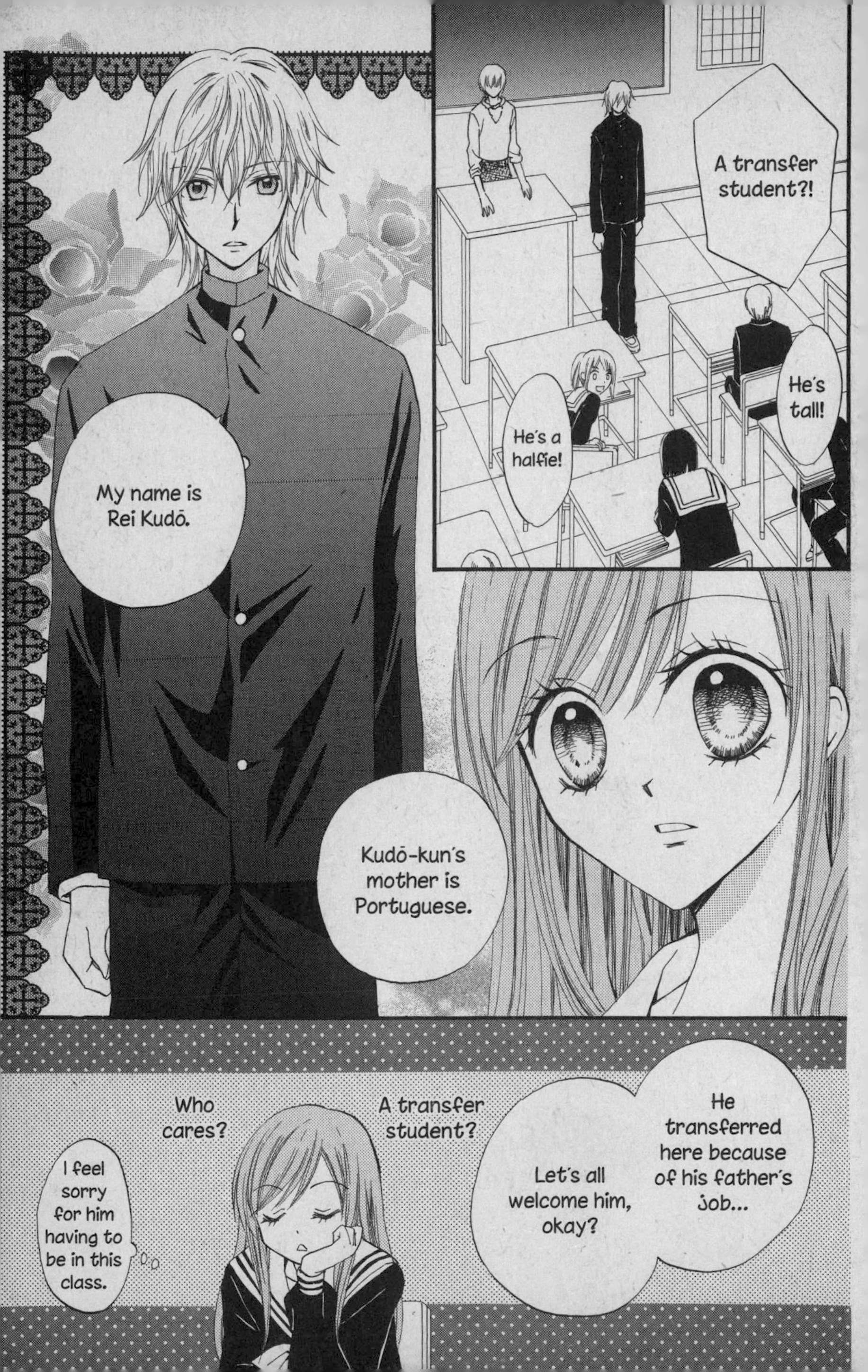
A transfer student?!
He's tall!
He's a halfie!
Kudō-kun's mother is Portuguese.
My name is Rei Kudō.
He transferred here because of his father's job...
Let's all welcome him, okay?
A transfer student?
Who cares?
I feel sorry for him having to be in this class.

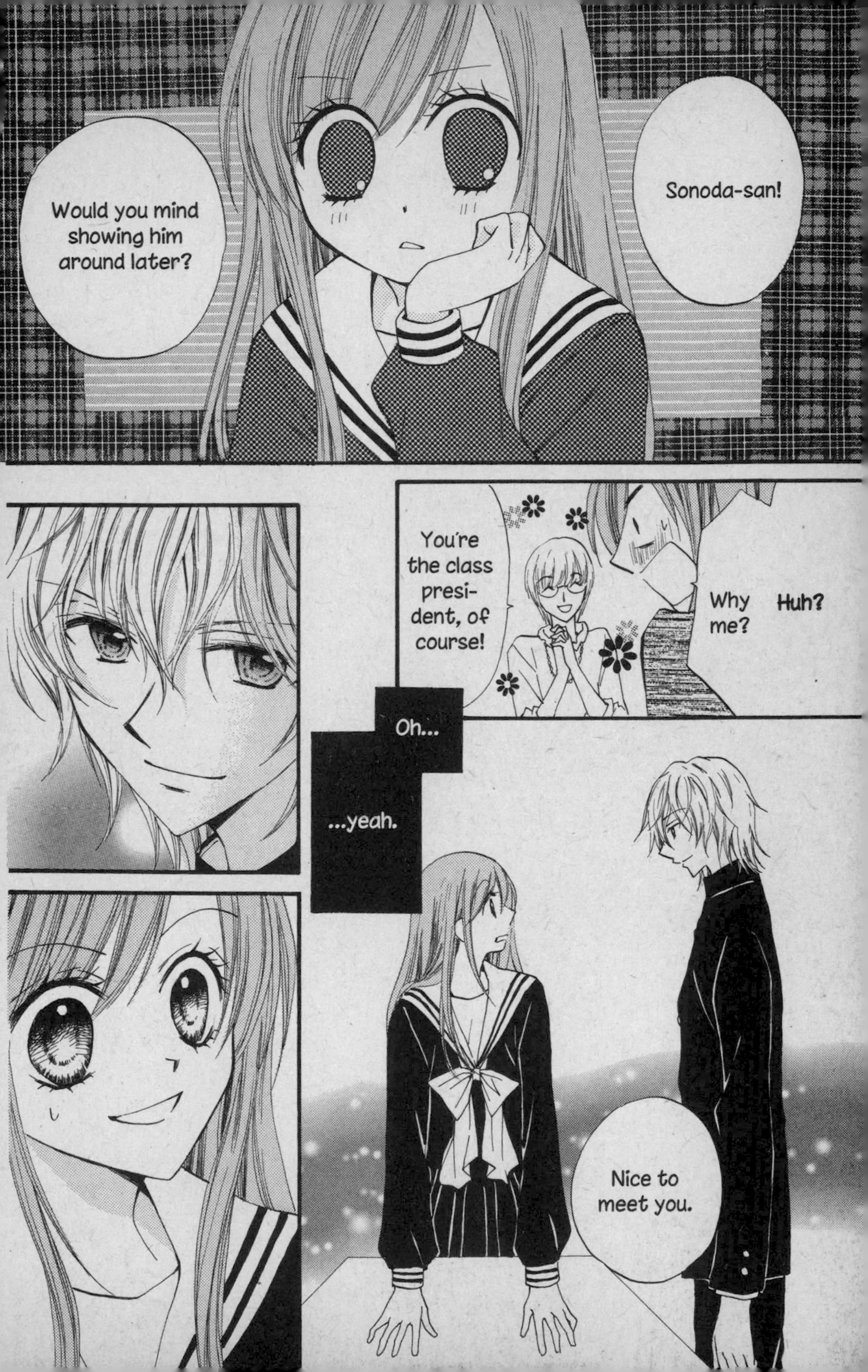
Sonoda-san!
Would you mind showing him around later?
Huh?
Why me?
You're the class president, of course!
Oh...
...yeah.
Nice to meet you.

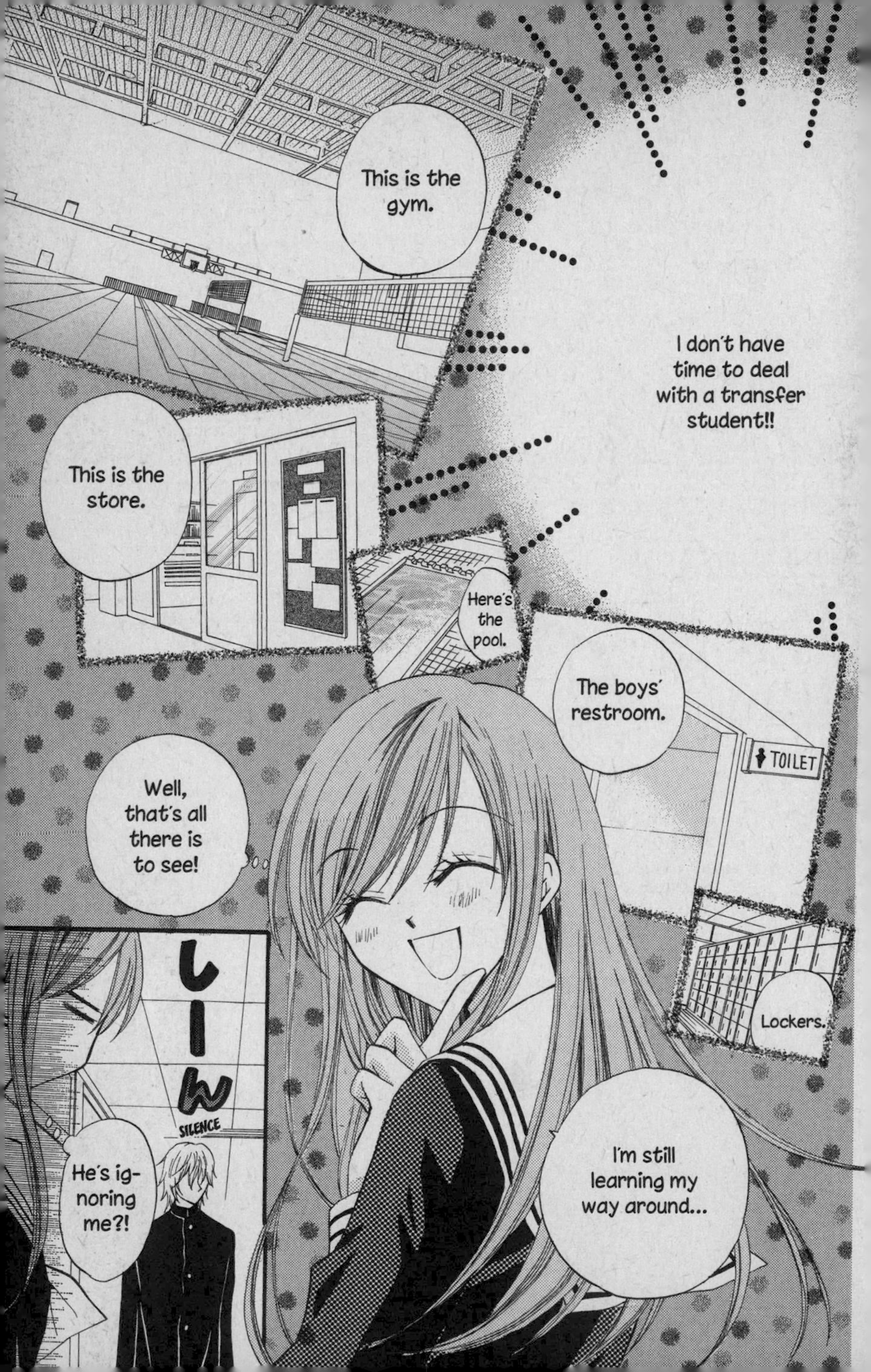
I don't have time to deal with a transfer student!!
This is the gym.
This is the store.
Here's the pool.
The boys' restroom.
TOILET
Lockers.
I'm still learning my way around...
Well, that's all there is to see!
SILENCE
He's ig-noring me?!

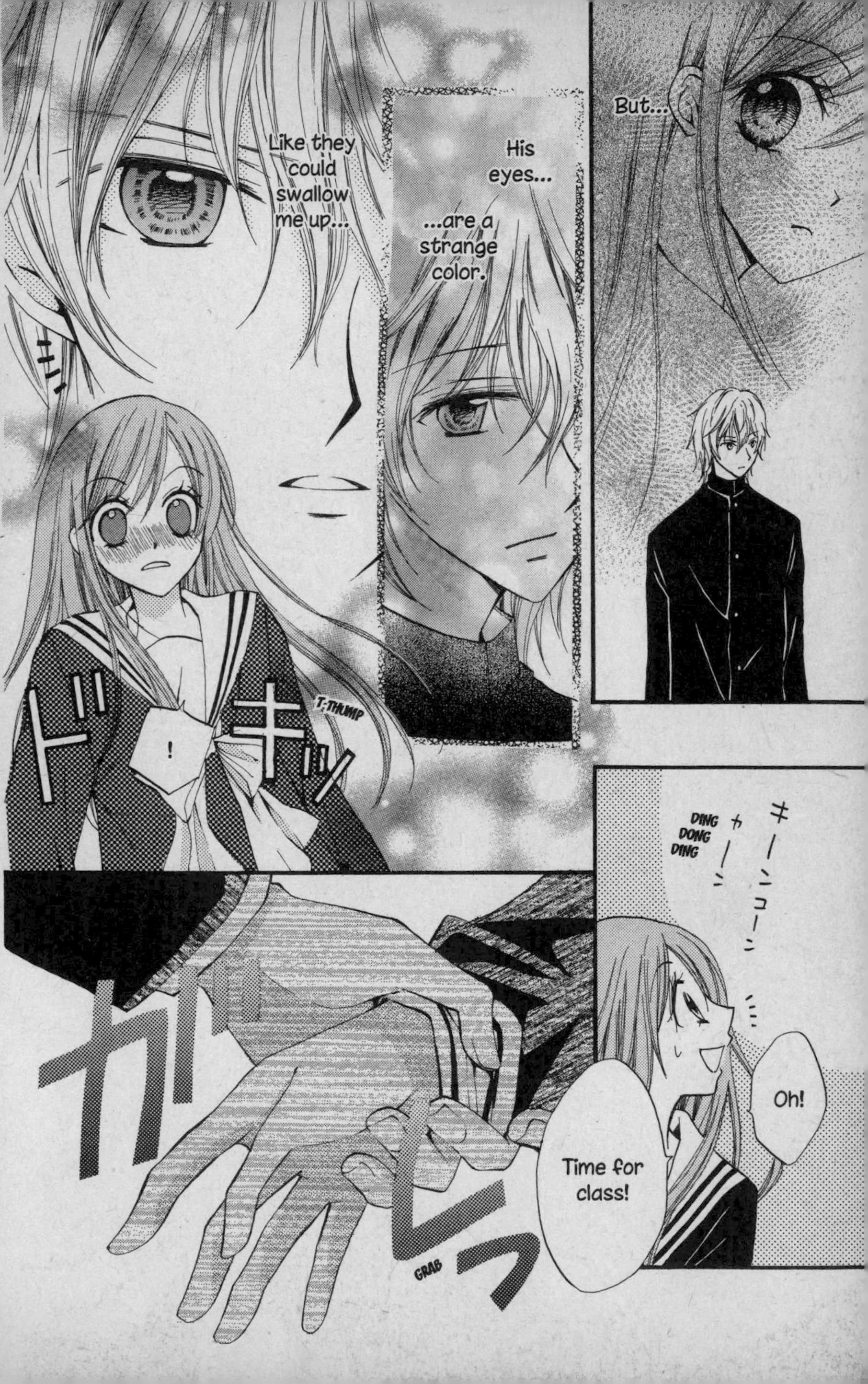

But...
His eyes...
...are a strange color.
Like they could swallow me up...
T-THUMP
!
DING DONG DING
Oh!
Time for class!
GRAB

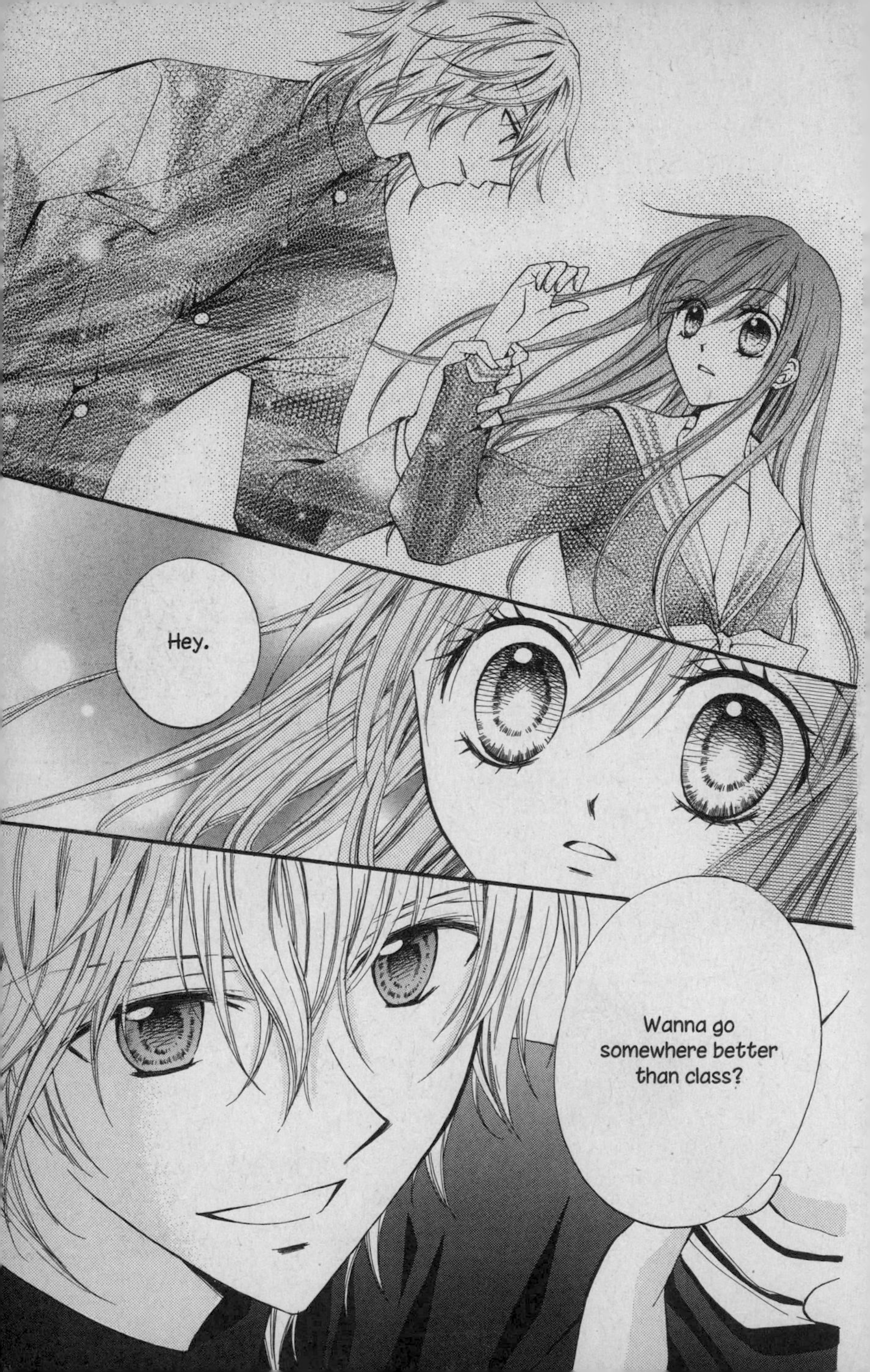
Hey.
Wanna go somewhere better than class?

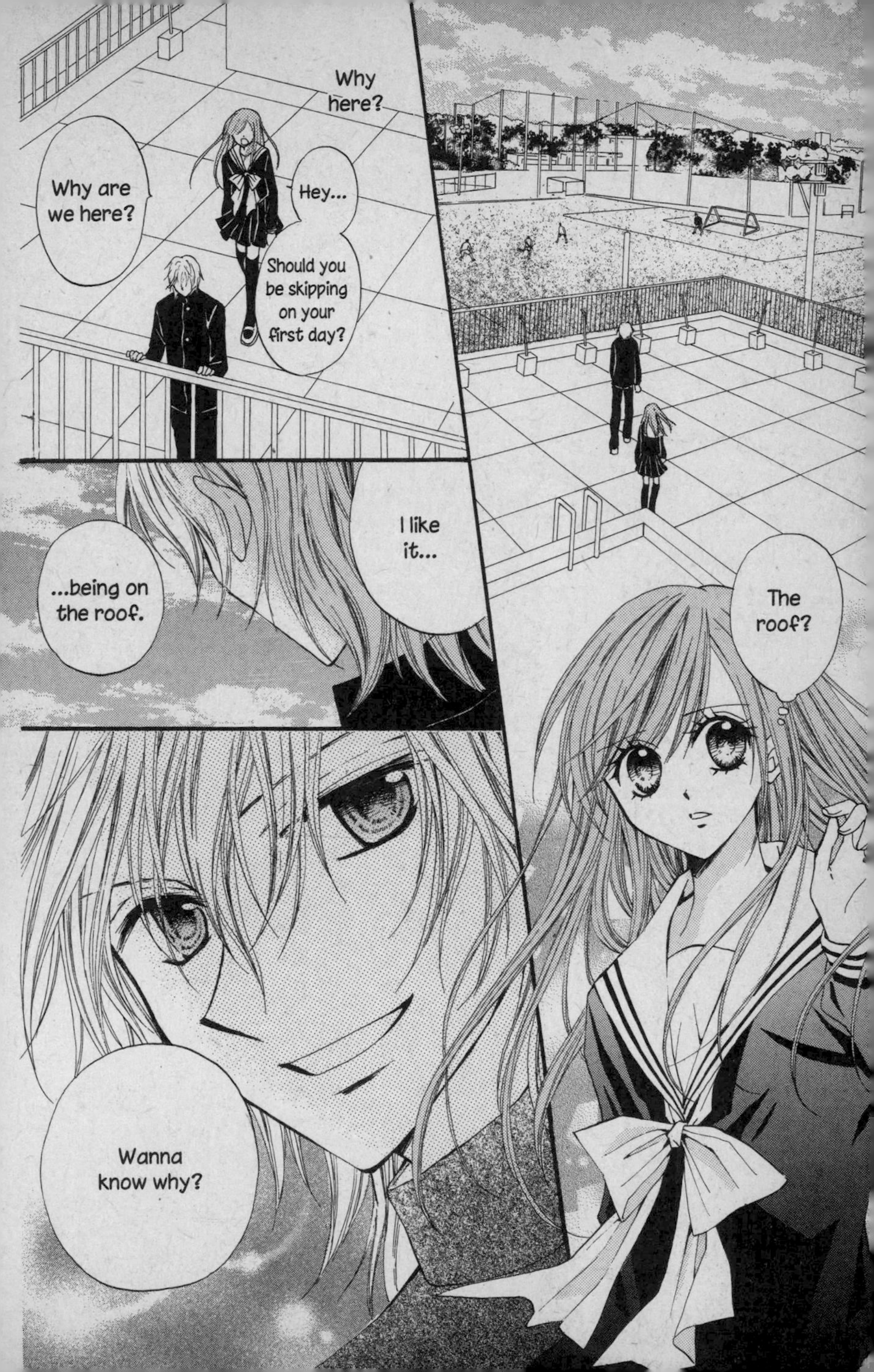

Why here?
Hey...
Should you be skipping on your first day?
Why are we here?
I like it...
...being on the roof.
The roof?
Wanna know why?

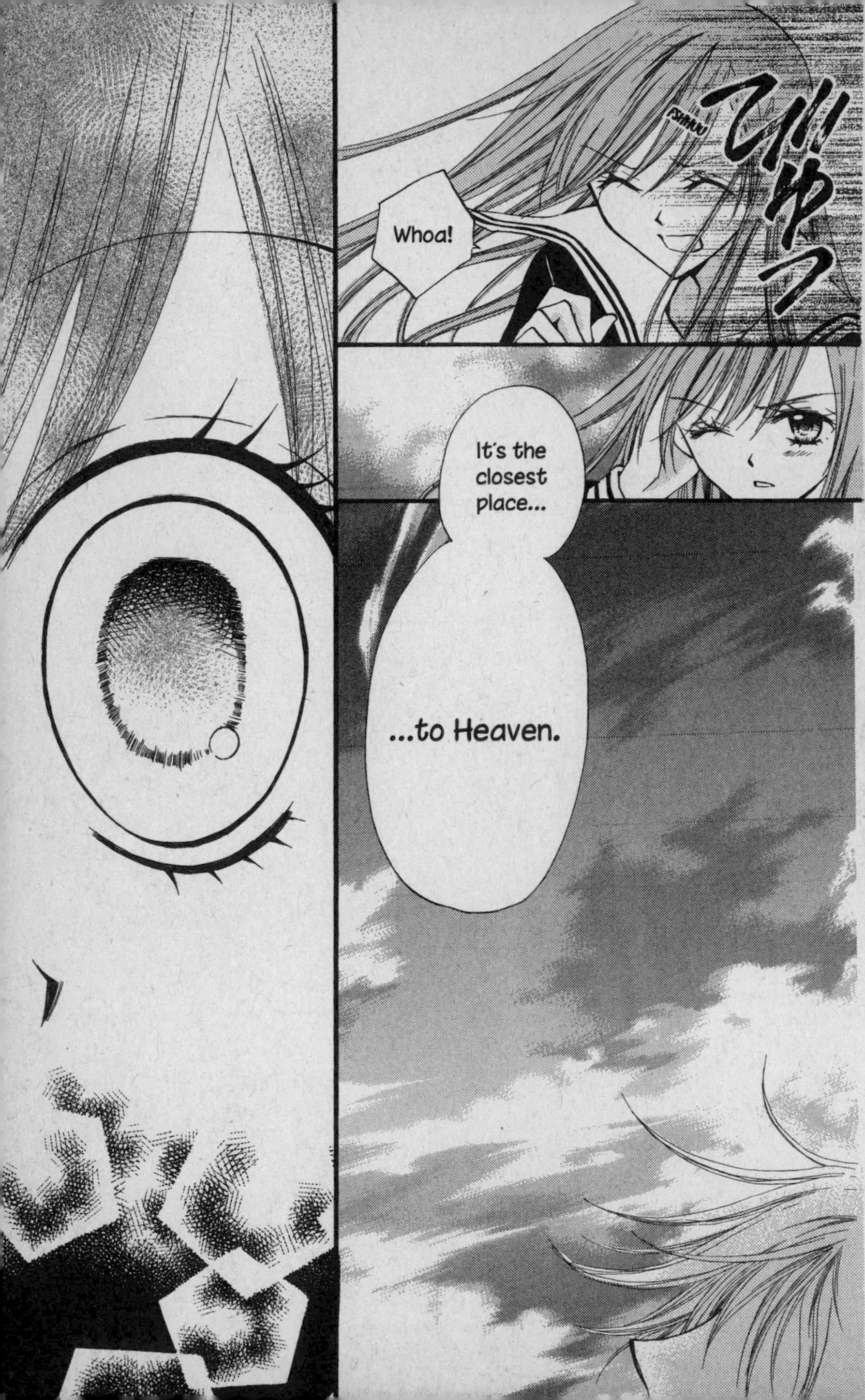
ひゅっ
FSHHUU
Whoa!
It's the closest place...
...to Heaven.

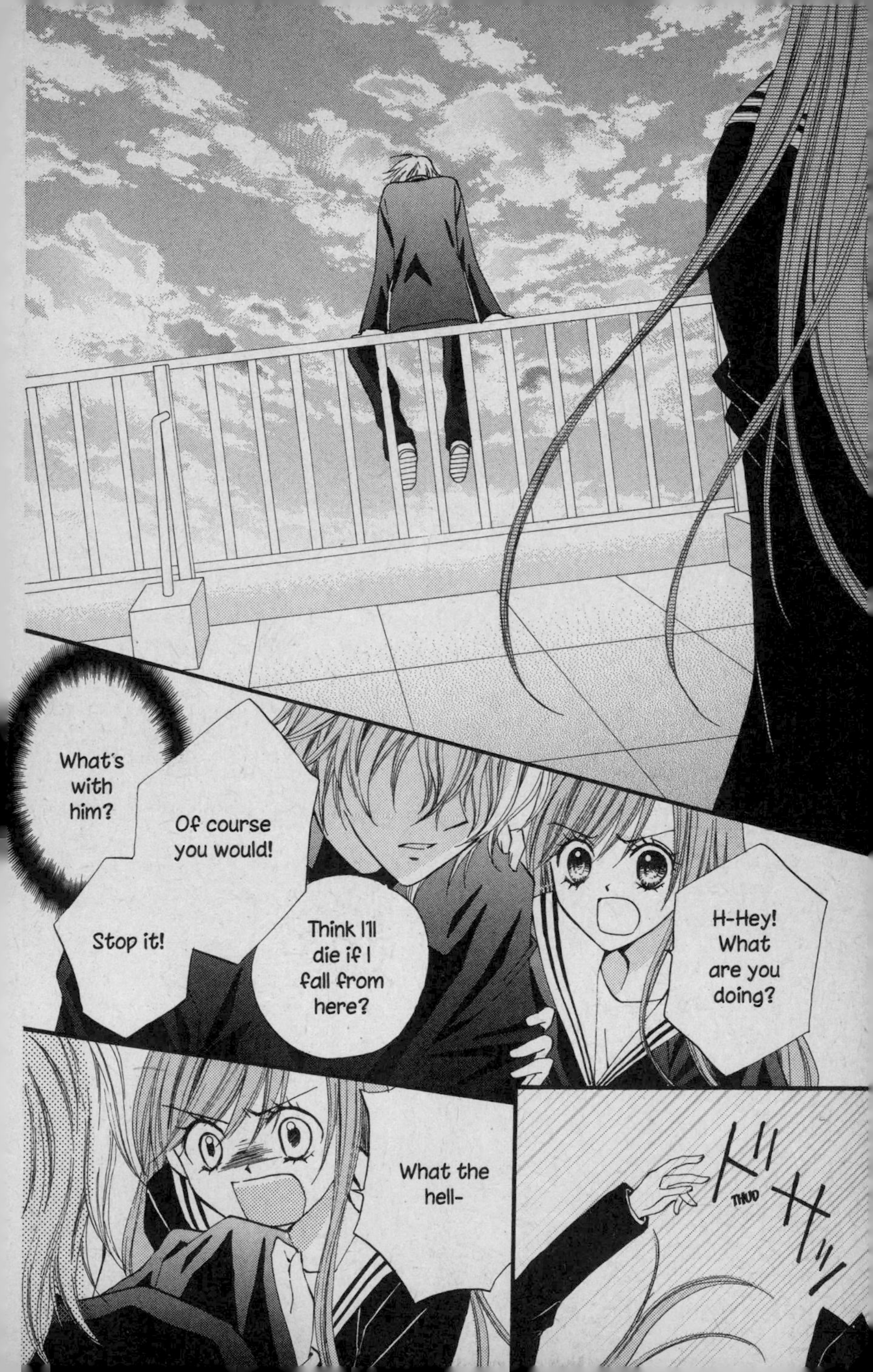
H-Hey! What are you doing?
Think I'll die if I fall from here?
Of course you would!
Stop it!
What's with him?
THUD
What the hell-

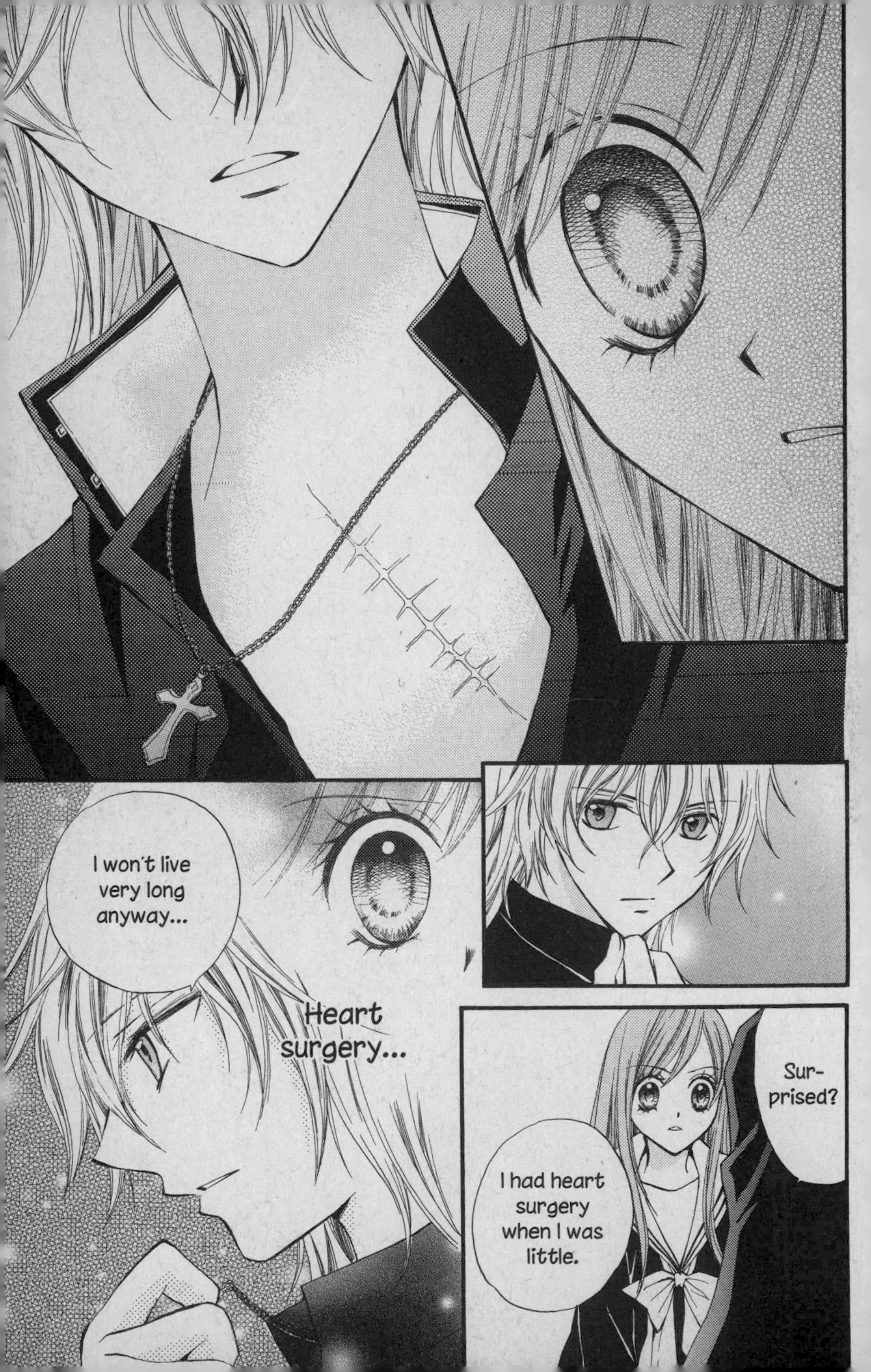
Sur-prised?
I had heart surgery when I was little.
Heart surgery...
I won't live very long anyway...

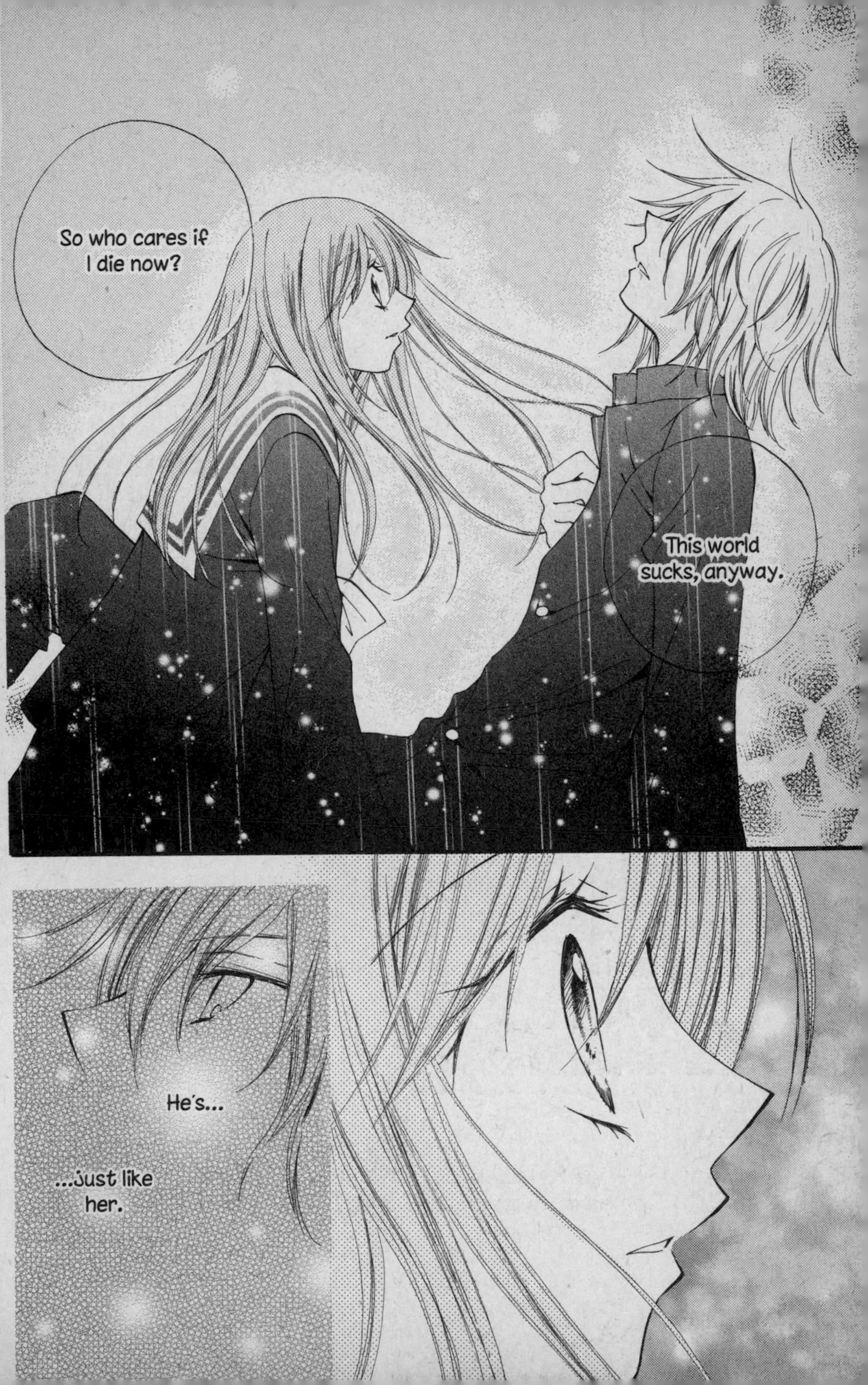
This world sucks, anyway.
So who cares if I die now?
He's...
...Just like her.

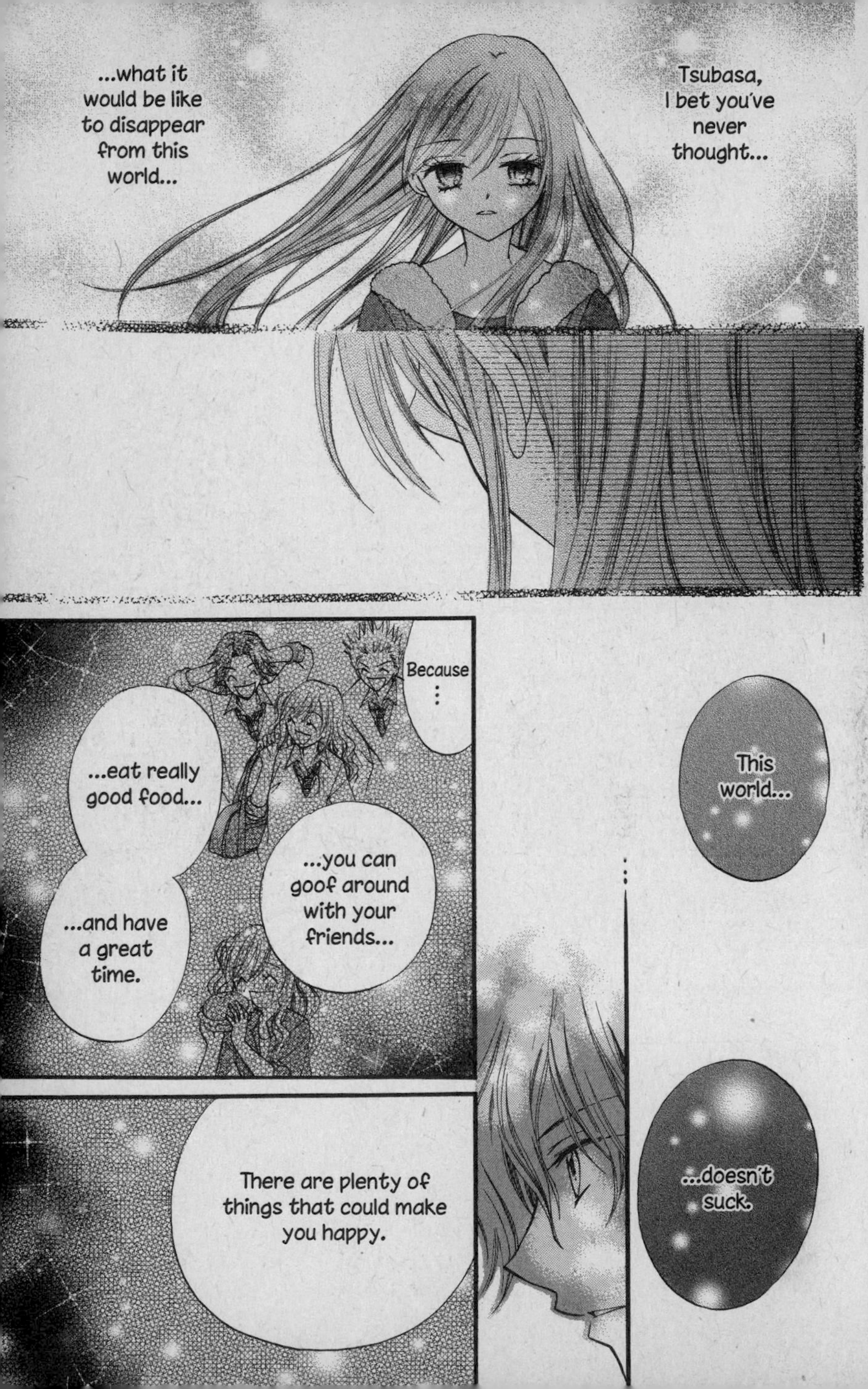

Tsubasa, I bet you've never thought...
...what it would be like to disappear from this world...
This world...
...doesn't suck.
Because...
...eat really good food...
...you can goof around with your friends...
...and have a great time.
There are plenty of things that could make you happy.

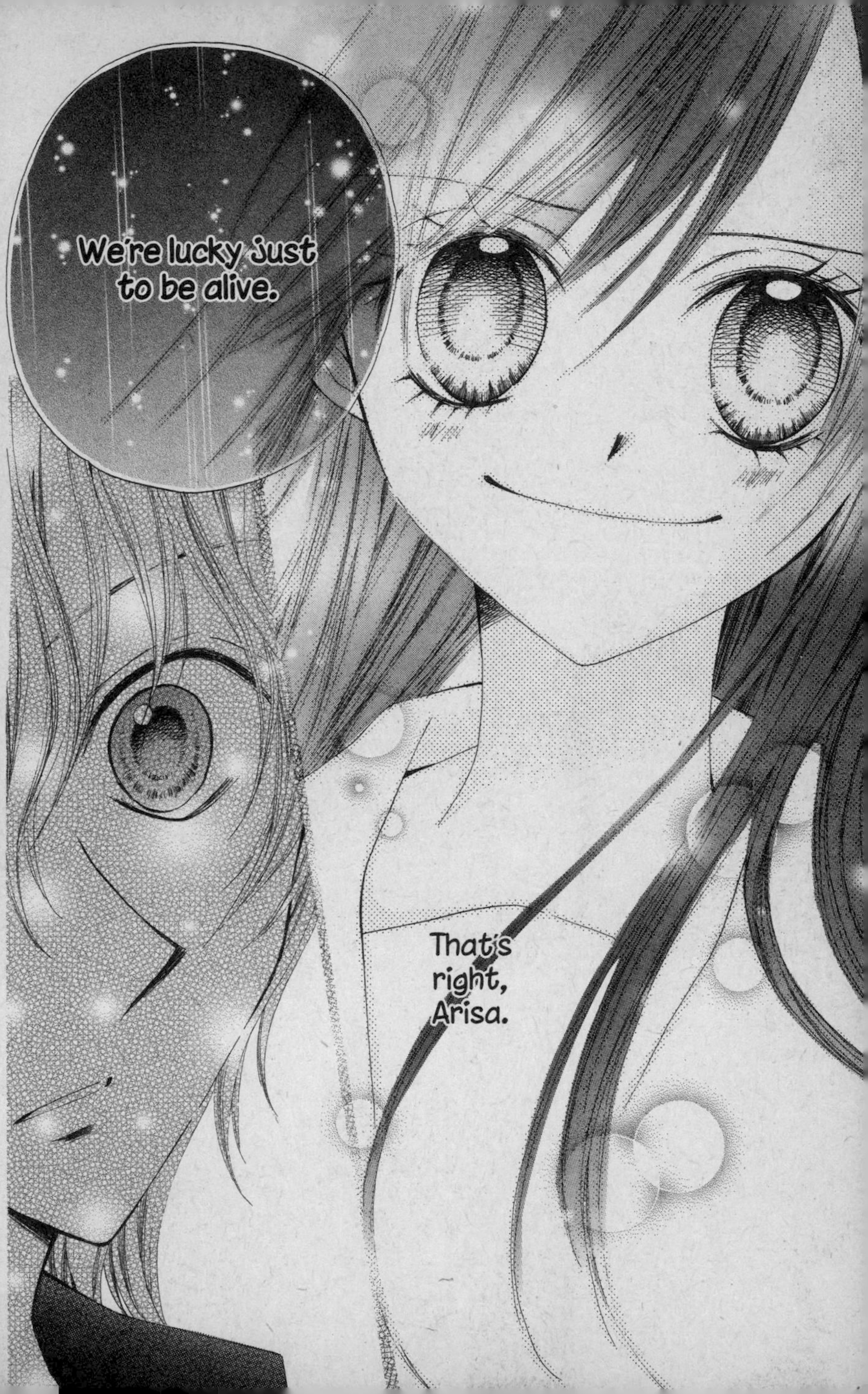
We're lucky just to be alive.
That's right, Arisa.

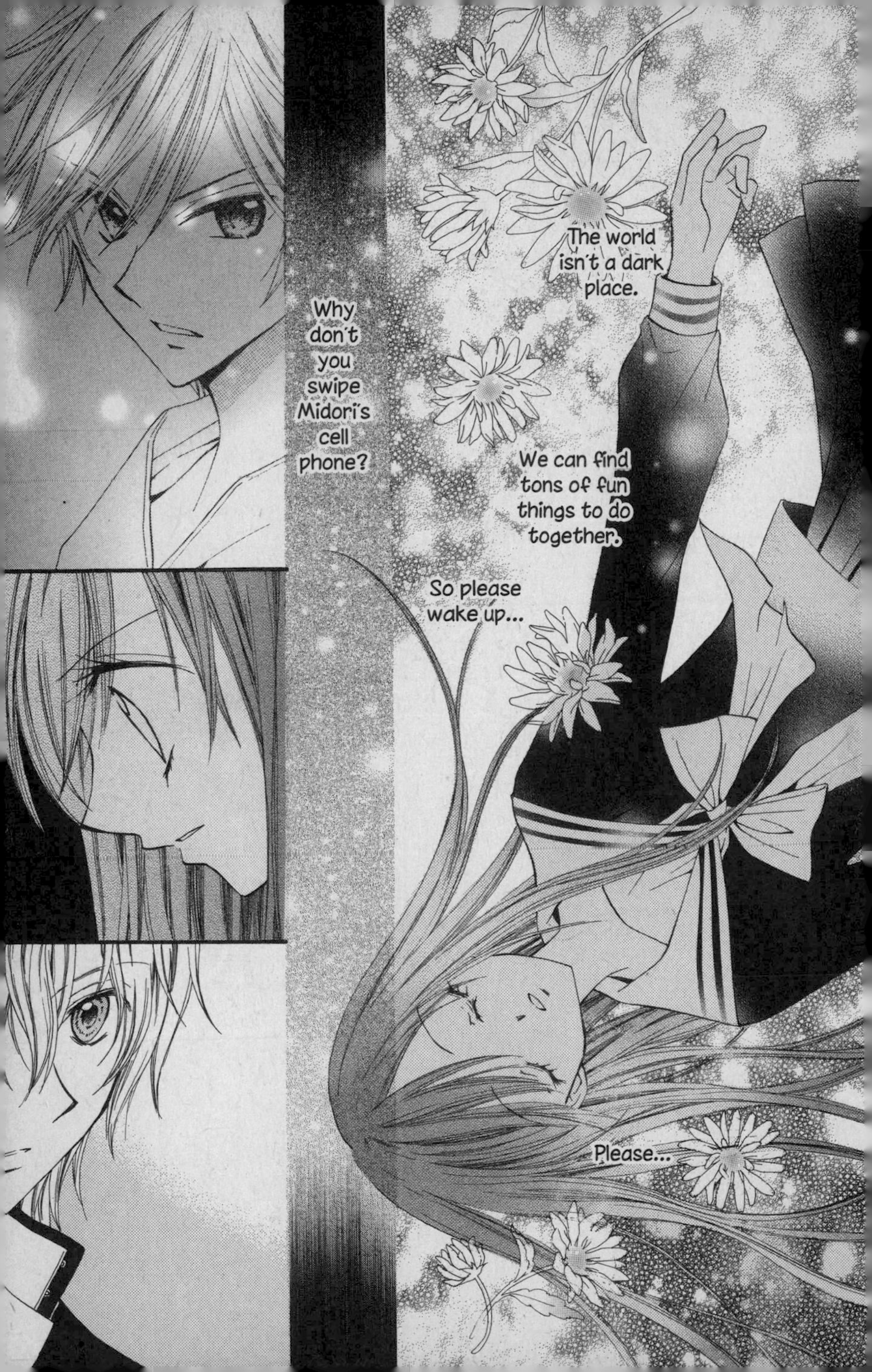
The world isn't a dark place.
We can find tons of fun things to do together.
So please wake up...
Please...
Why don't you swipe Midori's cell phone?

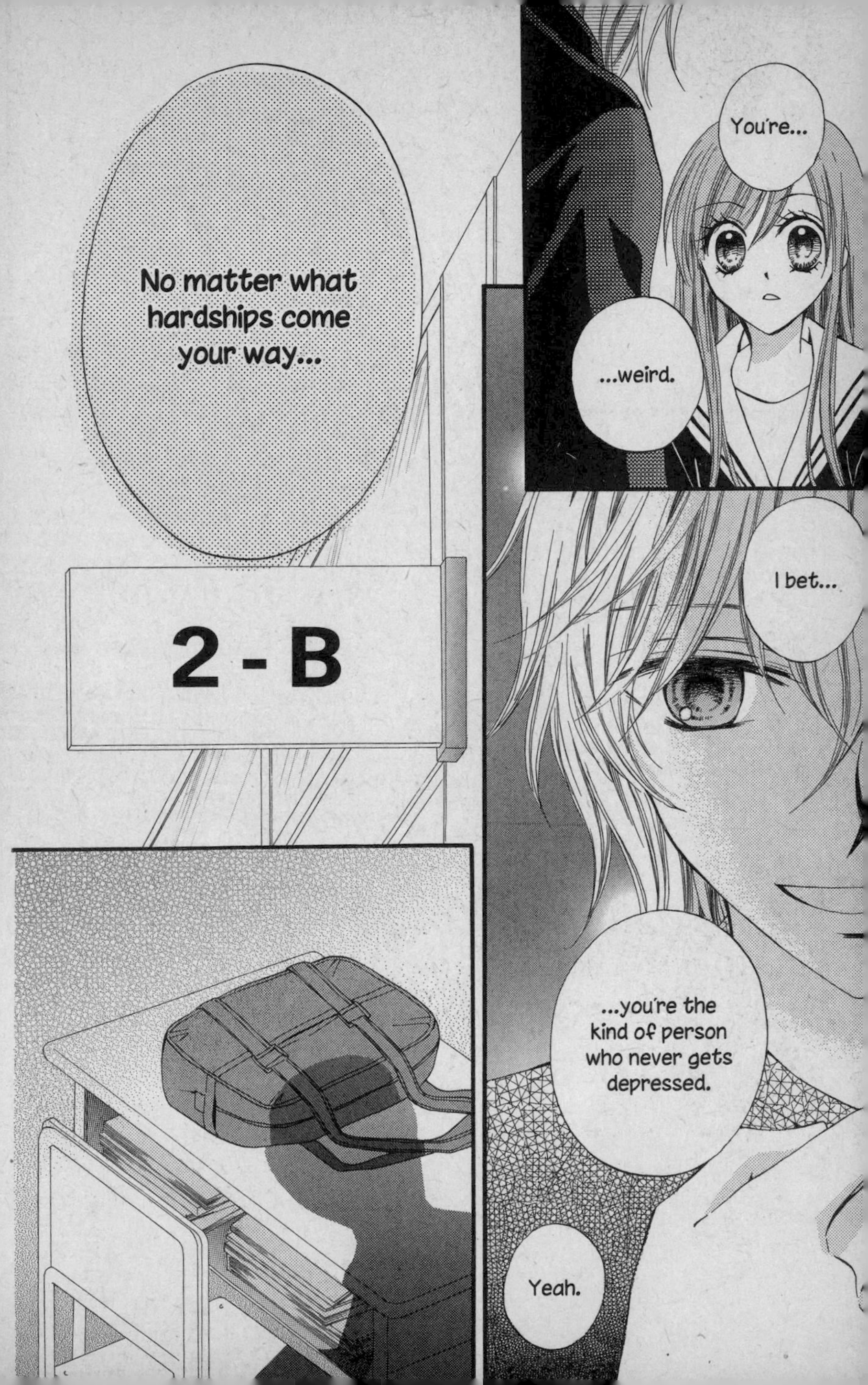
You're...
...weird.
I bet...
...you're the kind of person who never gets depressed.
Yeah.
No matter what hardships come your way...
2-B

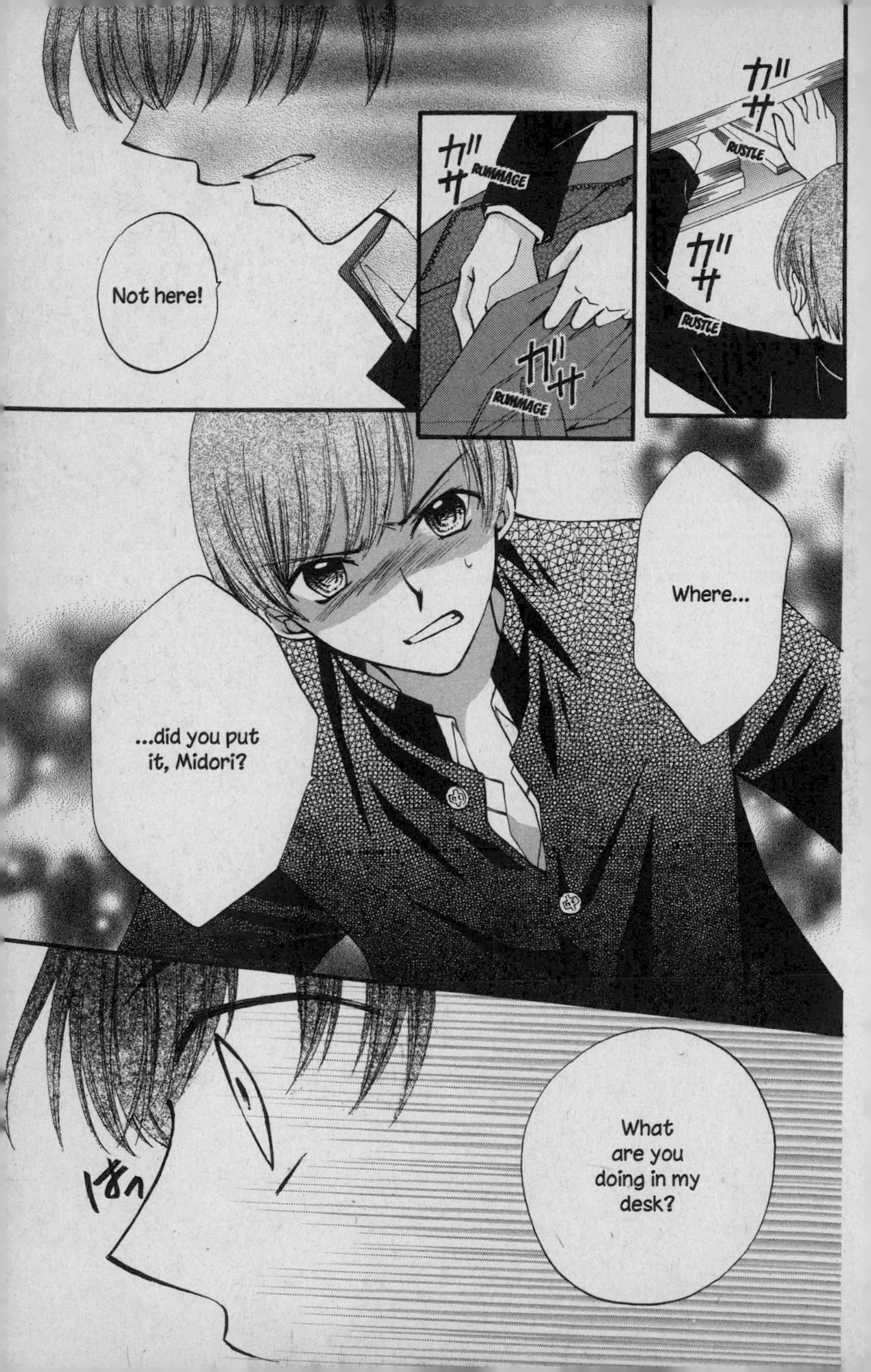
RUSTLE
RUSTLE
RUMMAGE
RUMMAGE
Not here!
Where...
...did you put it, Midori?
What are you doing in my desk?

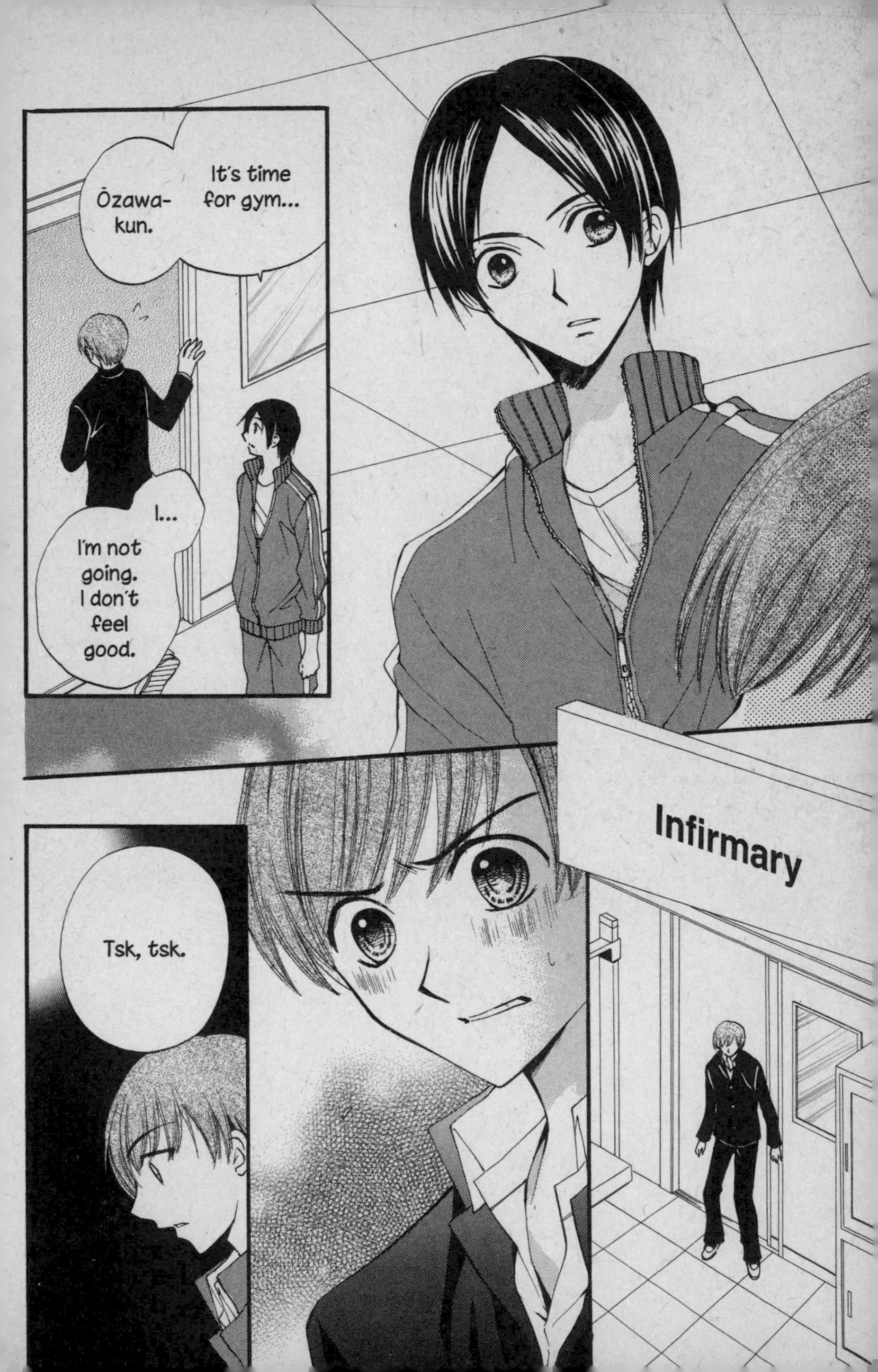
It's time for gym... Ōzawa-kun.
I... I'm not going. I don't feel good.
Infirmary
Tsk, tsk.

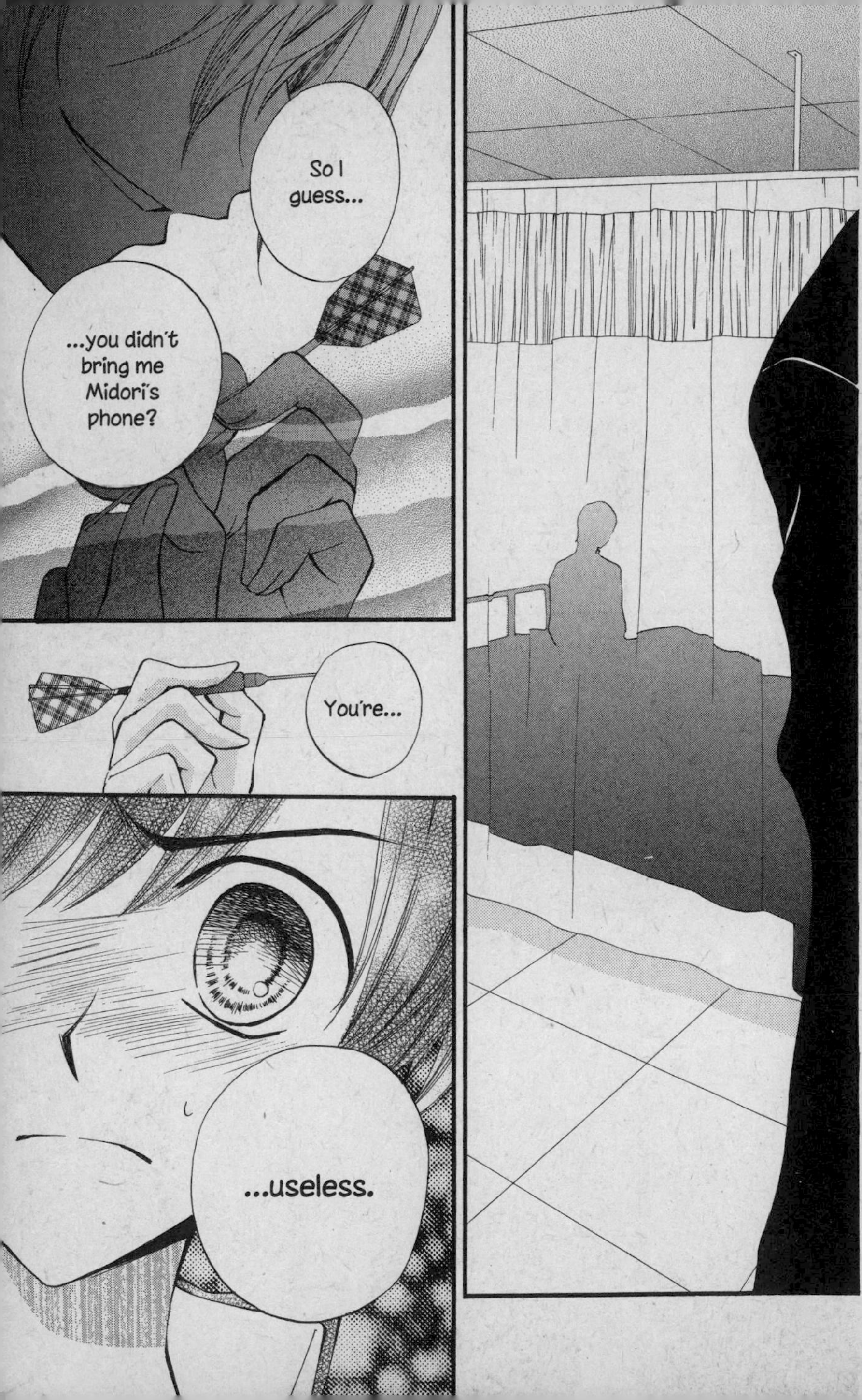
So I guess...
...you didn't bring me Midori's phone?
You're...
...useless.

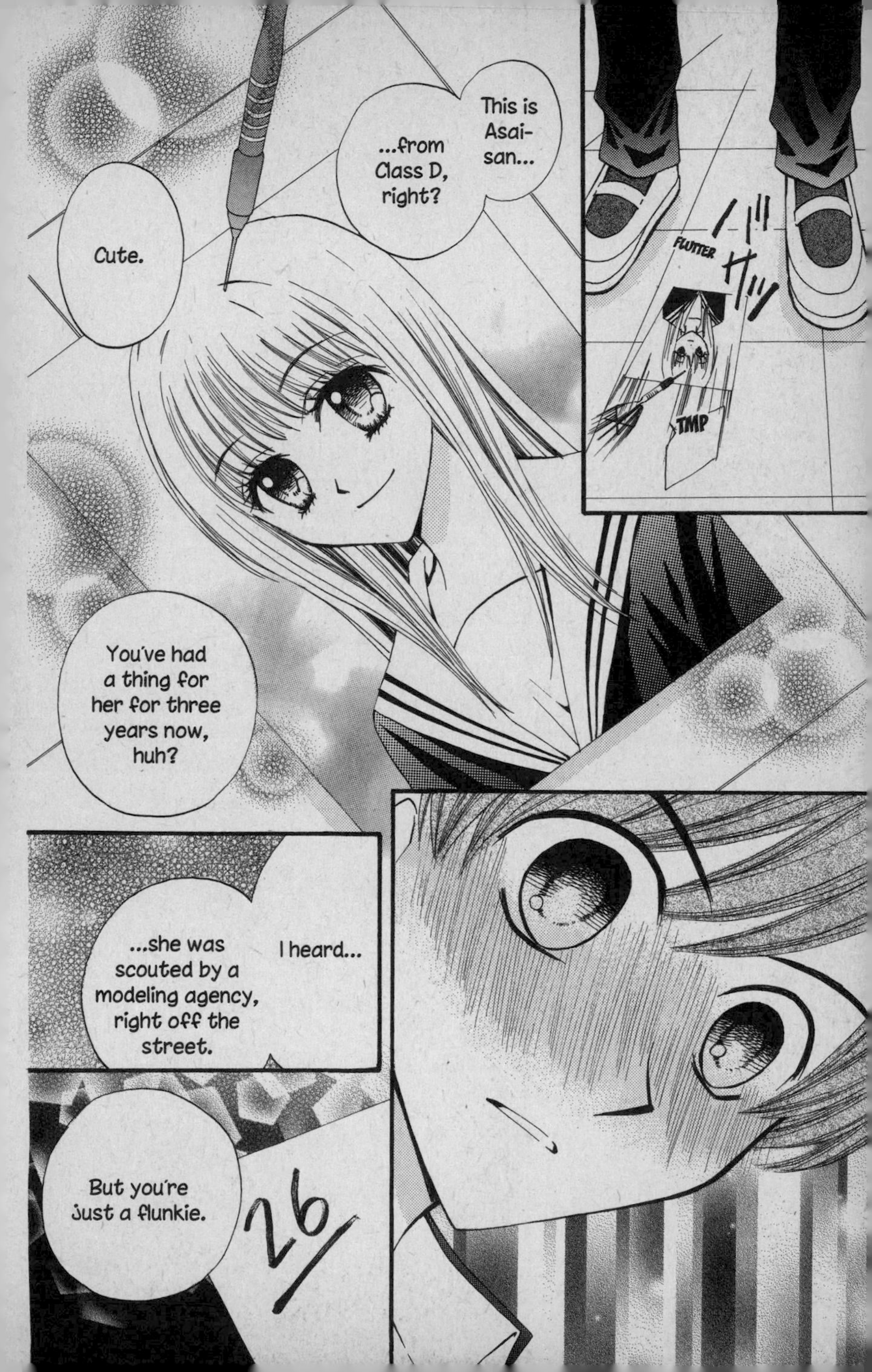
FLUTTER
TMP
This is Asai-san...
...from Class D, right?
Cute.
You've had a thing for her for three years now, huh?
I heard...
...she was scouted by a modeling agency, right off the street.
But you're just a flunkie.

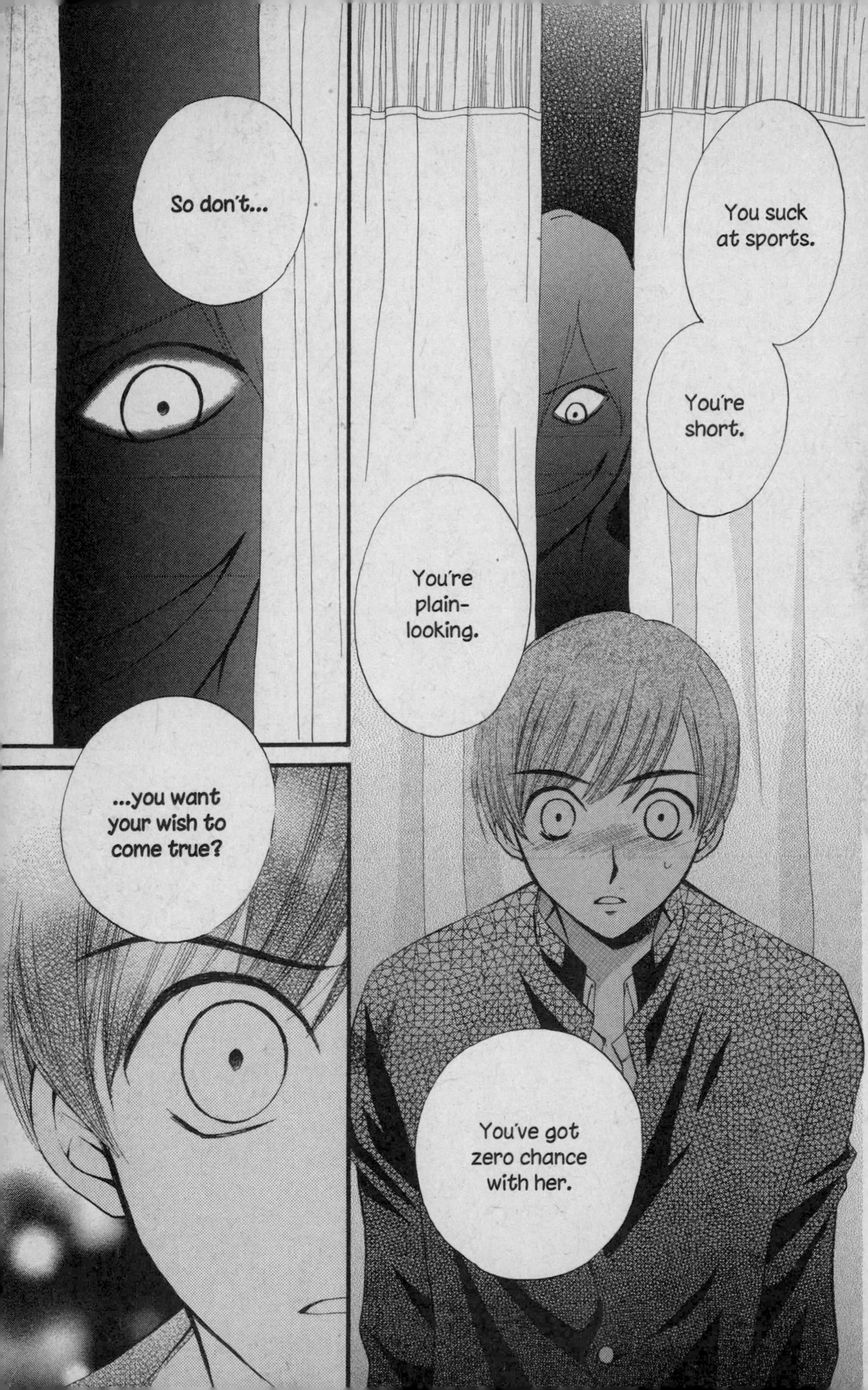
You suck at sports.
You're short.
You're plain-looking.
You've got zero chance with her.
So don't...
...you want your wish to come true?

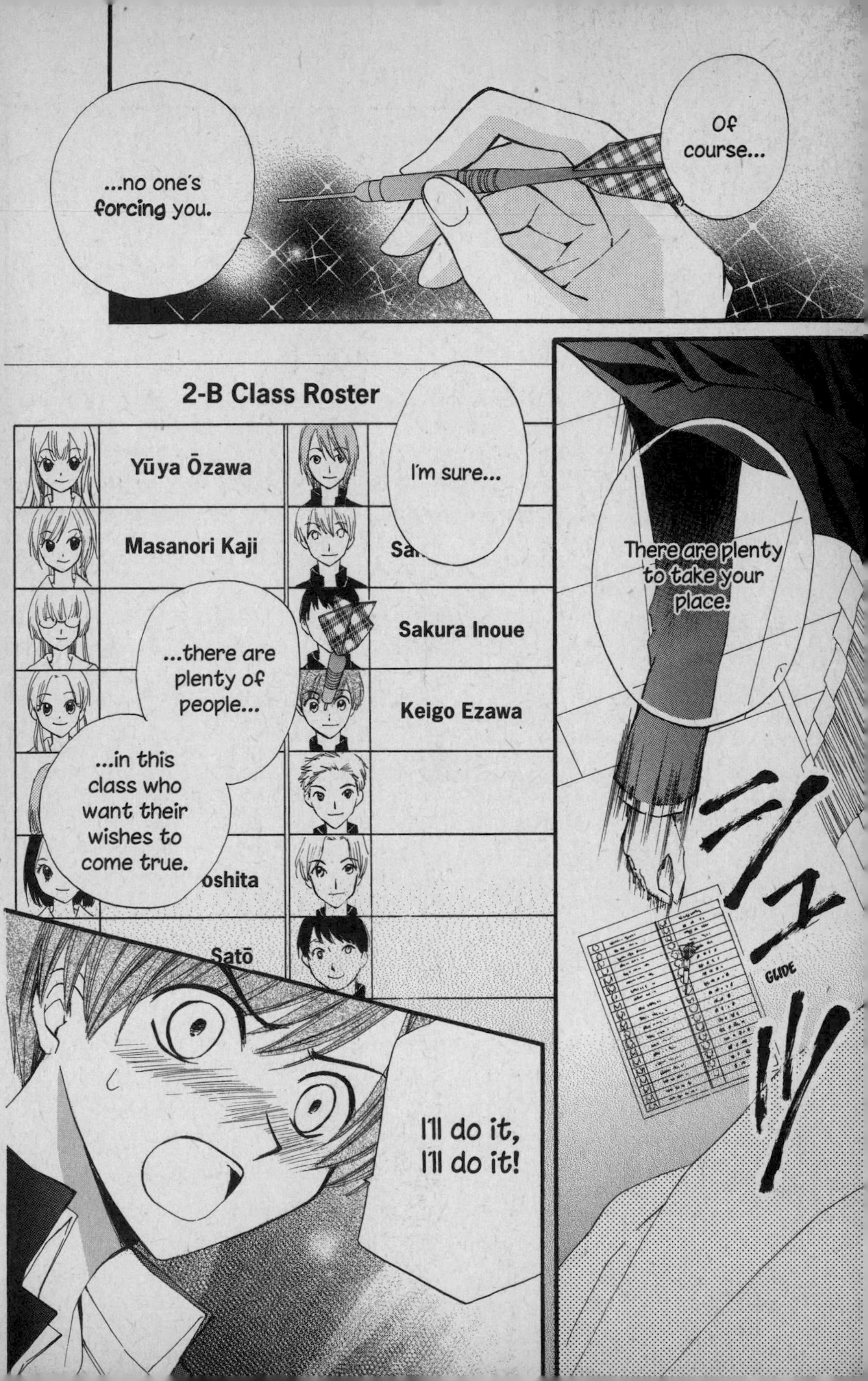
Of course...
...no one's forcing you.
There are plenty to take your place.
GLIDE
2-B Class Roster
I'm sure...
Yūya Ōzawa
Masanori Kaji
Sakura Inoue
Keigo Ezawa
...there are plenty of people...
...in this class who want their wishes to come true.
Satō
I'll do it, I'll do it!

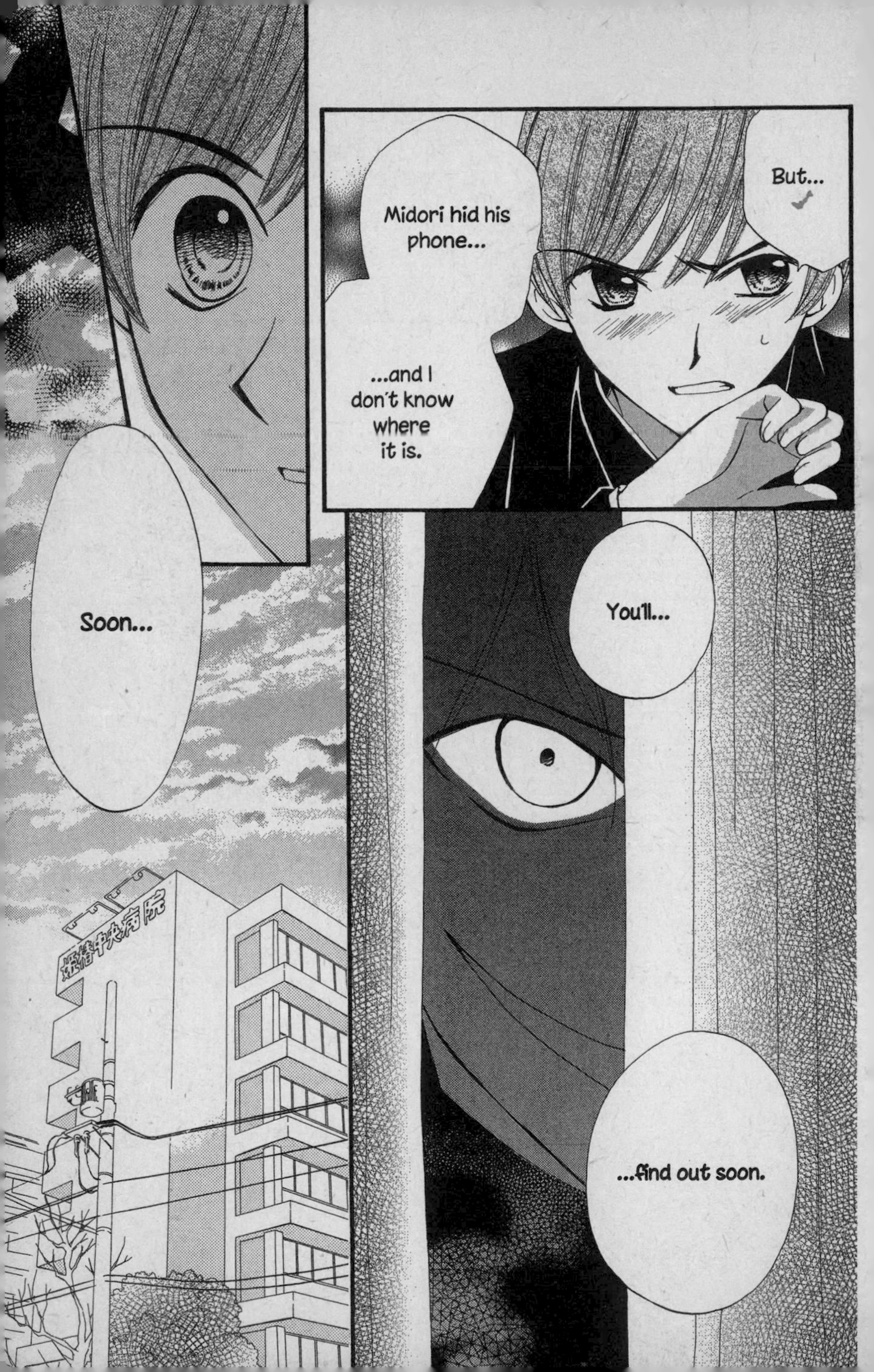
But...
Midori hid his phone...
...and I don't know where it is.
You'll...
...find out soon.
Soon...
姫椿中央病院

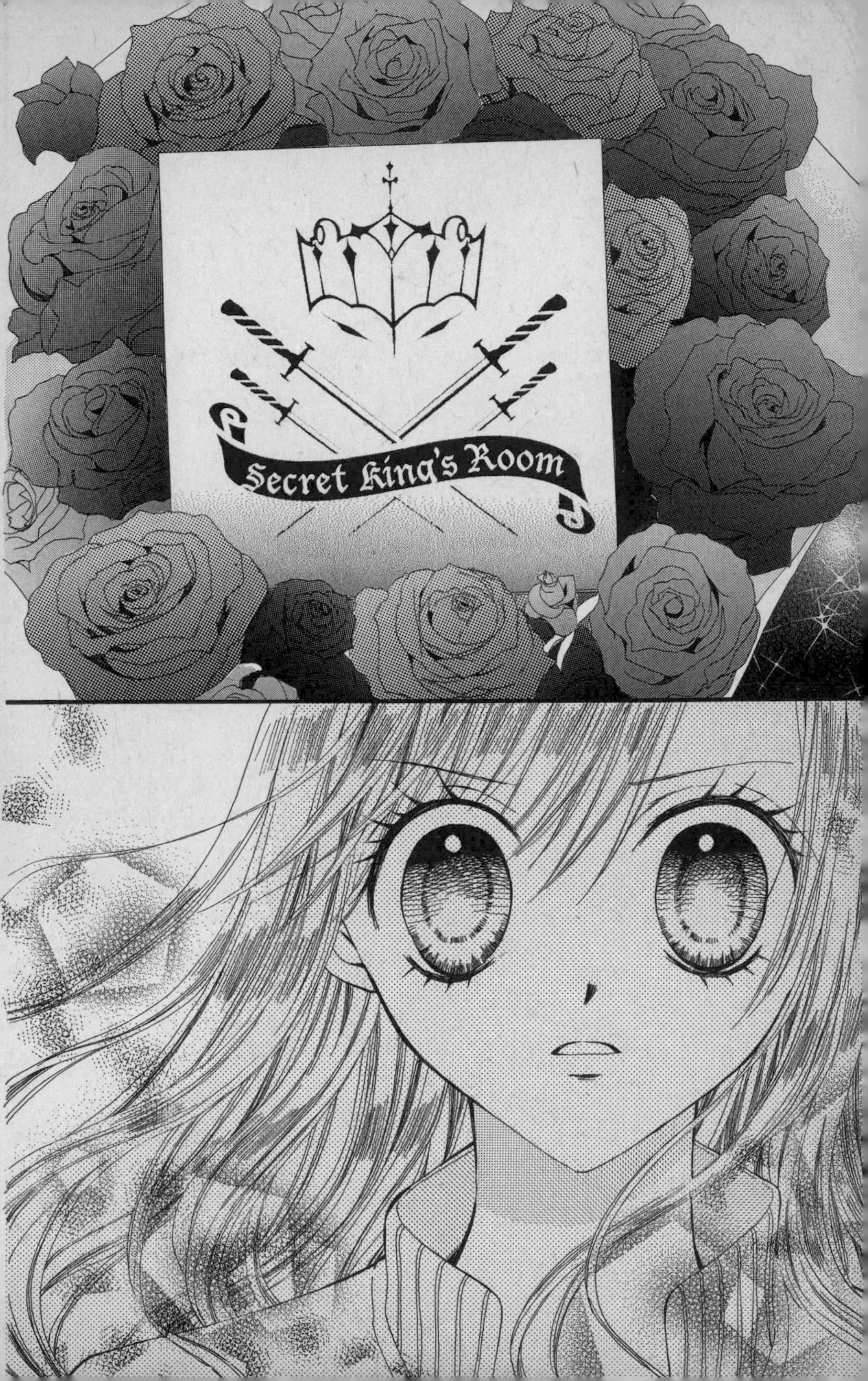
Secret King's Room

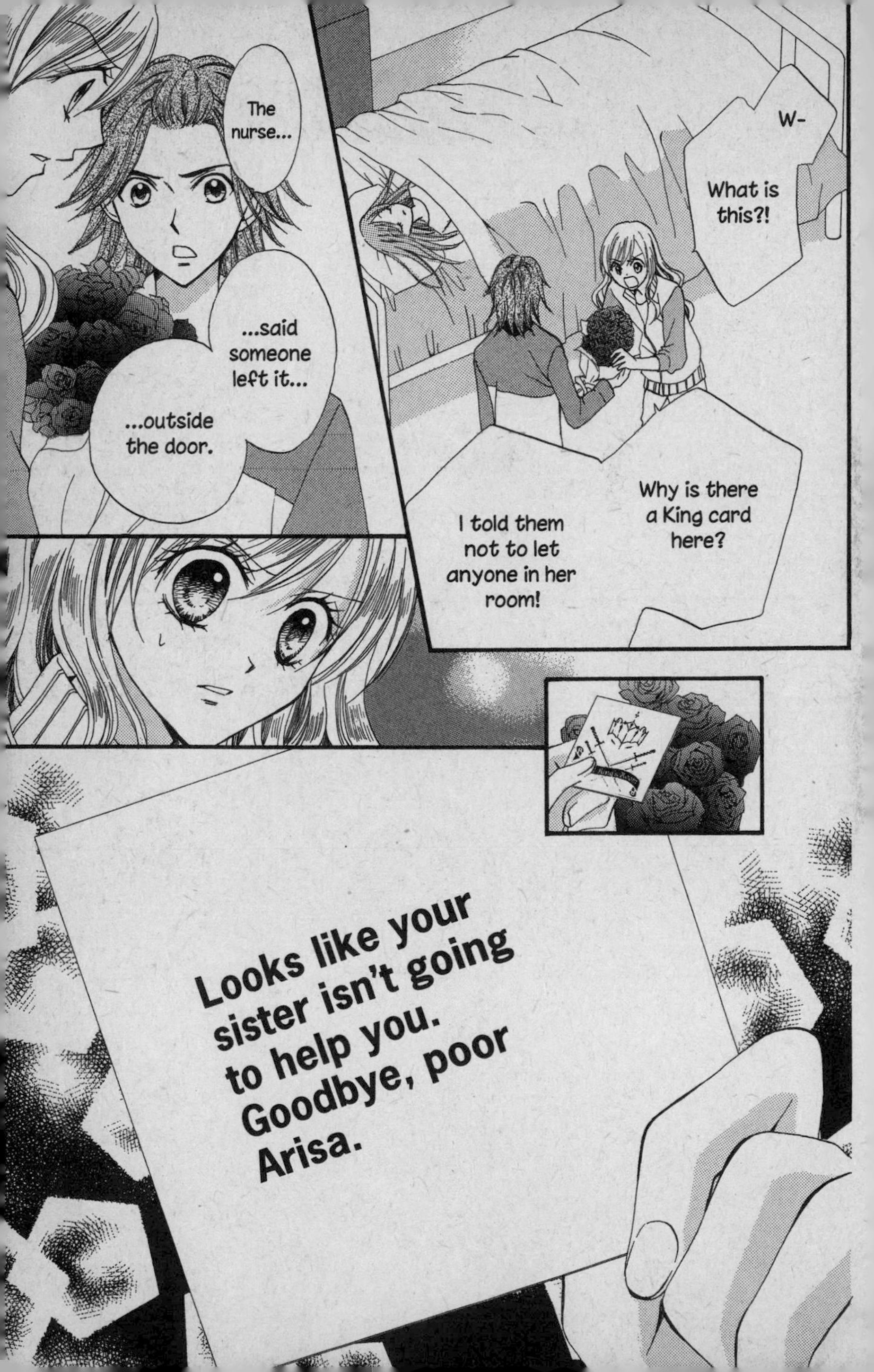
W-
What is this?!
Why is there a King card here?
I told them not to let anyone in her room!
The nurse...
...said someone left it...
...outside the door.
Looks like your sister isn't going to help you. Goodbye, poor Arisa.

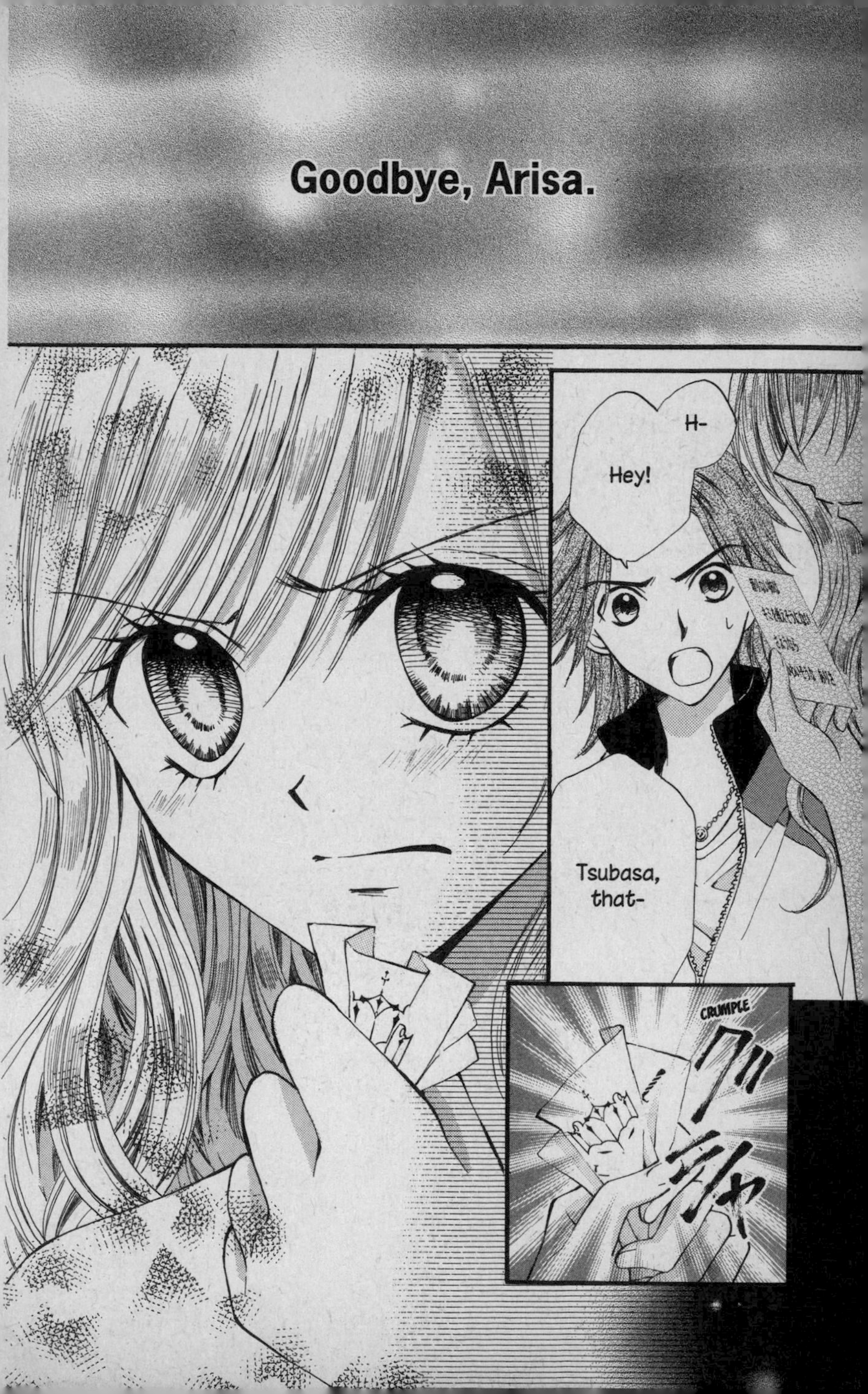
Goodbye, Arisa.
H-
Hey!
Tsubasa, that-
CRUMPLE

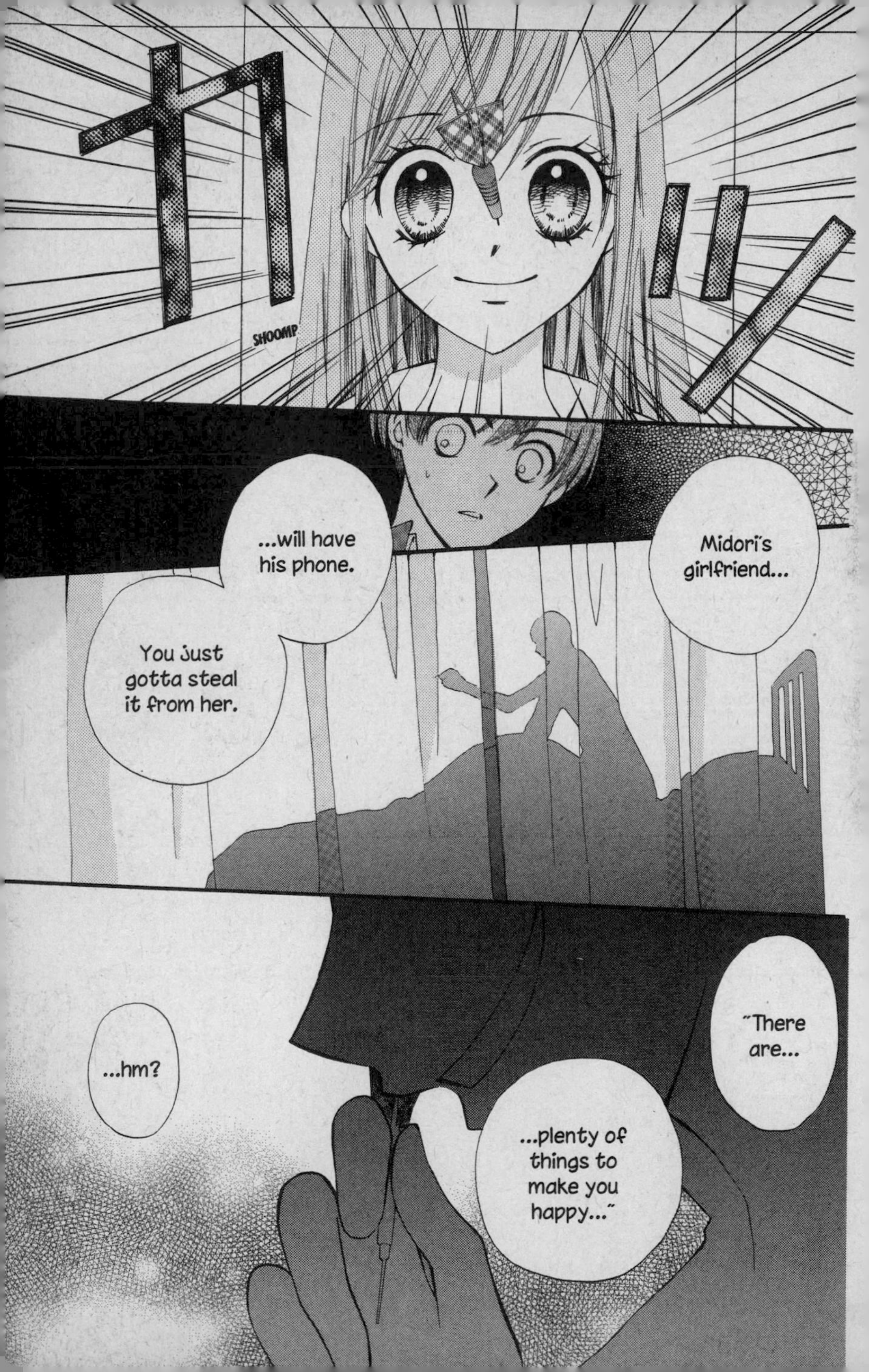
SHOOMP
Midori's girlfriend...
...will have his phone.
You just gotta steal it from her.
"There are...
...plenty of things to make you happy..."
...hm?

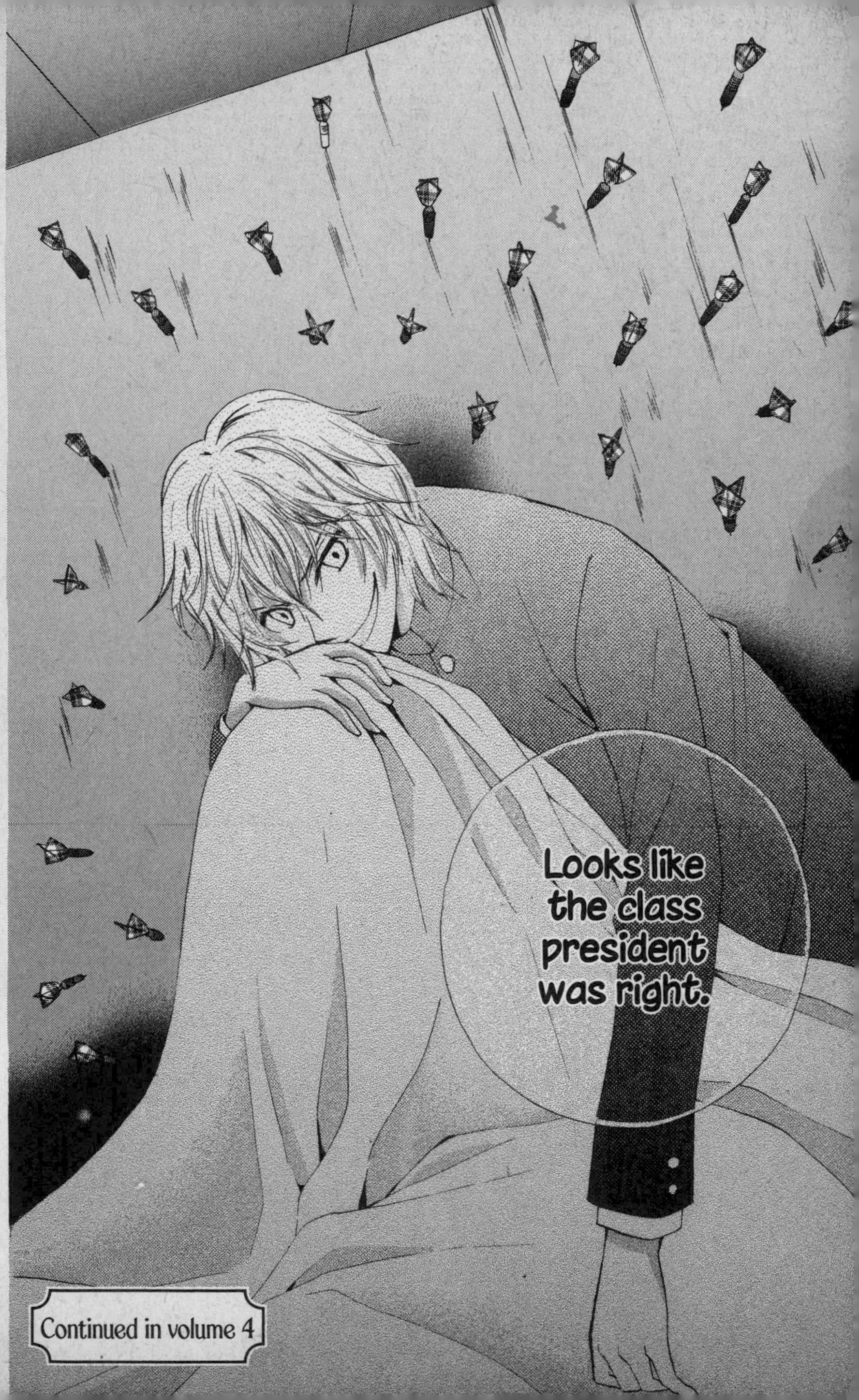
Looks like the class president was right.
Continued in volume 4

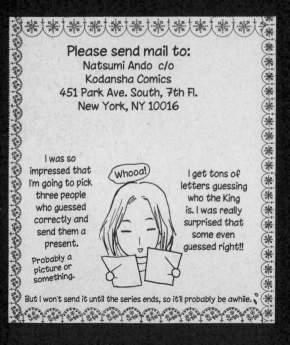

Please send mail to:

Natsumi Ando c/o
Kodansha Comics
451 Park Ave. South, 7th Fl.
New York, NY 10016

I get tons of letters guessing who the King is. I was really surprised that some even guessed right!!

Whooa!

I was so impressed that I'm going to pick three people who guessed correctly and send them a present.

Probably a picture or something.

But I won't send it until the series ends, so it'll probably be awhile.

~A letter from Mariko~

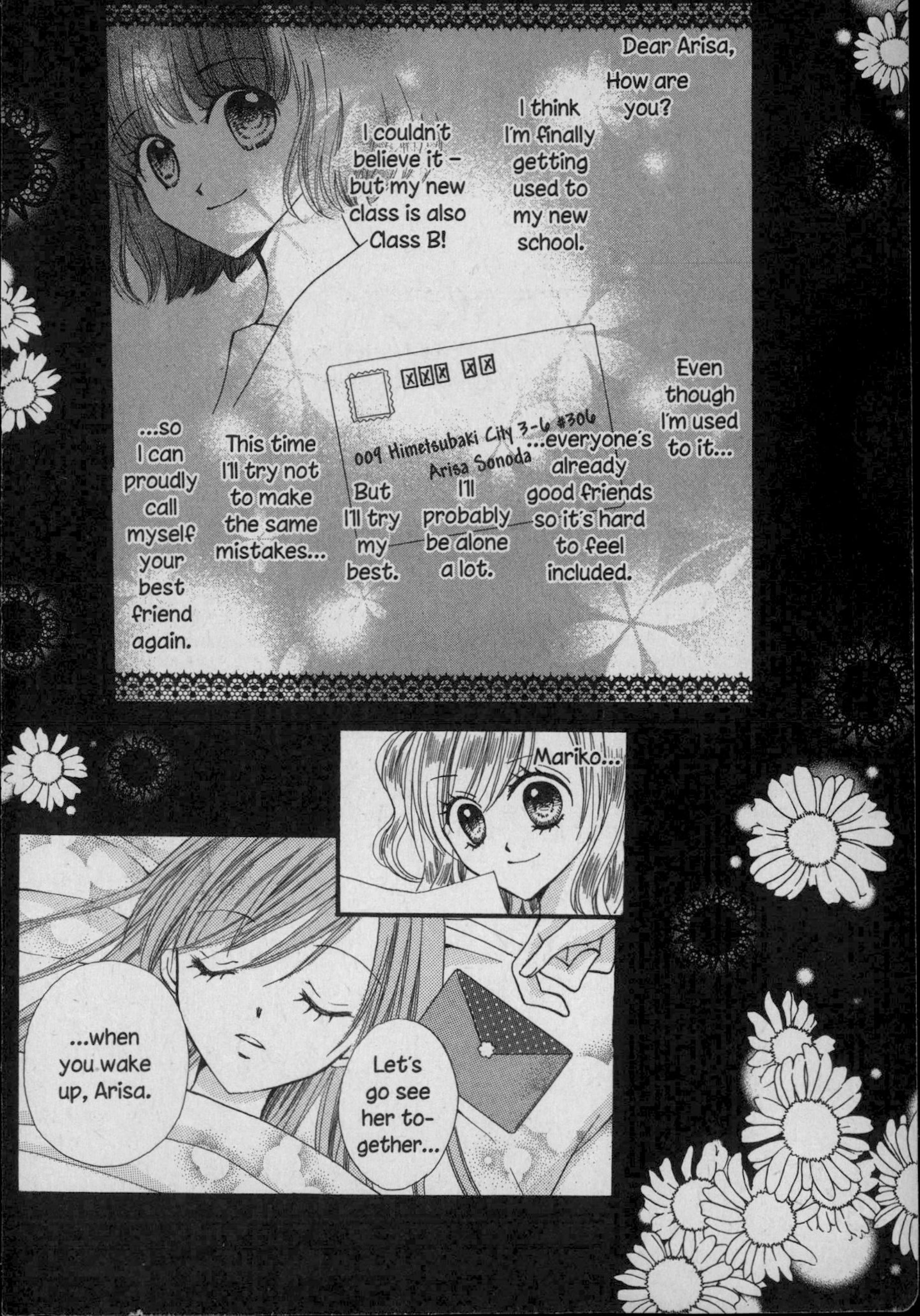
Dear Arisa,
How are you?
I think I'm finally getting used to my new school.
I couldn't believe it – but my new class is also Class B!
Even though I'm used to it...
...everyone's already good friends so it's hard to feel included.
I'll probably be alone a lot.
But I'll try my best.
This time I'll try not to make the same mistakes...
...so I can proudly call myself your best friend again.
009 Himetsubaki City 3-6 #306
Arisa Sonoda
Mariko...
Let's go see her together...
...when you wake up, Arisa.

Translation Notes

Japanese is a tricky language for most Westerners, and translation is often more art than science. For your edification and reading pleasure, here are notes on some of the places where we could have gone in a different direction with our translation of the work, or where a Japanese cultural reference is used.

The King

In Japanese, there is no pronoun used to refer to the King. It is not clear in the Japanese whether the King is male or female. This is more difficult in English, so the King is referred to as "he" in this translation. Keep in mind this does not necessarily mean the identity of the King is a male (or isn't).

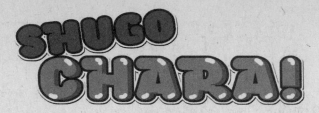

SHUGO CHARA!

PEACH-PIT

CREATORS OF *DEARS* AND *ROZEN MAIDEN*

PEACH-PIT
CREATORS OF DEARS AND ROZEN MAIDEN
SHUGO CHARA!
1

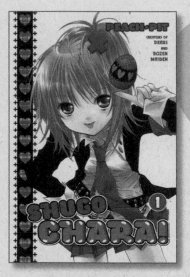

Everybody at Seiyo Elementary thinks that stylish and supercool Amu has it all. But nobody knows the real Amu, a shy girl who wishes she had the courage to truly be herself. Changing Amu's life is going to take more than wishes and dreams—it's going to take a little magic! One morning, Amu finds a surprise in her bed: three strange little eggs. Each egg contains a Guardian Character, an angel-like being who can give her the power to be someone new. With the help of her Guardian Characters, Amu is about to discover that her true self is even more amazing than she ever dreamed.

Special extras in each volume! Read them all!

VISIT WWW.KODANSHACOMICS.COM TO:

- **View release date calendars for upcoming volumes**
- **Find out the latest about new Kodansha Comics series**

KC KODANSHA COMICS

THE wallflower
YAMATONADESHIKO SHICHIHENGE

BY TOMOKO HAYAKAWA

It's a beautiful, expansive mansion, and four handsome, fifteen-year-old friends are allowed to live in it for free! But there is one condition—within three years the young men must take the owner's niece and transform her into a proper lady befitting the palace in which they all live! How hard can it be?

Enter Sunako Nakahara, the horror-movie-loving, pock-faced, frizzy-haired, fashion-illiterate hermit who has a tendency to break into explosive nosebleeds whenever she sees anyone attractive. This project is going to take far more than our four heroes ever expected; it needs a miracle!

Ages: 16+

Special extras in each volume! Read them all!

TOMARE!

[STOP!]

You're going the wrong way!

Manga is a completely
different
type of reading experience.

To start at the *beginning*,
go to the *end*!

That's right! Authentic manga is read the traditional Japanese way—from right to left. Exactly the *opposite* of how American books are read. It's easy to follow: Just go to the other end of the book, and read each page—and each panel—from the right side to the left side, starting at the top right. Now you're experiencing manga as it was meant to be!